A Manual of Clayshooting

CHRIS CRADOCK

A Manual of Clayshooting

B T Batsford Ltd, London

To Tommy and Joy
who made it all possible

ISBN 0 7134 5308 7

Text set in 10/12 pt Linotron 202 Times, printed and bound
in Great Britain at The Bath Press, Avon
for the publishers
B. T. Batsford Ltd
4 Fitzhardinge Street
London W1H 0AH

Contents

Foreword

Reading the proofs of this book my first impression is to admire the Author's courage in tackling such a wide subject at a time when the number of clayshooting disciplines has risen dramatically, thus increasing the technicalities. Chris ran a well-known shooting school and gun shop for a number of years, was the first National Coach and Safety Officer for the CPSA, acted as referee at many major Championships and is still the chief tutor for the Association's Coaching Committee, thus earning himself a life vice-presidency. Add to this his technical work for a monthly magazine, the contribution of a weekly page in another, and it becomes apparent that his knowledge and tenacity have faded little since he shot his first clay targets back in the 1920's.

The reader will quickly realise that he has, in one manual, filled a large gap in clayshooting information, catering for beginner, specialist shooter, administrator and, at the same time, produced a complete reference source for those who may need quickly to assimilate some clayshooting knowledge. I am not sure whether this has been achieved by the burning of much midnight oil, or innumerable hours of early morning brain racking, but certainly Chris has produced a veritable 'bible' for those interested in the sport at whatever level. It is an honour to pen a foreword to such a work since, as will be obvious, the author knows his subject to the full and has made available a hitherto untapped fund of knowledge.

Roy A Greatorex

President English CPSA
President, The British Clay Pigeon
Shooting Associations' International Board

Preface

I have written this book as a result of 60 years' experience of guns and shooting. None of it has been ghosted, yet in a way it has, because of my study of the many books published since 1800, and there will be much in these pages which confirms the conclusions reached by those long gone.

Over the years I have been privileged to watch, not only some of the world's best in action, but also Mr Average Shooter. From these people I hope I have learnt much. Because of this I believe I have now reached the state of knowing when I don't know the answer to a shotgun or shooter problem. This realization has greatly aided me to find an answer through my contacts and references.

Apologies are due to the ladies. I detest the word 'sportsperson', and have referred almost all the time to the shooter as a *he*. I also acknowledge, that anything in shooting a man can do, the ladies, given correct equipment and half a chance, will do as well and with less fuss.

Some photos show left-handed shooters, others right. Authors in the past have written for right-handers and told the sinistral to reverse everything. Although I have difficulty in knowing my left hand from my right, I have decided to treat all alike. If any reader looks at a photo and it is a mirror image of himself, and he is right-handed, the photo is of a leftie, i.e. exactly what a right-hander would see if he posed in front of a mirror. Of course, this will be vice versa for the left-hander.

Due to the fact that I have been writing for various magazines for around 30 years, some of the thoughts, opinions and conclusions expressed in the book may seem familiar, and for this, I crave my reader's indulgence.

1 Introduction

How it all began

Man's ancestor who rolled, dropped or threw that first piece of rock certainly started something. Especially the ancestor who having done so realized the implications and potential of such an action.

This was something which could help man to compete on more favourable terms with his quarry or enemy.

Inevitably more sophisticated methods of propelling hard objects such as pebbles, rocks, or even pointed sticks were evolved. The evolution of the spear, sling, ballista, bow and arrow, all helped man in his struggle to obtain sustenance. There was the added bonus that such weapons provided him with better protection from his enemies for both his dependants and himself. Finally gun powder was invented or discovered; now at last the little man could compete on equal terms with the big man.

The early guns were temperamental, to say the least, often proving a greater hazard to the person shooting them than to the quarry shot at.

In the late fifteenth century matchlock guns began to be used on the hordes of wildfowl which then lived in the East Anglian Fens and other parts of Britain. The next step forward came when Charles II and his courtiers returned to England and using flint lock guns introduced the French 'Art of Shooting Flying'.

In the early nineteenth century the percussion gun was evolved and developed, this in turn was followed in 1836 by the Lefaucheux gun, designed to be opened and loaded at the breech with pin fire cartridges. Lancaster's centre fire breech loader, using centre fire cartridges with percussion caps in their bases, was introduced in the early 1850s and the dangerous pin fire cartridge discarded.

It is interesting to read books of this period and to learn of the considerable opposition to the centre fire cartridge. The reason being because it was difficult to see if the gun was loaded. With a pin fire gun and cartridges one could see the pins projecting from the breech ends of the barrels. From then on progress was rapid.

The landed gentry in this country had the large acreages of land upon which almost unlimited game could be reared. They also had the money to buy the best guns available. The British gun trade had the vision and skills to evolve, design and produce, ever more efficient and beautiful shotguns. By the beginning of this century a pinnacle of excellence was reached in the design and manufacture of the side by side sidelock and boxlock hammerless ejector shotguns. The production and quality of these guns equalled, if not surpassed, those of anywhere else in the world.

With correct usage these high grade guns were almost everlasting. One famous side by side gun made by Boss and used in Birmingham for testing shotgun cartridges was credited with firing over a million and a half cartridges. All this usage only resulted in a barrel wear of less than one thousandth of one inch. So splendid were the materials used, so well made were these guns, and so long wearing were they proving, that the British gun trade is alleged to have looked around for new ideas, designs and improvements for its shotguns.

The side by side shotguns which the gun trade was making were simply lasting too long, being handed down from father to son or even grandson. The over and under shotgun, which had been made as a flintlock, was therefore rediscovered, redesigned, and brought up to date. This was hailed by the pundits as a great advance in the production of a more precisely pointing weapon.

The advertisements were full of the advantages, claiming that the shooting of an o/u gun was as precise as pointing with one finger. The shooting of the side by side gun then being likened to being as imprecise as pointing with three fingers. Surely, this must be one of the earliest examples of planned obsolescence.

In North America the vast quantities of wildfowl and game encouraged the development of both pump and semi-automatic guns. Both these types of gun usually had a capacity of four shots in the magazine and one in the barrel breech. They were much in demand and used by the market hunters. In addition the sport of shooting live pigeons released from boxes or traps was growing rapidly and many famous contests were shot between the leading marksmen of the time.

John Moses Browning (1855–1926), possibly the greatest of American gun designers, brought out his famous long recoil semi-automatic shotgun and had it made in Belgium. His final piece of shotgun design was the Browning Over and Under. The Belgium factory of FN tooled up for the production of this gun in the 1920s and even today the Browning o/u is still popular and rightly considered as a long wearing and hard shooting shotgun.

In the latter half of the nineteenth century the pastime of shooting live pigeons, starlings, and even sparrows was very popular. These birds were released by remote control from collapsible boxes called traps. Shooters were closely handicapped on their known form and shooting ability. This was done by 'yardage'. The less good shooters standing closer to the traps, shooters who won – and the prize stakes were often high indeed, being many thousands of pounds – were moved back further away from the traps. A similar system is used today, in the CPSA Down the Line handicap by Distance competitions.

By 1870 there had been many attempts to produce inanimate targets and machines to throw them. Glass balls, plain or stuffed with feathers; brass balls; small metal propellers; together with many other weird and wonderfully shaped targets had all been tried and found wanting.

In 1880 one Ligowski is alleged to have been watching some American youths skimming clam shells across the water. This gave him the idea of the saucer-shaped clay target. These were originally made from clay and fired in brick kilns. Because they were baked hard they were not easy to break, even when hit squarely with the 1¼ oz shot loads used at the time. Modern clay targets are manufactured from lime and pitch. The dimension for a standard target is 110 mm, with a tolerance of plus or minus 1 mm. Height is 25 to 26 mm and approximate weight 105 g with a plus or minus tolerance of 5 g.

Today we also have an assortment of clay targets which, although circular, are of different diameters and thicknesses. These are given various names such as mini-clays, midi-clays, battue, clay rabbits, through to the standard target.

Such varying targets may be used for FITASC or English Sporting clay target shooting. Clay targets were originally black, now they are produced in many colours. Shoot organizers try to provide targets of the required colour to allow such targets to be easily seen by the shooter, regardless of the background towards which, or against which, these targets are thrown. Any or all of these targets are thrown from a machine called a trap.

Basically a trap has a spring-loaded throwing arm, usually made of strong yet light alloy metal. The target is placed in its correct position upon the throwing arm. When a catch is released, or on some traps when the arm is pushed backwards over centre, the strong spring with which the trap is fitted causes rapid and partial rotation of this arm. The target then spins up and off the arm. Targets can be thrown for distances of up to 135 m. The spinning action imparted to the clay target by the trap arm and its running rail helps to maintain a reasonably stable flight trajectory, at least for the first 50 m.

In this country, the first ruling body of the sport was the Inanimate Bird Shooting Association – IBSA. Wimbledon Park was the scene of the first Championship in 1893. Each competitor shot at ten targets. The traps were usually set up in five banks of three traps, not unlike our modern Olympic Trench layouts, although the traps were generally set at ground level and shielded by sacking or hessian screens. Each competitor shot 'down the line'. That is, shooting at one target in turn from each bank of three traps. After this competitor had shot 'down the line' and killed or missed the five targets, a trapper ran forward and reloaded and cocked the five traps which had just been used. After which the trapper again retired behind the competitors. The next competitor then took his place on no. 1 firing point and shot 'down the line'. The traps being screened made it impossible for the shooter to know which trap of any bank of three was being used to throw the next target at which he had to fire; in addition he could not know the target's angle.

From this time onwards the progress of the sport of inanimate bird or target shooting was rapid. After a break for the 1914–18 war, clay target shooting started again in 1919.

Live pigeon shooting from traps was finally banned in this country in 1921, thereby encouraging the further development of clay target shooting. Automatic angling traps were introduced from the United States of America around 1923 and were soon being manufactured in this country under licence. The first Amateur Sporting Championship was held in 1925, and gave the sport another fillip.

The gunmaking firm of Holland and Holland has been running a shooting school since 1835. Sir Ralph Payne-Gallwey, a noted writer and authority on shotgun design and performance, had reported on the clay targets he had seen thrown when he visited Holland's school in 1896. The West London Shooting Grounds had also been in existence for some years at Perivale. All these factors encouraged the rapid growth of clay target shooting in two directions. We had the sport of clay target shooting as an end in itself. We also had the game shooter, who found clay target shooting both an enjoyable sport, as well as a great help towards his more accurate game shooting. Both King George v and his son, who was then Prince of Wales, used clay shooting to improve their game shooting skills, the Prince of Wales even having a clay trap installed on the stern of the battleship which he used when travelling overseas.

The first international match between England and Scotland was shot at Carlisle in 1925 when Scotland won. This was a feat which Scotland was to repeat some half a century later in another international.

With very few vicissitudes the sport has since grown continuously. Clay target shooting today – as with other sports – has many variations on an original theme and comes in many forms. Each form of clay shooting, or discipline as it is called, has its own rules, customs and taboos.

Down the Line

This is still the most popular clay shooting discipline. For this discipline we have a trap installed in an open-fronted house which has shot-proof sides, back and roof. This trap house is situated some 16 yd in front of a line of five markers or firing points, upon which the shooters stand. (See figs 1 and 2.)

All clays are thrown away from the shooter at a predictable height but at an unpredictable angle, travelling about 50 to 55 yd from the trap house. Two shots are allowed at each clay, a kill from the first shot scoring three points and one from the second, two points.

Double Rise

A variation of DTL, two clays being thrown simultaneously on fixed angles and predictable elevations. The shooter is allowed one shot at each clay. Scoring is five points for killing the two clays and two points for killing one clay of a pair. (See fig. 3.)

Although gun position is optional in both the above disciplines, the gun is usually mounted in the shoulder pocket before the shooters call for their clay target(s).

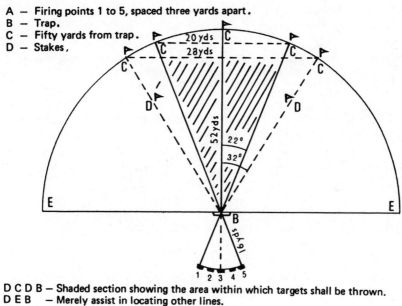

A — Firing points 1 to 5, spaced three yards apart.
B — Trap.
C — Fifty yards from trap.
D — Stakes.

D C D B — Shaded section showing the area within which targets shall be thrown.
D E B   — Merely assist in locating other lines.
B C   — Imaginary line.

1 Down the Line shooting.

A — Firing points 1 to 5,
   spaced three yards apart.

B — Trap.

2 Firing points for Down the Line.

Skeet

In Great Britain today there are three variations of Skeet shot. (See fig. 4.)

The International Shooting Union (ISU) or Olympic Skeet is shot with the shooter holding his gun butt at hip level and with a delay of up to three seconds occurring from the time the shooter calls for his target(s) until such target(s) are thrown. A round of Skeet consists of 25 targets

A   — Firing points 1 to 5, spaced three yards apart.
B   — Trap.
C   — Fifty yards from trap.
D   — Stakes.
D D B   — Shaded sections showing the areas within which targets shall be thrown.
F   — Arrows indicate the most desirable flights of targets.
G E B   — Merely assist in locating other lines.
B H   — Imaginary line.

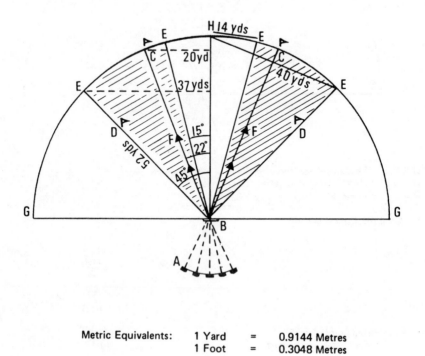

Metric Equivalents: 1 Yard   =   0.9144 Metres
                       1 Foot   =   0.3048 Metres

3 Double Rise shooting.

shot at from eight different firing points by each competitor. The clays are thrown a distance of 65 m at predictable angles and elevations.

American Skeet is shot over the same eight firing points as ISU. The target(s) are released immediately on shooter's call and are thrown a distance of 55 yd at predictable angles and elevations. Gun position is optional. A round consists of 25 targets.

In English Skeet the clay is released immediately on the call of 'Pull' or 'Mark' by the shooter. Gun position is optional. A round consists of 25 targets per competitor which he shoots at from seven different firing points. The clay targets are thrown 55 yd.

Olympic Trap or Trench

There are five firing points with three traps placed in the ground some 15 m in front of each point. The shooter may be thrown any one target

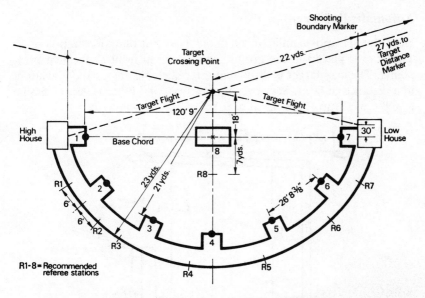

4 ISU Skeet layout. English Skeet omits Station 8 and target flight is 55 yd.

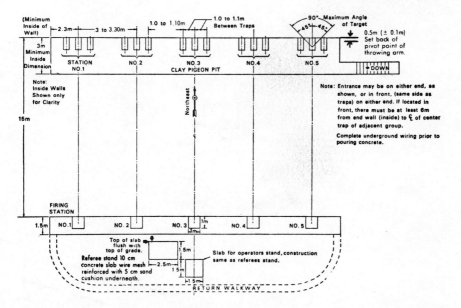

5 Olympic Trap or Trench.

from any one of the three traps. He is allowed two shots at each target. Scoring one point per kill, regardless of whether he kills with the first shot or the second shot. The clay targets may be thrown at set angles and distances of up to 80 m. Gun position optional. (See fig. 5.)

Automatic Ball Trap

Here the set-up is similar to Olympic Trap but only one trap is used. This trap is placed in the ground some 15 m in front of the five firing points. The clay target is thrown at unpredictable angles and elevations to a distance of 80 m. Scoring, gun position, and other rules are similar to Olympic Trap. (See figs 6 to 9.)

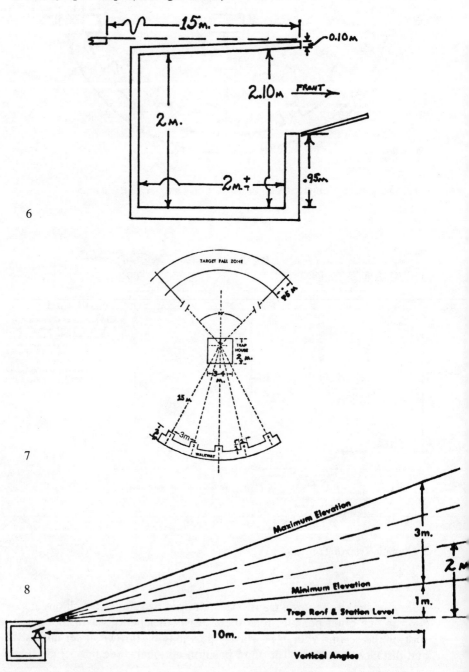

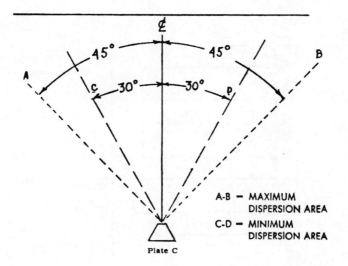

A-B — MAXIMUM
DISPERSION AREA
C-D — MINIMUM
DISPERSION AREA

Plate C

9

6–9 Automatic Ball Trap. (8) shows the target elevations and (9) the horizontal angles.

Universal Trench

This is very similar to Olympic Trap. There are five firing points, but only five traps. The shooter may be thrown one target from any one of the five traps. This discipline is very popular in Europe. Scoring, gun position, and other rules are similar to Olympic Trap or Automatic Ball Trap. (See figs 10 and 11.)

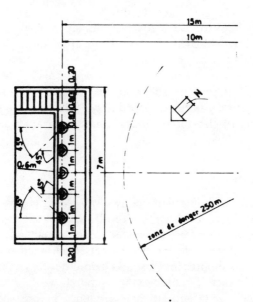

10 Universal Trench, plan view of a trench and supports for the traps.

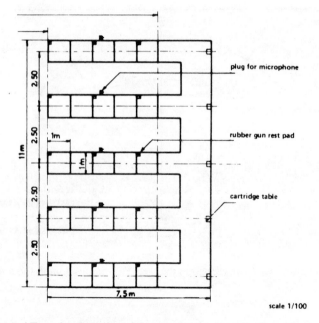

scale 1/100

plug for microphone

rubber gun rest pad

cartridge table

11 Universal Trench, plan view of the shooting stations at 10 m, 12 m and 15 m, and the points for microphone plugs.

Sporting Clays

These are clay targets thrown on trajectories which simulate live bird shooting in the field. For instance, a target may be thrown almost vertically into the air in front of the shooter, and would be classified as a 'springing teal'. Targets may be thrown as singles or in pairs from behind a high bank of earth towards the shooter, the shooter being placed in a protective cage to prevent him from turning around. Such target(s) are called 'driven partridge'. Targets may be thrown off a high tower of up to 120 ft to simulate 'driven pheasants'. It will be realized that there are an infinite number and variations of target heights, speed and flight which may occur in Sporting clay shoots. In addition, today (1983) a variety of clay targets may be used, with such names as mini, midi, battue, rabbits, etc.

FITASC Sporting

An even harder discipline with its own rules, and is possibly the most exciting and demanding discipline of all. Special sporting layouts are designed. The shooters are squadded. Each squad goes around one layout with a referee and scorer. Targets from each firing point are shown to the first shooter in the squad before he shoots. The rest of the squad follows in turn. On the next firing point, another member of the squad is shown the targets in their sequence before shooting. After which the rest of the squad members shoot in turn. No competitor is allowed to watch targets being shot by members of another squad. Targets are thrown silent rise and the gun butt must be visibly out of the shoulder pocket until the target is visible in the air.

ZZ Target Shooting

The final discipline is zz target shooting. This was first seen in 1963, being designed to supplant live pigeon shooting in Monte Carlo. The zz target usually has a white plastic central disc, set in a circle to which are attached two wings of propeller shape. There are five traps set in a line in front of the shooter similar to the five traps used to house live pigeons. Each of the five traps has an electric motor which has the zz target mounted on its spindle. When the shooter is ready the trapper switches on all five motors and the targets begin spinning. At the same time the motors and zz targets are spinning they are also oscillating. When the shooter calls for his target, a zz target is released at random from one of the five traps. The released target can, and does, go almost anywhere, due to the angle of the motor, the spin of the target and the prevailing wind. The shooter is allowed two barrels at any one target. He has to knock out the target's centre white disc which has to fall inside a perimeter boundary fence. Gun position is optional.

Handicaps are carefully designed to allow shooters to compete on reasonably equal terms. However, luck must play a part, due mainly to wind variation. Most competitions are shot over ten targets, shoot-offs, on a system of sudden death, or miss and out, are the rules.

It is an exciting sport to watch but has not yet become popular in Britain. National championships have been staged at the Blandford and Dorchester Gun Club. For most people, however, it takes too much time and costs too much money.

The CPSA

The ruling body of the sport is called the Clay Pigeon Shooting Association (CPSA). This has been in existence for over half a century. The president is Roy Greatorex, an ex-shooter who gave up competitive clay shooting to devote much more than his spare time to the needs of the Association.

Peter Page has recently retired as the director, February 1985, he had been associated with the CPSA ever since 1937. He had a break for war service, rejoining on demobilization. He became assistant secretary in 1946, joint secretary in 1956, and secretary in 1962. Finally he was made director in 1970, a position that he filled with distinction until his retirement.

The new director is Keith Murray, one of our most active and best known clayshooters. A member of the CPSA since 1961, he has had much to do with the growth of the sport. He has organised clayshooting events from local charity shoots to world championships, studied ISU Skeet coaching in the USA, was a member of the British shooting team 1974 and 1976 and was team manager on two overseas tours. He also served as Chairman of the International Board 1977–84. His enthusiasm, personality and extensive experience will bring much to the sport.

There is an Executive Committee composed of people who have had wide experience of clay target shooting in many parts of the world. These people give freely of their time and the experience they have gained. The year-by-year growth of the Association is due largely to their activities.

The CPSA offices are now in Buckhurst Hill, Epping. Here a small but dedicated staff often work long and unsocial hours administering the sport and looking after their members. The inevitable computer is in use, this means that the CPSA bible or book of members' averages seems to be published earlier and earlier every year.

Michael Alldis, the first development officer, resigned in May 1983 to found and run his own shooting school, 'The Essex'. The present development officer is Brian Hammond, who, with Clarrie Wilson, the current national coach, organises courses for would-be clay shooting coaches, referees, and safety officers nominated by affiliated clubs.

Any query regarding clay target shooting has only to be sent to the CPSA address at the back of this book and a large SAE enclosed. Usually the enquirer will receive a prompt reply. The normal literature he will receive includes the pamphlet *Score with your Bird*, the CPSA *Ten Commandments for Safer Clay Shooting*, and a booklet *How to Start a Clay Club*. Rule books for the different disciplines are available to members who send £1.50 per book plus a large SAE.

All paid-up members of the Association are covered third party insurance for up to a million pounds on any one claim. Such an insurance is vital for all clay shooters. Guns can be lethal instruments and anyone can make a mistake. Therefore, I stress, that the CPSA clay target insurance scheme for members is a fine thing. Membership of the Association with its very modest fee must be very worthwhile for this insurance alone.

The Welsh and Scottish CPSA are also very good go-ahead organizations. Both Associations have the welfare of their members paramount.

Periodicals

The official organ was the *Shooting Magazine*, published monthly. Therein one can still obtain time and place of CPSA affliated club fixtures. Also shoot reports, tests on various new guns and cartridges, answers to clay and rough shooters' questions, reports on CPSA coaching courses, referees' courses, safety officers' courses, etc., plus Association news. In addition, many clay clubs and shooting grounds advertise their activities, as do numerous specialist gun, clay trap, cartridge and clothing suppliers.

The Shooting Times is an old established weekly. For many years it was the official organ of the CPSA. At the present there is a half page devoted to CPSA news and events, plus a page of clay club fixtures each week. Tests on guns, cartridges and equipment appear frequently. Photos and reports are given on the bigger national and international shoots. There are many pages of advertisements covering clay or game shooters' requirements. Another feature is a monthly page of advertisements for shooting schools.

Sporting Gun is a monthly magazine catering for clay and game shooters, providing clay club fixture lists, photos and reports of many shoots, and tests on guns and cartridges. Advice is given on gun maintenance, with many advertisements from gun, cartridge, clay trap, clothing and accessory suppliers, plus details of shooting schools.

Guns Review is a monthly magazine giving detailed gun tests, together with some advice on clay shooting. Also advertisements from most suppliers of gun and shooting requisites.

CPSA clubs

CPSA affiliated clubs run registered shoots for members only. Members' scores in registered shoots are returned by the clubs to the Association and then fed into the computer. The end product being the CPSA *Annual Averages Book*. By this means members are classified according to their average scores during the year in the different disciplines in which they have shot. The idea being that members of like performance compete against each other. This is an attempt by the CPSA to preserve the equity of any competition which clubs may run.

At the present time clay target shooting is booming as never before. In Britain it must be increasingly rare for any prospective clay shooter not to be able to find a club, in fact several clubs, within easy motoring distance of his home. Most clubs shoot on Sundays, plus the odd evening meeting during the week for practice, training and coaching.

Some fortunate clubs have floodlights installed, and hardy souls that their members are shoot in the evenings, even throughout the winter months, regardless of the daylight hours. The larger clubs have full facilities including restaurants, toilets and club rooms with television for the families and friends who have come with club members.

Resident coaches, safety officers, and other officials of the club are always in attendance. Some clubs have gun shops on the premises allowing prospective customers to try various guns under expert supervision before buying.

The better clubs, and they are in the great majority, have the best interests of their members at heart, regardless of how well a member shoots. What all club officials and members insist upon is that the members shall be *safe* and be seen to be *safe*.

Any new member who is unsure how to behave safely should ask an official, who will be glad to help. As one club puts on its advertising posters, 'It is not how good a shot you are – it is how *safe* you are'.

Mercifully, the CPSA records of accidents with shotguns are very rare indeed, and everybody connected with clay shooting should try and keep it that way.

2 Modern Shotguns & Cartridges

Shotguns

It is not possible in the space available to provide full details of all the guns on sale today for clay target shooting. There are five main types of shotguns.

1   Single barrel, single-loading guns.

2   Double barrel, side by side guns.

3   Double barrel, over and under guns.

4   Single barrel, semi-automatic or self-loading guns with magazine capacities for up to seven cartridges.

5   Single barrel pump guns with magazine capacities of up to six cartridges.

The single and double barrel guns can have either box or sidelock actions with internal or external hammers or tumblers. They can be fitted out as either ejector or non-ejector guns. Briefly the specifications for modern shotguns together with some of the options available are as follows.

1a   Single-barrelled Hammer Guns with or without Ejectors
These are rarely used for clay target shooting in this country.

1b   Single-barrelled Hammerless Guns
Either box or sidelock, with or without ejectors, with or without solid or ventilated ribs.

In the United States, and in other parts of the world where DTL shooting is strictly single barrel, the specialist single barrel shotgun with a long barrel, ventilated rib and correctly fitted stock is rightly popular. High grade guns, such as the American single barrel Ithaca with its ventilated rib and long barrel, can command a high price on the secondhand market. There is also a demand for new guns of this type which has led to them being again manufactured.

The Italian Perazzi and Belgian Browning are also producing o/u guns with an extra single barrel to fit the same action. Until the British DTL rules are changed there will be little need for these single barrel guns in this country.

2   Side by Side Hammer Guns, with or without Ejectors

There are available imported, low-price, non-ejector hammer side by side guns. As for hammer ejector guns, these are rare birds indeed. The Italian firm of Famars is producing a self-cocking hammer ejector gun. Using a combination of modern high-quality steels, sophisticated machinery and top-class workmanship, this gun has old-fashioned and pleasing lines coupled with a performance on clay targets equal to that of any modern hammerless side by side shotgun.

Side by side hammerless guns may be ejector or non-ejector. The barrels may be any length from 25 to 32 in., chambered and bored as required. The locks can be side or boxlock. The triggers can be double or solid, or double with the front trigger articulated. Single non-selective or single selective triggers are also available. Ribs can be swamped, single raised, raised ventilated, and of varying widths.

The top surface of the rib may be smooth, matted, cross-milled, or file-cut as specified.

Stocks can be straight hand, half or full pistol grip. Combs can be sloping or Monte Carlo. Butts may have natural surfaces, be fitted with recoil pads, or composition heel plates. Fore-ends can be splinter, half or full beavertail. A few side by side guns are still in use although the most notable exponent of such a gun no longer shoots.

This gentleman is the legendary Percy Stanbury. He bought a side by side Webley and Scott boxlock hammerless ejector gun with single trigger, 30 in. barrels, bored full and full, with raised file cut rib, in the 1920s. Since that time he competed with no other. His record with this gun is remarkable. He represented England in international matches 26 times, he won National Skeet, Sporting and DTL championships many times.

Stanbury with his Webley and Scott gun was an almost unbeatable combination over many years. Their record is a fitting tribute to a fine shooter and an equally fine English-made shotgun.

Stanbury told me recently that at one time he was shooting some 500 cartridges per week and that his Webley and Scott had fired some hundreds of thousands of cartridges while in his possession.

At the present time those shooters who have the time and money can still obtain top-quality side by side hammerless ejector guns built to almost any specification. The British gun trade can still produce the best there is – at a price and given time. For those who are short of either of the above commodities but who still wish to have a specialist-built, side by side gun, all is not lost. The Italian makers of Beretta, Famars, Perazzi and Piochi, together with the Spanish Aya and Ugartechea, will still build high-performance, top-quality guns, capable of standing up to years of hard work.

Such guns will not be cheap and almost inevitably there will be a waiting time; if so, it is usually months and not years. Guns of this quality can be taken into any company. The importers advertise in the shooting press and will be delighted to quote and supply.

Lower down the price scale Japanese Miroku and Italian Fabarm and

Winchester also build side by sides, either box or sidelocks. Guns of this quality are readily available, give little trouble and, like the great majority of new guns today, are good value for money.

3   The Over and Under Shotgun

Possibly the most popular clay target gun at the present time in use in Great Britain. Available to almost any specification. Barrel lengths from 25 to 34 in. Chambered and choked to suit, or supplied with interchangeable screw-in chokes. Top ribs can be solid, ventilated, flat, or stepped in various widths and top surfaces. Side ribs are solid, ventilated or non-existent. Action is box or sidelock, ejector or non-ejector. Triggers are double, single non-selective or single selective, with fixed or detachable and interchangeable trigger assemblies. Stocks can be to almost any specification, with straight hand, half pistol, full pistol, with or without recoil pad, which may be solid or ventilated, adjustable or non-adjustable. Stock comb can be normal or Monte Carlo, cast off or on as required. The fore-end can be splinter, schnozzle or beavertail. The clay shooter who cannot find today a gun to suit his specification and pocket among the o/u range must be choosey indeed.

4   The Single Barrel Semi-Automatic or Self-Loading Shotgun

Still produced abroad in large quantities at a reasonable price, these guns are rightly popular among clay target shooters.

Interchangeable barrels can be obtained in lengths from 25 to 34 in., chambered and choked to suit. Alternatively, barrels are available with chokes that screw on, like the Breda. Those which screw in, like the Winchester and Perazzi, or those which drop in like the Beretta. There is also available the Cutts compensator which can be fitted to semi-automatic barrels by specialist firms. These compensators have a full range of choke tubes which screw in, from spreader to full. Barrel ribs can be solid or ventilated, stepped or flat, floating or fixed, of varying widths, and with varying anti-reflecting surfaces.

Stocks can have straight hand, or pistol grips, and combs can be sloping or Monte Carlo. Recoil pads are available of composition, solid or ventilated rubber. Stocks are usually straight or have little cast off or on. For left-handers who find the empty cases thrown across their faces off-putting, Remington semi-automatics are now available which load and eject on the left-hand side.

Semi-automatics can be slightly more choosey concerning ammunition than normal guns. Nevertheless, correctly maintained, used with suitable cartridges, these guns have won many competitions including the 1981 FITASC Sporting World Championship and are justly popular among clay target shooters. Their design does seem to spread the apparent recoil, making them popular with shooters who are recoil sensitive. For clay target shooting in Great Britain only two cartridges are permitted to be loaded at any one time. When not in use the bolt should always be back in the open position.

5 Pump Guns

These guns are similar to the semi-automatics described above. Specifications for barrels, chokes, ribs, stocks, etc., are very much the same. The main difference between pump and semi-automatics being that the shooter himself, by tromboning or pumping the fore-end on its slide, ejects the empty case and feeds in the second cartridge.

These guns are not often used in this country, although there have been a few notable shooters who have done well with them. They are still very popular for Single Barrel DTL shooting in the United States.

Special Guns

Disabled shooters, or disabled would-be shooters, whether due to loss of hand, arm or leg, arthritis, rheumatics, even those confined to a wheelchair, seldom realize how guns can be tailored to meet their personal needs. These guns can be easy opening, balanced to suit the shooter, and for one-armed people have anatomically formed and well-fitted pistol grips.

A skilled gun fitter working in harmony with gunmaker and shooter can nearly always produce a suitable special gun. The subject is too vast to cover in this book, but those interested are advised to visit a gunmaker and take full advantage of his knowledge. Holland and Holland of London who now own W. & C. Scott of Birmingham, and Purdey of London have centuries of experience between them. The writer knows many disabled shooters whose specially designed and fitted guns have given them great pleasure, both in ownership and performance.

Finally, let it be clearly understood that a modern shotgun of good quality and well maintained, which can be loaded and fired with two cartridges, will prove to be far more consistent in performance than its owner.

With barrels correctly bored, stock correctly fitted, championships have been won and will continue to be won, by side by sides, over and unders, and semi-automatics. This is regardless of the country in which such guns were manufactured.

Cartridges

The most popular cartridge in this country for clay shooting is of 12 gauge. These cartridges can be obtained with shot loadings ranging from $\frac{7}{8}$ oz through to $1\frac{1}{4}$ oz. Shot sizes allowable and available range from English size 6, with its shot pellets diameter of .100 in., approximate metric equivalent 2.60 mm, through to English size 9, pellet diameter .080 in., approximate metric equivalent 2 mm.

The cartridge case can be of paper or plastic. The plastic case can be a simple tube with a base wad plus a metal head. Or it can be compression formed with a plastic head and tube all in the one piece. The heads of both cases are metal covered.

Advantages and Disadvantages of Paper and Plastic Cases

The paper case, although water resisting, can be an unmitigated nuisance in really wet weather conditions. An example of note was at the European Championships some years ago. A foreign team was using foreign paper-cased cartridges, which were swelling in the damp conditions prevailing. In fact, so much so, that the team manager had a large screwdriver with which to lever out the swollen cases. The team, however, still won major honours in spite of this trouble.

Plastic cases are usually waterproof and perform well. There can be problems for shooters who use them for Turner team type shoots. The reason being that static can build up and with some guns and some plastic-cased cartridges the ejectors will malfunction. For all other types of clay target shooting this does not matter.

Case Crimp
Modern cartridges, whether plastic- or paper-cased, are usually pie crimped. The crimp may be of six or eight segments, both of which are efficient. The pie crimp does away with the overshot wad, which was the cause of many blown patterns in the past. So much was this so, that the Americans claimed a big increase in perfect scores in Single Barrel 27 yd Distance shooting when the pie crimp was introduced and the overshot wad discarded.

Percussion Caps
For many years the chemical used in the cap was responsible for much corrosion and rusting of gun barrel interiors. Today most of the cartridges available in Britain have non-corrosive caps. Even so the prudent shooter, if in doubt, should check with his usual supplier. Caps used to be made of copper, now the material is more likely to be steel. There have been troubles due to this; if the cap is too hard, misfiring may occur. If too thin, the striker pin may rupture the cap, thereby allowing a super hot jet of burning gas to hit the end of the firing pin. Even one ruptured cap can cause erosion and pitting of a firing pin and subsequent misfiring. Having said all that, experience over the last 50 years has shown that weak or damaged main springs, short or incorrectly contoured striker pin noses are much more likely to be the cause of cartridge malfunction than hard or soft percussion caps.

Powder
The bigger cartridge manufacturers have been making cartridges by the million for many years. Their powder is manufactured in batches and each batch code numbered. When a factory switches on to a new batch of powder, test loadings are always made and the resulting cartridges fired through a special pressure barrel. Careful reading of the pressures and velocities produced are noted. The powder load is adjusted until the pressures produced are correct, only then will cartridges be loaded for sale to the public.

Guns with English proof and $2\frac{1}{2}$ in. chambers were proof marked for pressures of 3 tons to the square inch and the usual maximum shot load was $1\frac{1}{8}$ oz. Guns with English proof and $2\frac{3}{4}$ in. chambers were proof marked to $3\frac{1}{4}$ tons to the square inch and the shot load was $1\frac{1}{4}$ oz. Both the $1\frac{1}{8}$ oz shot load for $2\frac{1}{2}$ in. chambers and the $1\frac{1}{4}$ oz shot load for $2\frac{3}{4}$ in. chambers were considered safe and all was well until some years ago. Then the competition rules were changed and the old Olympic Trench load of $1\frac{1}{4}$ oz was no longer permitted for any discipline except FITASC Sporting. However, modern shooters demanded a new cartridge with a $1\frac{1}{8}$ oz shot load similar in performance to the $1\frac{1}{4}$ oz load and as cartridge manufacturers are in business to provide what the clay shooter requires, they produced a high-performance $1\frac{1}{8}$ oz shot load cartridge. The new Eley Olympic Blue is an example. This cartridge with $1\frac{1}{8}$ oz shot load is designed to be used in $2\frac{3}{4}$ in. chambered guns and a proof pressure of $3\frac{1}{4}$ tons to the square inch. It is not suitable, nor was it designed, for use in $2\frac{1}{2}$ in. chambered guns proofed for 3 tons to the square inch pressures. English cartridge makers print these facts on their cartridge boxes. Should a shooter have any doubt he should seek advice from his supplier.

Wads
The majority of cartridges today use a plastic wad. These come in many shapes and as a rule tend to produce slightly tighter patterns than the old type of felt or fibre wad. Even so, there is at least one Skeet cartridge on the market which has a plastic wad, and yet the patterns thrown are equally as wide as those produced by felt- or fibre-wadded cartridges.

For DTL, Olympic Trench, and similar types of disciplines the plastic or mono wadded cartridge is at present most popular. For Skeet, the felt or fibre wad is still in favour. This holds even more true with the retro-choked type of gun barrel.

Lead Pellets
The rules state lead pellets, spherical, with sizes ranging from English size 6 shot to English size 9 shot being allowed. Such shot may be nickel plated in an attempt to increase its hardness and therefore resistance to malformation when being fired up the barrel.

Considerable research has been done on shot sizes and hardness. Kynoch – now Eley – did a lot of work in the early part of this century and Eley still carries on this tradition in its search for perfection. Major Sir G. Burrard also experimented after World War I (see his book, *The Modern Shotgun*). The American and Continental makers have been, and still are, similarly engaged. Peters, the great American cartridge makers, spent much time and money in the 1920s on the stringing of shot and produced spark photographs illustrating the formation of shot charges in flight. Some of the latest work to be published has been done by Bob Brister, an American shooter and an avid shotgun experimenter. He, by using a station wagon which towed a long trailer with pattern sheets on the side, has shown the advantage of hard shot and plastic wads for long distance shooting. He also demonstrated the advantages of soft, easily deformed lead shot and trumpet chokes for increasing the shot string for Skeet and other short-range shooting. The patterns he produced are illustrated in his book, *Shotgunning: the Art and the Science*.

Any modern shooter should be able to obtain a suitable cartridge to suit his barrel chokings and produce patterns of sufficient pellet density to break any target at which he shoots. See Chapter on Shotgun Patterns.

Storage of Ammunition

The manufacturer's advice should be followed. Modern cartridges are wonderfully stable and consistent in use. They should, however, be stored at temperatures around 60° to 65° F. They should not be stored in the airing cupboard, or near heaters, especially in modern, high-temperature, centrally heated houses. Nor should they be left in a closed car boot in the sun. High-temperature storage can produce high pressures when such cartridges are fired. These high pressures are due to shooter negligence and he can blame nobody but himself.

Really cold conditions, and by this is meant refrigerator-type temperatures, should be avoided. The writer has only once had trouble, this was in the winter of 1928/9, when the problem cartridges had been stupidly stored in an outhouse for many weeks during intense frost. Again the poor results obtained were due entirely to shooter negligence.

Storage Life

Well-made, correctly stored cartridges can be expected to be kept successfully for at least ten years, after which time they will usually still out-perform the shooter.

Other Gauges

The same basics hold generally true for smaller gauges. At the present time there is a small upswing towards lighter guns and smaller gauges. This is nothing new; it is a shooting fashion which happens once a decade and is usually short-lived.

The modern 12-gauge cartridge has been carefully evolved over many years. The laws of action and reaction are exactly the same as they have always been. W. W. Greener's formula of a 96 to 1 ratio of gun weight to shot load still holds good. Those shooters who are sensitive to recoil would, I believe, shoot far better and in much more comfort if they used for their clay shooting the heaviest gauge gun they could handle, in conjunction with as light a load as possible.

Experience has proved that the combination of a heavy gun plus a lightly loaded cartridge, such as the Eley 1 oz Impax, or Hull Cartridge $\frac{15}{16}$ oz, has produced many good scores in the past. This marriage of heavy gun and light load makes for a stable pointing gun which keeps swinging easily. The low recoil from the light load helps the shooter to be more accurate with his second shot.

I cannot understand the logic of marrying a light 20-bore gun, of possibly less than 6 lb weight, with a 3 in. cased heavy load cartridge.

Such marriages usually prove painful to the shooter and are best avoided.

The shooter should eventually, by experiment and experience, correctly marry up his gun and cartridge to suit a particular discipline. He can be sure, however, that good-quality modern cartridges, like their equivalent in modern shotguns, will prove to be far more consistent in performance than any shooter.

3 Gun & Cartridge Specifications for the Various Disciplines

The Going-away Disciplines

The Gun

All shotguns, including semi-automatics, may be used, providing the calibre does not exceed 12 gauge. The four disciplines of Olympic Trap, Automatic Ball Trap, Five Trap Universal and British Down the Line are all concerned with targets thrown away from the shooter on mainly angling and rising trajectories. The target distances thrown can vary from 75 m plus for Olympic Trap, to 50 m for DTL. Two shots are allowed at each target. Modern trap guns are stocked straight in the hand with a comb height which will give the shooter a high sighting plane. This should allow him to see a fair amount of rib. Trap guns of this specification should print their pellet patterns slightly above their point of aim. The idea of all this is to enable the target to be kept in view and above the muzzles at all times. A quick second shot can then be taken, should be first shot result in a miss.

Shooters who use a low or flat shooting trap gun do, I believe, handicap themselves. To break the target they have to blot out the sight of it with their gun muzzles when firing their first shot. If a miss results, the shooter will not know until the rising and unbroken target reappears once more above the gun muzzle. He has then, once more, to blot out the target before firing his second shot. All of this makes for time-consuming, uncertain shooting. The further a target travels the more irregular will be its trajectory.

To ascertain correct comb height and stock dimensions see Chapter 4 on the try-gun, gun fitting and gun stock alterations.

Barrels and Barrel Lengths

Long barrels do seem to enable most shooters to point more accurately. For the disciplines in question accurate gun pointing is essential.

Going away targets incorrectly read will invariably be missed. Any inaccuracy in gun pointing when shooting at these targets will result in the divergence of the shot flight compared with the target trajectory. The further the target and shot pattern travels away from the shooter the greater will be the error and divergence. A missed target will be inevitable.

The most popular barrel length for trap guns today is 30 in. The 32 in. is, however, becoming more popular, especially among our younger and stronger shooters.

Top Ribs and their Widths

Championships have been won with ventilated ribs of almost every height and width. The essentials are that the top rib should be well ventilated to reduce mirage or heat haze around the rib and above it. The top surface of the rib should be anti-glare. This can be achieved by cross-milling, file cutting, and many other methods which result in a non-reflecting surface, even when the gun is pointing towards the sun. Ideally, of course, clay target layouts should not face the sun. Unfortunately, this desirable state of affairs is not always practicable.

Top rib widths can be anything from 3 to 18 mm. Good scores have been and still are shot with narrow 3 mm width ribs, with midi 10 mm width ribs, and wide 18 mm width ribs. Basically, I believe, the choice of top rib width is a personal one, depending upon the individual shooter's preference, or, even, his idiosyncracies. It has happened many times that a shooter changing from narrow to broad ribs may find his score improved. The reason for this being that the broader rib and sight picture ensures a greater lateral lead being given to the target. This enables the shot string to be placed more on the leading edge of the target. However, within a very short time the average shooter will be back to his old evil ways, and once more hitting the trailing edge of his targets with the leading edge of his shot patterns. This action of his will ensure that the slightest check will result in a miss behind.

Side Ribs on Over and Unders

These may be solid, ventilated, or even non-existent. In my experience, guns with no side ribs keep cooler. They swing more easily, especially in cross-winds.

Sights

The front sight can be white, red, green, yellow, fluorescent, or whatever colour the shooter fancies. Some shooters copy the tricks of yesteryears' live pigeon shooters such as the Hon. S. R. Beresford. He used a different sight to suit different light conditions and backgrounds. Too bright a front sight can be a distraction to some shooters; similarly, too small or too dark a front sight can also cause problems. The choice is there for the shooter and only he can obtain the correct answer.

Intermediate or Centre Sights

These, if fitted, are small and usually white. They can assist in two ways. When the gun is mounted correctly the two sights should be in line laterally. If not, the shooter should correct his gun mount. This should take care of gun canting, poor head and cheek to gun comb relationship. The position of front and centre sights in a vertical plane should produce a sight picture similar to an upside down figure-of-eight. The front sight should be sat upon the small centre sight. All of which should assist in consistent and accurate gun mounting and help to reduce the variables.

Barrel Chokings

Due to the excellence of modern cartridges and the absence of that producer of cartwheel patterns, the overshot wad, barrel chokings can now be more open. Years ago full choke was standard, in fact in the 1920s Major Sir G. Burrard proved mathematically that even 1¼ oz shot, size 7, in a full choke barrel was inadequate for DTL shooting.

Now we have champions who shoot and win at the more demanding Olympic Trench or Automatic Ball Trap disciplines while using guns bored half choke first barrel, and full choke second barrel. Some shooters even have guns bored as open as quarter and three-quarter choke. Much of course depends upon how quickly the shooter performs. It is better for our beginners to commence with three-quarter and full choke if using a double-barrelled gun. For semi-automatics full choke barrels should be the first choice. Eventually, the shooter himself will ascertain the best and most suitable choke or choked barrel to suit his speed and style. Chokes can be easily opened and regulated by a skilled barrel borer to suit a specific cartridge, shot size and shot load. Unfortunately, the chokes of a gun can be just as easily ruined irrevocably by a barrel boring gun butcher.

Type of Action

Double-barrelled guns can be obtained with either box or sidelock actions. It used to be generally agreed that the sidelock action properly tuned provided better trigger pulls, i.e. light and crisp, than the boxlock.

Today I firmly believe that either type of action correctly designed, with sears and bents properly angled and hardened, can be adjusted to have light, short, and crisp trigger pulls. Furthermore, they will hold their tune indefinitely. Even the modern semi-automatic tuned by an expert gunsmith should have good trigger pulls.

Single or Double Triggers

Regardless of popular opinion double triggers can be released just as quickly as single triggers. Modern single triggers are very reliable and very fashionable but World Championships have been won with double-triggered guns. Again, this must be a matter of personal choice and usage. (See Chapter 12 on loss of form.)

Mainsprings, Coil or Vee

Both types of main springs are very reliable. It used to be claimed that the Vee spring was quicker. Now we have guns like the Remington 3200 which claims super fast lock times for their coil mainspring actions.

Ejectors

These are nice on a cold day when one's fingers have no feeling but they are not really essential. The Russians with their Vostok non-ejectors seem to win Championships well enough. Non-ejectors when open should lift cartridges or cases far enough out of the barrel chamber to allow even gloved fingers to remove same without fumbling. All double guns, whether side by side or o/u should have actions which stay open at full gape. This gape should be wide enough to allow easy loading and unloading. It is regrettable that some double guns due either to faulty design or assembly do have a considerable amount of overrun. This defect causes the gun to close partially after being fully open and will cause loading difficulty. If due to poor assembly a skilled gunfitter can usually rectify quickly. If due to poor design the gun should be left in the gun shop, unbought.

Safety Catches

These should be manual. To prevent unauthorized interference some competitors mechanically fix their safety catches permanently in the firing position. Guns such as the Krieghoff are supplied with a hidden locking screw.

Gun Weight

Competitions are shot over four stages of 25 targets. Therefore, a shooter may shoot 100 to 150 cartridges during a day's competition, with the possibility of another 30 to 75 cartridges if he becomes involved in a shoot-off.

As has been explained, there are immutable laws of action and reaction. The lighter the gun weight the lighter should be the shot load. Excessive recoil will in turn create problems resulting in bruised cheeks, sore muscles, gun headache, head lifting and eventually produce the dreaded twitch or flinch (see Chapter 12). A gun weight of $7\frac{1}{2}$ to $8\frac{1}{2}$ lb is usually recommended. I personally would always choose and shoot the heaviest gun that I could handle with comfort.

Suitable Cartridges

Maximum shot load is $1\frac{1}{8}$ oz or 32 g. Maximum shot size English 6. Pellets must be spherical and are of hardened lead and may be nickel plated. Cartridges for the foregoing disciplines are usually loaded with plastic or mono wads. The mono wad protects the pellets as they travel up the barrel and the harder shot will suffer less deformation. All of which results in a high performance and tightly patterning cartridge.

In the years when DTL was almost the only going away discipline shot with targets travelling a maximum distance of 55 yd, shot deformation mattered less.

The traps in use were the Black Diamond or equivalent and were hand-loaded by the trapper. Correctly maintained and operated these traps were smooth functioning. This allowed targets to be manufactured which could be easily broken by a few shot pellets. All this has changed. ABT and OT layouts are numerous. The targets thrown are spun off the trap arm at speeds of maybe 90 mph and thrown distances of 80 m or more. Some traps today are automatically loaded, the targets being dropped onto the trap arm. There is often also a certain amount of inbuilt trap vibration. For these and other reasons target manufacturers have been compelled to produce harder targets to withstand these increased stresses. The modern target is therefore harder to break than those of 20 years ago. With the older, softer target some shooters even used size 9 shot cartridges for their first barrel, with 8, 7½ or 7 shot sizes for their second barrel.

Today possibly the most popular shot size for first barrel shooting is 7½, with 7 or even 6½ size shot in use for the second barrel. The present-day competitor can, however, still rest assured that modern good quality cartridges with shot sizes 6½, 7 or 7½ of either hard lead or nickel shot produce enough energy to break targets more consistently than the shooter. He should also derive comfort from the fact that the shot charge is travelling much faster than even the fastest clay target. Therefore, if this shot charge is fired on a correct course in relation to the target's trajectory, the pellets will always catch up with and break the target. This is regardless of whether the shot size is 6½, 7 or 7½.

The Skeet Disciplines

The Gun

All shotguns, including semi-automatics, may be used providing the calibre does not exceed 12 gauge. Changing of guns between stations or firing points during a round is not permitted unless the referee has accepted a gun malfunction which cannot be repaired quickly. Skeet targets are usually taken at distances from a few feet up to 25 yd. Station 1 high or Station 7 low targets may be shot legally at distances of up to 40 yd by novices or very slow shooters. Ideally, most competitors try and kill their targets near to the crossing point. This ensures, except for Station 8, that the majority of targets will be taken at a distance of 21 yd. Championships have been won in the past with side by sides, o/us, semi-automatics, and pump guns.

Today the o/us or the semi-automatic shotguns are the most popular, with the side by side or pump gun rarely seen in the big competitions.

The remarks made earlier in the chapter on the going-away disciplines concerning gun actions, lockwork, trigger or triggers, safety catches, ejectors, rib widths and sights, hold equally true for Skeet guns.

The essential criteria for an ideal Skeet gun are as follows – butt shape, stock fit, balance, barrel lengths, ribs and borings.

The majority of shooters require their guns to shoot flat and true to point of aim. For the English and American Skeet discipline, where gun position is optional, there are shooters who, by premounting their guns, can achieve good scores even with an ill-fitting gun. For ISU Skeet, the unpredictable time of target release, plus the extra speed of the targets, together with the rigidly defined gun-down position, places a premium on smooth, speedy, and accurate gun mounting. The slightest mismount can result in a missed target.

The butt shape should fit the shooter's shoulder pocket accurately. The comb height should fix accurately the shooter's eye position, so that it is looking straight along the barrel rib. All this applies when the gun is correctly mounted.

Gun Balance

This has been usually at or about the hinge pin with double guns. Fashions change, and some top shooters now prefer to have their guns slightly muzzle heavy. This they rightly believe helps their guns to keep swinging without check.

Barrel Lengths

Again fashions change, today the most popular length is $27\frac{1}{2}$ to 28 in., with a few shooters still using $26\frac{1}{2}$ or even 30 in. The theory, again borne out in practice, is that $26\frac{1}{2}$ in. barrels result in a gun which is too lively, very easy to start swinging, and just as easy to check or even to stop that all essential 'follow through'.

Barrel Rib

Rib widths, ventilation, and sights are similar to those required on a trap gun. Only the shooter can decide what width and sight combination suits him. The rib surface is very important and should be the best non-glare obtainable.

Skeet targets are shot from seven firing points placed around the perimeter of almost a half circle. Modern Skeet shoots are well attended and may continue throughout the daylight hours. This makes it almost inevitable – especially in the winter months – that on some firing points the sun will be a nuisance. One of the best non-glare ribs now available has a cross-milled surface with the milling slightly curved. Such a surface will show up as a dead black line when the gun is pointed towards the sun.

Chokes

Experiment and experience seem to prove that a barrel choking which provides an even spread of pellets with 70 per cent in a 30-in. circle at 21 yd is ideal. There is, however, much more than that to be considered.

Skeet rules state that cartridges may not be loaded with spreader devices and that the shot pellets must be spherical and of 2 mm diameter. This is fine, but there are at the present time no restrictions concerning the internal shape of gun barrels.

Therefore it is possible to produce a choke which will by its very contours change the shape of a fair number of the pellets in a shot load. This can produce a slightly longer shot string. The American Cutts compensator choke with its spreader choke tube was one of the first to achieve this result. Today we have also the trumpet-type choke, this is similar in shape to the Cutts. In addition, some trumpet chokes also have a raised ring inside the middle of the choke, which can result only in even more battered shot.

One very famous firm of Italian gunmakers has a fixed clay trap together with a fixed gun cradle, the gun placed in the cradle. The target

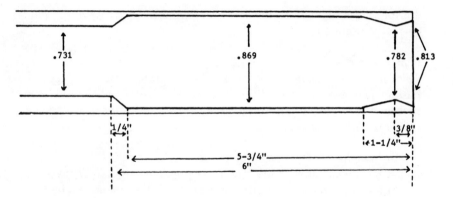

12 Trumpet chokes.

and gun are fired electronically and the expert gun choke regulator will alter the length of the shot string thrown by working on the contours of the trumpet choke.

Furthermore, rifled chokes are now obtainable. My friend, Gough Thomas Garwood, designed a rifled choke tube which screwed onto the end of a semi-automatic gun barrel. When we tested this rifled choke, even with mono-wadded cartridges, we were obtaining wide even patterns of 50 in. diameter. Whereas with a true cylinder-bored barrel we were obtaining only a spread of 32 in. diameter at the same distance of 21 yd.

Miroku is producing a Skeet gun with rifled chokes. This gun produced patterns approximately to those we obtained with the G. T. Garwood rifle choke tube.

Perazzis also have slots in both barrels in their Skeet choke. Krieghoffs have anti-recoil slots in the bottom barrel of their Skeet guns.

Gun Weight
A gun weight of $7\frac{1}{2}$ to $8\frac{1}{2}$ lb is advised, the reasons being the same as those given for the going-away disciplines.

Suitable Cartridges
Maximum shot load $1\frac{1}{8}$ oz or 32 g. Shot size English 9 or 2 mm. Each round of Skeet to be shot with cartridges of one type only. Many, many are the Skeet cartridges available. As a very rough guide, conventionally bored Skeet guns will shoot good patterns with almost any good Skeet cartridge, regardless of the wadding used.

The trumpet-choked Skeet guns do seem to be slightly more choosey and generally perform better with fibre- or felt-wadded cartridges. The Skeet shooter aspiring for that perfect marriage between his gun and cartridge can achieve this only by trial. The pattern plate will show the pellet patterns, and the size of the pellet marks on the plate will also show the strength of pellet blow. A few rounds of Skeet should show how the pattern breaks the targets and what the recoil of the gun with a particular cartridge is like. Firing the gun over a smooth stretch of water will provide an indication of shot string length. After which the best combination of gun and cartridge should be noted and rigidly adhered to.

Rifled Chokes
Police authorities have ruled that shotguns with any type of rifled choke are classed as Part 1 Firearms and can only be held on a Firearm Certificate.

'English Sporting'

The targets which are legal for this discipline can be standard, midi, mini, battue and rabbit. They may be black or coloured to suit background conditions, and can be thrown in any direction and trajectory deemed safe. Distances thrown are dependent upon the shoot organizers' discretion and the capabilities of the traps in use. At one shooting ground, the Apsley, targets on one stand are thrown 140 yd.

Legal targets can be singles, with full use of gun, i.e. two shots allowed at each single target. Two targets with the second target thrown or released upon report of gun. True doubles with two targets thrown simultaneously from either a doubles arm on one trap, or from two traps which may or may not be set up to throw the targets at the same speeds or trajectories. It is normal to have to shoot targets at any distance from a few feet up to 50 yd or more.

The Gun
All shotguns, including semi-automatics, may be used providing the calibre does not exceed 12 gauge. Championships have been won with side by side, over and under, also semi-automatic shotguns. Extremely popular in the 1920s, the side by side has become of late years unfashionable, but during the past two or three years, due mainly to the Eley special side by side competitions, these guns are making something of a comeback. The remarks on the going-away disciplines and the Skeet disciplines regarding gun actions, lockwork, safety catches, ejectors, rib widths and sights hold true for guns suitable for English Sporting.

There are at present no restrictions on the number of guns a competitor may choose to use for this discipline. In Chapter 2 the options of guns, extra barrels, choke tubes, etc., are described. The permutations are endless in order to enable the shooter to match target trajectories and barrel chokings, it being possible to have a veritable arsenal, subject to the depth of the shooter's pocket and the physical strength of his wife or girlfriend who would be expected to carry them around!

Barrel Length
In the early 1920s barrel lengths of 28 to 30 in. were mainly used but the

influence of the newly introduced discipline of Skeet from the United States of America, plus the introduction by Robert Churchill of his 25 in.-barrelled guns encouraged the use of 25 to 26½-in. barrels. Now that Sporting targets are being thrown farther and faster than ever before, the 30 in. barrel(s) are again in use, being more pointable and swinging more smoothly. Some of our younger and fitter shooters are even using 32 in. barrels.

Ribs
It is essential that the top barrel rib is well ventilated. As many as five pairs of targets may have to be shot in succession on one firing point and such shooting can result in very hot barrels and rib mirage.

There will inevitably be some firing points where the targets will have to be shot either going into or across the sun. Therefore the ideal rib top surface should be glare-free and of like specification to that advised for a Skeet gun.

Rib widths obtainable can vary from narrow – 6 mm, through midi – 12 mm, to wide – 16 mm, according to the shooter's wishes or whims.

Barrel Chokings
For a semi-automatic one-gun owner, using one barrel with a fixed choke, half choke should be suitable. With interchangeable chokes he can choose the choke tube most suitable to the target's trajectory.

For a shooter using one double gun with fixed choke, the choice of quarter choke in one barrel and half choke in the other is a useful compromise. A shooter using one double gun and a full range of screw-in choke tubes will usually watch carefully the targets being thrown on a firing point. He will then select suitable choke tubes to match such targets' trajectories.

A similar procedure will be followed by all those shooters who have provided themselves with a selection of alternative guns, spare barrels, chokes, and so forth.

Triggers
On double guns two triggers allow instant choice or selection of which barrel to fire first. Single non-selective triggers can cause problems where the barrels are bored with different chokings. For instance, on one firing point the first target thrown may be a close incomer with the second target a wide crosser. Ideally, one would fire the open-bored barrel first. If, on the next firing point, one had a wide crosser followed by a close incomer, one would wish to fire the tighter-choked barrel first. One cannot do this when using a single non-selective trigger. For English Sporting the single selective trigger will be more versatile. This holds equally true for double guns with screw-in chokes. It is, of course, possible to switch choke tubes from one barrel to another on such guns. It is much quicker and easier to alter the firing sequence by means of a single selective trigger.

Stock, butt shape, fit, balance and barrel length requirements are similar to those for a Skeet gun. The fact that the gun stock must be out of the shoulder pocket when the target is called for requires a well-fitted and fitting gun. Such a gun can be smoothly and accurately mounted into the same place in the shoulder pocket with consistency. As with most guns a miss-mount will usually result in a missed target. With the gun stock correctly mounted the pattern placing should be slightly high, most Sporting targets are rising and the above pattern placing will help the shooter. (See Chapter 4 on gun fitting.)

Gun Weight

As advised for the going-away disciplines, $7\frac{1}{2}$ to $8\frac{1}{2}$ lb, for similar reasons.

Suitable Cartridges

The biggest gauge allowed is 12. The maximum shot load is $1\frac{1}{8}$ oz. Shot sizes from English 6 through to 9 are legal. Shot must be spherical of normal production lead and can be plated. Disperante or spreader cartridges are at present allowed. The most useful shot size to use on the going-away and wide crossing targets is $7\frac{1}{2}$, with size 9 for the close-driven incomers.

Modern cartridges available for this discipline have a superb performance with high velocities and consistent patterns. Most have been designed for use in guns with $2\frac{3}{4}$ in. chambers and proofed for pressures of $3\frac{1}{4}$ tons.

The shooter should spend time patterning his gun(s) on a pattern plate (see Chapter 13 on patterns). He should also shoot at the different types of Sporting targets, observing carefully how the targets are being broken. Only thus can he ascertain accurately which make of cartridge and shot size suits his gun and his shoulder. Some high-performance cartridges produce much recoil and only the shooter himself can decide what is acceptable to himself and his shoulder.

Having thus ascertained by practical trial the most suitable gun(s), chokings, cartridges and shot sizes, all, and I repeat all, the shooter has to do is to match this with his own performance.

FITASC Sporting or Parcours de Chasse

Targets

The specification for legal targets, their trajectories, whether such targets are thrown as singles, doubles on report, or true doubles are similar to those for English Sporting. However, electric targets may also be included.

Target trajectories are fixed by the shoot organizers who have to establish such trajectories in calm air. A course or round consists of 25 targets per shooter. No training or practice is allowed on such a course prior to a competition. Squads can consist of up to six shooters.

The Gun

All weapons, including semi-automatics, are allowed, providing the calibre does not exceed 12 gauge.

The remarks for the going-away and the Skeet disciplines on gun actions, lock work, etc., apply equally to guns used for FITASC Sporting.

There is one difference in FITASC rules which states, 'Any changing of weapons, or parts of weapons which functions normally is forbidden during the shooting of any one layout. The exception to the foregoing rule is if a shooter's gun jams or breaks down, and when such a malfunction is not due to shooter error. In such cases the referee *may* allow the shooter to change his gun.

Before a competition begins all shooter's guns are marked as a check against unauthorized substitution.

Barrel Lengths and Ribs

The criteria for these are the same as described for English Sporting.

Barrel Chokings and Chamber Length

There is no unanimity in choice of chokings. World championships have been won with double guns bored Skeet and Skeet, also with a single-barrelled semi-automatic bored half choke. One veteran shooter who has been consistently in contention for many years shoots a double gun with both barrels bored cylinder. With this gun in 1981 he won the Veterans World Championship.

For our Mr Average or beginner who chooses to shoot a double gun my advice is to have this gun bored quarter choke in one barrel and half choke in the other. Should he choose to shoot a semi-automatic, half choke barrel is suggested. Any of these chokes can be opened at a later date if subsequent experience proves they are too tight.

Barrels should have $2\frac{3}{4}$ in. chambers (70 mm), be English Proofed at $3\frac{1}{4}$ tons or the Continental equivalent. This will enable $1\frac{1}{4}$ oz shot load to be used.

Triggers

Shooters using a double gun with identical chokings in both barrels can obtain no advantage by using either double or single selective triggers. Shooters using double guns with different barrel borings will find it advantageous to opt for either double or single selective triggers. The reasons for this are the same as those given for English Sporting.

Stock fit, butt shape, balance, barrel length requirements are the same as advised for guns used for shooting ISU Skeet or English Sporting. (See Chapter 4 on gun fitting.)

Gun Weight

This must be sufficient to keep recoil down to an acceptable level; $7\frac{1}{2}$ to $8\frac{1}{2}$ lb is advised.

Cartridges

The biggest gauge allowed is 12. The maximum shot load allowed is heavier than for English Sporting and may not exceed 36 g or 1¼ oz. The shot must be spherical and of lead. Shot sizes can be anything from 2.6 mm down to 2 mm, which approximate from English size 6 through to size 9. No dispersal or abnormal loading of cartridges is permitted.

Matching the shot load and shot size to a particular gun and chokings to provide optimum performance should be done as advised for English Sporting.

4 The Try-Gun, Do-It-Yourself Fitting & Stock Alterations

The Try-Gun and How it is Used

A try-gun is a shotgun with an articulated stock. It can be mounted and fired as a normal gun. It may be a single barrel, semi-automatic, pump or double-barrelled gun bored full choke.

The stock is articulated to enable the gunfitter to:

a   Move the stock laterally to the *left* in relation to the line of the barrel top rib. This will provide *cast on* which may be required for a left-handed shooter who mounts and fires his gun from the left shoulder.

b   Move the stock laterally to the *right* providing *cast off*, which may be required for a right-handed right-shouldered shooter.

c   Move the stock vertically up or down in relation to the line of the barrel top rib. This will decrease or increase the amount of stock *bend* or *drop* from comb through to heel.

d   Shorten or extend stock length.

e   Shorten or extend heel or bump of stock. Shorten or extend toe of stock. These adjustments will alter gun *pitch* or *standout*.

Gun Fitting

The basic principle of successful shooting is that moving targets are shot with a moving or swinging gun. A shotgun is pointed and not aimed. Mr Average can be expected to point the forefinger of his extended arm at any specific object at which he is looking. He will have been using this pointing action for most of his life, an action which will be as natural to him as breathing.

A skilled gunfitter will so adjust the stock of his try-gun to enable his client to mount and shoot the gun smoothly, accurately and comfortably. The measurements are then taken from the stock and the client's own gun is altered to match these measurements. Only when the client has mounted such a fitted gun in exactly the correct place in his shoulder pocket, with comb snugly up into his cheek, will the barrels lie correctly in his front or pointing hand. Both hand and barrels will then be pointing exactly where the shooter is looking.

It is unfortunate that many people fail to get the best out of their correctly fitted guns. The reason is because even after being shown how to mount such a gun correctly they persist in sloppy gun mounting, slam banging the stock butt anywhere in the general direction of the shoulder pocket, shoulder point or even biceps. The old dictum that a miss-mount invariably results in a missed target is still only too true. Clients who cannot be bothered to mount their fitted guns properly will rarely shoot well except by accident.

Fitting Procedure
The fitter will first ascertain whether his client is left or right handed. Right-handed people usually shoot from the right shoulder and left-handed vice versa. The gunfitter will take his try-gun and visually demonstrate to his client that the gun is empty. It cannot be stressed too often that it is essential that the try-gun is mounted correctly when fitting is taking place. The client's head should be held normally, comb of stock brought firmly into cheek, butt of stock pulled back into shoulder pocket, with heel of stock level with the top of the shoulder. Should the client be a newcomer to shooting the fitter will himself position the try-gun correctly as above to enable preliminary tests and measurements to be taken.

Testing for Master Eye
The fitter will close the empty gun and have the client mount it. The fitter will then stand facing his client at a distance of about 6 ft. Holding the tip of his forefinger immediately below his right eye, he will instruct his client to keep both eyes open and point the try-gun at the finger tip. Right-handed clients with a right master eye should then have this eye looking directly down the barrel top rib and the gun muzzles should be pointing exactly at the fitter's finger tip. Right-handed clients with a left master eye will find their left eye causes their gun muzzles to deviate to the left. Their left eye will be lining up their gun muzzles with the finger tip. When this happens the client is instructed to close his left eye while the gun is still mounted. This action allows the client's right eye again to take complete charge of pointing and enables the client to understand clearly which is his master eye.

The course of action when clients aiming of master eye and trigger hand are in unison is straight forward; this is to alter cast of stock – if required at all – giving *cast on* for left-handed clients, and *cast off* for right-handed clients. The amount will vary from nil to half an inch perhaps.

The fitter will take up a similar position facing his client as for establishing master eye. The client will then mount and point the empty try-gun at the fitter's forefinger. By altering the stock to give more or less cast the muzzles should eventually be pointing exactly at the forefinger.

The course of action when trigger hand and master eye are not in unison: the fitter will consider well the client, his age, build, shooting experience and character. Usually then, after consultation with the client, he can advise the adoption of one of three techniques:

a   A client of determined character with a 'will to overcome' will be advised and encouraged to shoot from whichever shoulder is on the same side as his master eye. A few minutes' concentrated dry mounting practice each day, morning and night, in front of a large mirror and using a correctly fitted gun, will in the space of one month literally work wonders. Such dry practice will produce 'muscle mastery' and 'muscle memory', thereby ensuring correct and smooth gun mounting and pointing. Such clients invariably become excellent shots.

b   A client who insists on continuing to shoot from the wrong shoulder in relation to his master eye must also embark on a planned course of action which enables his non-master eye every aid to control the pointing of the gun. This can be achieved by various means, by winking the master eye while gun mounting, by fitting a blinker on the side of the barrels, by using special spectacles with a frosted patch on the master eye spectacle lens. By raising the comb height to enable the eye placed directly behind it to see more easily.

c   Should the foregoing fail, the last resort of the gunfitter is to measure for and provide a gun with a cross-over stock which will enable the shooter to mount his gun on the opposite shoulder to that of his master eye. Such guns are expensive, difficult to fit well, often uncomfortable to shoot, especially when using heavy loads; also they are usually difficult to sell once no longer required.

Stock Bend or Drop

This is most important for accurate shooting. When correct, the amount of comb drop at the point where the client's cheek makes contact should be equal to the measurement from the client's eye pupil to that part of his cheek which is touching the comb. Strangely enough this cheek to eye pupil measurement varies little between shooters, at the most a variation of between $1\frac{1}{2}$ to $1\frac{5}{8}$ in.

   Fitting procedure is similar to that for cast. The empty gun is given to the client, who points and mounts as previously. The drop of stock is altered until the client's eye is looking flat down the rib when the gun is correctly mounted.

Adjust Length of Stock

The gun, empty, is handed to the client. The fitter stands sideways to client's left shoulder if he is right handed and vice versa if he is not. The client mounts gun, pointing at any distant object, the fitter checks the distance on the side of the stock between trigger hand fingers and thumb, to client's mouth and nose. This distance should be $1\frac{1}{2}$ to 2 in. and stock length adjusted until this is so.

Adjust Pitch of Butt for Comfort

This final aspect of gun fitting is possibly the most neglected and misunderstood. The old idea was to provide a stock with a long toe, in the belief that a high shooting gun would result. This idea has been and still is hotly disputed. What cannot be disputed, however, is that a long-toed stock can be very uncomfortable to shoot, such a long toe will naturally transmit much of the gun's recoil to a very small area of the shoulder. Therefore, in modern times most fitters take great care to so shape the butt to enable it to bed evenly on the client's shoulder pocket contours, giving a slight chamfer on the inside edge of the butt as well. Such a shape should assist in accurate and smooth gun mounting.

The above principles are even more important when fitting a female client, here a short toe, rounded edge, and the toe slightly twisted outwards can really help to make shooting a pleasure and not a penance. To provide a lady with a gun, the butt of which has a nasty sharp pointed long toe and with flat sharp edges, is not only an abuse of the try-gun but also of the lady herself.

When the fitter has arrived at an approximate fit with the try-gun, the next step is a session at the pattern plate. This can be fairly straightforward if the client is an experienced shot and a few minor adjustments will be all that is required before a session at clays takes place. The tight boring of the try-gun now helps, and the small spread of shot pattern will show up sloppy pointing, bad mounting or even bad gun fitting.

If the client is inexperienced the fitter must now act as coach and teach the client how to shoot. Half an hour's session with a snap cap and a simple, straight incomer series of clays, practising gun mounting, swing and follow through, will enable the fitter to see whether the gun is following the line of the target and whether the client is pulling the trigger at the correct time.

The use of a snap cap instead of a live cartridge saves money, the absence of muzzle blast enables the client to know better what is going on, also mounting should be easier to practise without the fear of recoil.

When the fitter is satisfied that the novice client is mounting, pointing and swinging correctly, he will allow live cartridges to be used. Adjustments to the try-gun *will not* be made because of poor shooting due to bad gun handling, and it may well take three to six months of constant practice before a novice has become accurate enough in gun mounting and pointing to enable the gunfitter to produce the final stock measurements required. Even more important, it may well take another 18 months' hard work practising and shooting by the novice before he becomes good enough to take even 60 per cent advantage of his well-fitted gun.

These basic principles for try-gun adjustment and stock fitting apply equally to guns for all kinds of clay shooting. Each section of clay shooting ideally requires a specialist type of gun and fitting.

Competition has become so keen that one point in the final score can make all the difference between a Gold Medal win and a runner-up position.

DTL guns are usually stocked and fitted so that the client can see the target all the time and such guns will usually throw their patterns high. The gun is mounted before the target is called for, therefore the butt can have a serrated pad fitted to help check butt movement on shoulder between first and second shots.

Skeet guns are normally fitted to throw their patterns level, and stocks are usually slightly shorter than for DTL guns. Butt shape, especially for ISU Skeet, can be critical and the butt is normally fairly smooth faced, measurements from toe to trigger centre are usually about equal to that from bump to trigger centre.

Guns for Sporting clays are stocked similar to Skeet guns, as in both ISU Skeet and Sporting clay shooting the gun butt is not allowed to be premounted in the shoulder pocket when calling for the target; this places a premium on smooth and accurate gun mounting.

Trench guns are usually stocked as for DTL although some shooters prefer a gun which does not throw its pattern quite as high as for DTL; this is because some Trench targets are thrown at a much flatter angle of rise than others.

Fitting guns for any keen clay shooter can mean hours and hours of work for the fitter, the higher class the shooter the more rewarding it will be for the fitter, and he can be assured of the fullest co-operation from such experienced people. They are completely dedicated and expect and accept only the best.

Therefore the whole subject should be studied: choking, barrel length, ribs, sights, balance, size of grip, correct positioning of both hands and of trigger finger, trigger pulls, contour of butt, etc. The basic rule with these clients is to hasten very slowly, once a gun has been found which suits, and measurements obtained which are almost correct, the pattern plate must be brought into full use. The gun should be fired by the shooter in strings of about six shots, the plate is not whitewashed between these shots, after a string has been fired the six patterns superimposed will often show a slight bias away from the centre of the aiming mark on the plate. After the placing of the six shots has been studied, the plate should be whitewashed and only one adjustment made before shooting another string of shots. When, and only when, the pattern is consistently placed on the required position on the plate should actual clay shooting take place.

Different brands of cartridges can produce varying amounts of recoil, this can effect the amount of muzzle flip and the pattern placement. Therefore trap guns should be tested with only one brand of trap cartridge at a time. The same would apply to Skeet guns and Skeet cartridges. A shooter deciding to change from his usual brand of cartridge will be well advised to test the new batch, as above, before using them in competitions.

The client should now be secure in the knowledge that the gun is putting its pattern in the required place, knowledge which gives him confidence in his equipment, thereby leaving his mind and body free to treat each and every shot with the full concentration that is so essential in top class clay shooting.

Do-It-Yourself Gun Fitting

There are those who wish to do their own gun fitting. Among them are those who can and do alter their gun stocks successfully without the use of a try-gun. By sticking bits on or whittling bits off, or by both, they eventually come up with a stock which fits correctly. Unfortunately, there are many others who are not so capable. Guns can be seen at shoots with stocks of weird and wonderful shapes. A large proportion of these stocks began life on a gun as a beautifully shaped piece of walnut, a fine tribute to the stocker's art. Subsequently they have been bent, twisted and butchered at the whim of their owner until the beautiful stock has been transformed into something resembling an ill-shaped piece of fire wood. The following notes are intended to assist those who wish to press on regardless in their quest for a do-it-yourself well-fitted gun.

Equipment Required
A stock measuring board
Tape measure
A roll of plastic tape, or Scholl's moleskin tape
A set of rubber comb raisers
A rubber or leather slip on stock boot
A full length mirror

The DIY person should first measure his gun and record the stock length, bend or drop at comb through to heel on the measuring board. Also pitch or standout. Any subsequent alterations should also be checked and recorded.

The mirror enables the shooter to observe himself and his gun mounting and has to take the place of the professional gunfitter. He will

Required: a plank of wood 60 X 10 X 1 in.; a piece of wood 10 X 2½ X 1 in. and a piece of wood 42 X 21½ X 1 in.

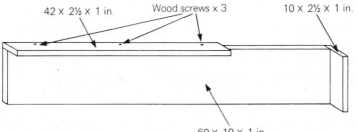

This board may be used for measuring the stock drop at comb and bump of heel. Also to ascertain the standout at muzzle or pitch at toe.

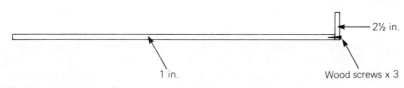

13 A measuring board.

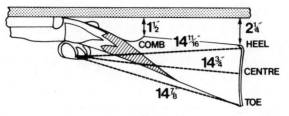

14 The measurements of a gun. Standard stock measurements with a cast of ¼ in to right or left.

stand facing the mirror at a distance of 6 to 9 ft and will adopt his normal shooting stance.

A right-handed shooter will close his empty gun and line up the muzzles with his right eye as seen in the mirror. Then, while keeping both eyes open he should smoothly and slowly mount his gun. By observing where the muzzles are pointing in relation to his right eye in the mirror he should be able to obtain his own answers concerning master eye, some indications on any alterations of cast, bend or drop required. Stock length and fit of butt in shoulder can be observed by him standing with first his left and then his right side to the mirror.

The problems of gun fitting and the reasons and remedies as set out in the previous section should be clearly understood by the DIY person. He should then apply this knowledge to his own gun fitting.

Course of Procedure
Having established which eye is master and decided from which shoulder to shoot, the DIY person can then begin to make any adjustments he may think required. The importance of correct gun mounting cannot be stressed too strongly, the professional gun fitter will always insist on this. Now, however, the shooter is on his own and must by his own efforts and observations make absolutely certain that he really is mounting his gun as explained in the previous section. Those people who cannot be bothered to do this will be basing their stock fitting measurements on false premises and cannot hope for success.

Stock Length
We have seen that a gap of 1½ to 2 in. is advised between mouth/nose and fingers of trigger hand. There are many shooters who shoot well whose stocks have as short a gap as ½ in., others whose stocks are so long that there is a gap of 3 in. Such shooters' success is simply a matter of long practice and much shooting. As long as the shooter's face is not being bruised by the trigger hand, a stock need not be considered too short. Similarly, if the shooter can smoothly and accurately mount even a very long stocked gun, it need not be considered as too long. So much is this so that one of our most successful colts has shot super scores at Skeet and Sporting with a gun whose stock is so long that there is at least a 3 in. gap between fingers and face. One of our finest gun fitting

coaches usually specifies a set of measurements giving a stock length producing about a 2½ in. gap. He is himself an extremely good shot and his own guns are similarly stocked.

If the DIY person decides his stock requires lengthening he can achieve this by the use of the stock boot. This is simply placed over the butt, if the stock is still too short, packing can be inserted inside the boot to increase the length. Also the amount of packing can be increased or decreased at heel or toe, for improved and more comfortable butt placement on shoulder. This packing will also increase or decrease stock pitch.

Should the stock require shortening, and is fitted with a butt plate or recoil pad, these can usually be removed with a screwdriver. If still too long, the stock will have to have a piece cut off it. This is easy enough to do, but if subsequently it is found to be too short and the sawn-off portion has to be replaced, the look of the gun is ruined and its resale price lowered.

Stock Bend or Drop
When the gun is mounted the shooter's master eye should be looking straight down the barrel top rib with the pupil in clear view.

A stock which when cheeked allows the eye to come below the rib line has to have the comb lifted or the stock straightened through the hand.

To lift the comb line is easy. Strips of tape or moleskin can be placed along the comb until the eye position is correct. Or a rubber comb raiser can be used. These come in three sizes, any one of which can be taped on the comb to obtain a correct fitting.

To straighten the stock through the hand is a job for a skilled stocker.

A stock which is too high in the comb can be all too easily lowered by removing wood off of the comb. Such alterations should not be lightly undertaken as wood once removed cannot easily be replaced. Such butchery again results in lowered resale value.

Having by this time arrived at a reasonable stock length, butt pitch and comb height, the next step is the use of the pattern plate. Ideally such a plate should be 6 × 6 ft in size or larger. This plate is whitewashed immediately before a cartridge is fired at it. The impact of the pellets can easily be seen on the wet whitewashed surface, enabling both pellet pattern and pattern placement to be observed. There are many such plates, both at clay club grounds, and of course, at shooting schools. The DIY person must be capable of shooting accurately at a pattern plate. If he cannot do this, and nine out of ten shooters can't, he must practise until he can. The easiest way to achieve this expertise is to load the gun with a snap cap. The pattern plate will have an aiming mark in the centre. The shooter will premount his gun correctly, just as is done for DTL. The muzzles should be pointed about 12 in. below the aiming mark and in the same vertical plane. Slowly bringing the muzzles up towards this mark and pulling the trigger just before the muzzles are centred on it should produce accurate results. There being no muzzle blast or recoil, because of the snap cap usage, the shooter should be able to practise pulling the trigger without producing snatch or barrel flip. When he can do this simple exercise properly, he can begin to use cartridges and obtain consistent pattern placings.

To check for bend or cast is now easy. The plate should be whitewashed and once again have an aiming mark placed in its centre. With a tape, a firing point should be measured exactly, and placed 16 yd from the plate. Assuming a distance of 36 in. from master eye to muzzles, the errors of stock cast or bend will be increased 16 times on the pattern plate. Six shots should be fired in succession, using the premounted technique previously described. The six superimposed pattern group can then be studied in relation to the aiming mark. Therefore, a pattern placed 4 in. low will require the comb lifted or stock straightened ⅛ in. A pattern placed 4 in. high is usually regarded as correct for most shooters. A pattern group placed 4 in left, would involve an increase in cast off by ¼ in. A pattern group placed 4 in right would involve a decrease in cast off by ¼ in.

Any assessment of stock measurements as indicated by the above pattern placement should be viewed with extreme caution by DIY person. By his own observations a skilled gunfitter will know how much error in pattern placement is due to incorrect gun fit and how much due to client error. Lacking such a skilled observer the DIY person should now co-opt the services of a friend who is willing and competent to stand closely behind him and observe the moving barrel/target relationship and eventually the shot pattern and moving target relationship.

The shooter and his friend should then visit a gun club, of which they are fully paid-up members, on a practice night. The shooter will shoot at various targets thrown on consistent trajectories, as straightaways, straight incomers, full right- and full left-hand crossers. From observation the competent friend should be able to tell where the DIY person is actually shooting. All this can then be used to further check gun fit measurements. Unfortunately, competent friends are few. Many DIY people are not good shots, even worse, they mount their guns inconsistently. Because of these variables they can easily waste time and money in butchering their guns while trying to achieve their ideal of a well-fitted gun.

In many cases the DIY person would be better served in the long run by obtaining the advice so freely available in a gun shop. After full discussion there, he should meet their gunfitter-coach at a clay club or shooting school, together with a selection of guns as advised. The end result should eventually be a happy customer, shooting well with a correctly fitted and comfortable gun.

Errors in Gun Fitting and Mounting

CAUSE	EFFECT
Too short a stock	Bruised nose, mouth, face, first or second finger of trigger hand

Too long a stock	Bruised shoulder point, bruised biceps
Ill-shaped butt, too narrow, too large, too sharp edges, too long and/or too sharp a toe	Bruised chest, shoulder, or biceps
Excessive bend or drop of stock	Bruised face, gun shooting to left due to low right eye position
Ill-shaped rear bow of trigger guard	Bruised second finger of trigger hand
Too narrow a stock hand or grip	Bruised face, bruised second finger of trigger hand
Too light a gun or too heavy a cartridge load	Excessive recoil with bruising of face, shoulder and chest

Slovenly gun mounting particularly when holding the gun loosely can also result in any of the above effects.

Gun Stock Alterations

Problems of Altering Stock Cast or Bend
Double guns made in Great Britain usually have their stock and actions held together by means of two screw pins which pass vertically through the stock hand or head. One screw pin has its head positioned in a countersunk hole in the action top strap underneath the top lever. The pin screws downward usually into some part of the trigger plate. The other pin has its head positioned in a countersunk hole at the rear end of the bottom strap. This head and hole are usually concealed by the trigger guard strap. The pin screws upward into the top strap just behind the safety catch thumb piece.

To alter cast or bend on these guns can usually be done by a skilled stocker. He will heat the hand or grip of the stock by means of steam, hot oil or infra-red lamps until the hand of the stock is pliable. He will then by cramping in a jig alter cast or bend as required. The stock and action will be left in the jig until it has cooled. A good quality stock with the grain running straight along the hand should present little difficulty when treated as above. A stock which is short in grain, i.e. has the grain running across the hand, can and easily will crack even when correctly heated. Because of this it is normal practice in the gun trade to accept stock alterations only for cast or bend at customers' own risk.

A further complication can arise on guns, the actions of which have been excessively oiled and subsequently stored upright. This oil will often drain down into the stock head and hand from the action, causing the stock to become 'oil rotten'. Most stockers will refuse to work on such stocks.

A straight hand stock is easier to alter than a stock with a large pistol grip. With the latter there is much more wood to heat and it may take two or three applications of heating and cramping to achieve what is required.

Altering Cast or Bend on Imported Guns

Imported double guns usually have stock and action held together by a stock bolt. It is often believed – even by gun shop salesmen, who should know better – that stocks fitted with a stock bolt cannot have cast or bend altered. This is not so. As with English guns it is a job for a skilled stocker, but it can be done. Previous remarks on wood grain, straight hand or pistol grip stocks, hold equally true for imported guns. The stocker will enlarge the hole in the stock through which the stock bolt passes. He will then make cast or bend alterations in the normal manner but without having the stock bolt in situ. When the stock has cooled he can either replace the stock bolt with a bent stud bolt or he can use an offset washer under the head of the existing stock bolt.

After any alterations which require heating, cramping and cooling, the gun will have its stock removed. Then it will be stripped, cleaned and reassembled before being returned to the customer.

It is unfortunate that some amateurs alter their gun stocks fitted with a stock bolt, by heating and cramping while the bolt is in position. Such brute force must result in a bent stock bolt which cannot then be removed. Nor can the action be stripped and cleaned. Guns with stocks so treated can only be brought back to normal condition by restocking.

Alterations not Suitable for Heating and Cramping

Due to poorly grained wood, some gun stocks cannot be subjected to heating or cramping. Some increase of cast can be obtained by having the stock face swept out. Some decrease can be obtained by having extra wood inlet. The comb line can be made higher by cutting off the existing comb, replacing this with a larger matching piece of wood which is glued and pegged in place. The stocker will then round off and reduce as required and will also blend the contours of new comb and stock.

Stock Length Alterations

Before any stock lengthening or shortening is attempted the balance of the gun and its moment of inertia should be carefully checked and noted.

Stock Lengthening

This can be achieved by the addition of rubber recoil pads, plastic pads, ebonite blocks, white line spacing washers or wood. Rubber recoil pads come in many shapes and thicknesses, and can be solid or ventilated. The surface can be matted or smooth. The butt end of the stock is flattened and a pad of suitable thickness screwed or glued thereon. The new pad can then be buffed down to match the stock shape.

Ebonite blocks are available in thicknesses of up to 1 in. The method for fitting is as for recoil pads. When fitted and shaped, the end surface can be chequered or lined as required.

Lengthening in Wood

It can be difficult to obtain a matching piece of wood. If a matching piece is found, it is usual to refinish both stock and extension.

Stock Shortening

For stocks with existing heel plates or recoil pads, these are removed. The stock is shortened by cutting off the amount of wood required, the plate or pad refitted and buffed down to size.

Any alteration which increases or decreases stock weight will alter both gun balance and its moment of inertia. The stocker will, by drilling holes in the stock and removing wood, lighten it, or by drilling holes and inserting lead, make it heavier. By these methods he will eventually produce a gun which although its stock shape and length has been drastically altered will still have the same balance as it had before alterations began.

This rebalancing is especially important if the altered gun belongs to a shooter who, because of advancing years and stiffness, is having the stock of his favourite gun shortened. If not rebalanced, such guns will be muzzle heavy and slow moving.

Finally, when all alterations have been done the stock surface can be refinished as required.

5 Buying a Gun, Suitable Clothing & Useful Equipment

The Gun

As with any business, gun shops rely on profits for their existence. The most successful shops provide before sales expertise, plus an after sales service to their customers. There are many good shops in Britain, and if the prospective gun buyer has one locally he should first pay it a visit. Before buying a first gun, or any gun, the clay shooter must possess a valid Shotgun Certificate (see Appendix II). He should also consider the following questions:

1   What is the cost of clay target shooting?

2   How much money is he prepared to spend?

3   How long and at what level does he hope to participate in the sport?

4   Age and health limitations.

The following information provides some of the answers to aid a buyer in his deliberations.

Cost

Targets at present cost approximately £1.50 per 25. Cartridges bought in bulk are £2 per 25. This will result in a total cost per round of £3.50 to £4.50 when shooting practice starts.

A competition round of 25 targets with prize money will cost:

Skeet, Olympic Trap, or DTL: £2.50 to £4.

English Sporting: £2.50 to £5.

FITASC Sporting: £4 to £10.

The organizers may return up to 50 per cent of these fees as prize money. Added to the above costs will be £2 to £3.50 per round for cartridges, plus the expense of food, travelling and any overnight accommodation.

At one level of the sport there will be those who, maybe once a month, shoot one practice round at a total cost of £3.50. At the top level there will be the dedicated competition shooter who may shoot 100 targets in competitions every week in the year, plus another 100 per week in practice or training. Shooting at this level can cost £1000 to £2000 per annum, plus other expenses for travelling, subsistence or accommodation. For the handful of top shooters who can rely on winning prize monies to allow them to break even or shoot at a profit, there are thousands who can't, and never will.

Age and Health Problem

A normally healthy person in his twenties can expect to continue shooting for many years. Statistics show he will arrive at his peak in his late thirties, after which time his standard of performance will slowly decline. The writer is 74 years old, and shoots as often as he can afford, and still breaks enough targets to make his shooting an absorbing and pleasurable sport.

Choice of Discipline

It is advisable to select one discipline only. The local gun shop will usually have an arrangement with a nearby gun club and can introduce the novice. The gun shop manager together with the club coach can provide a gun of approximate fit suitable for whichever discipline the novice fancies. The club coach can then give some elementary instruction in safe gun handling and the shooting of easy targets.

There is no easy discipline. For his first choice the novice will be well advised to choose DTL, English Skeet or English Sporting. Concentrating solely on one of these he should soon be breaking 50 per cent of his targets.

Having chosen a discipline the local gun shop should again be visited. The novice buyer should allow at least one hour for this. To park one's car on double yellow lines, rush into the shop, expect to jump any queue of customers, attempt a reasoned discussion and buy a gun in five minutes is unrealistic and can prove to be an expensive and unrewarding experience. The novice should take the time to explain his choice of discipline, and the amount of money he has available for purchase of a gun. The salesman can then show a suitable gun or guns within this price range. Even then one should hasten slowly.

There are many questions to be asked and answered:

Can the chosen gun be tried at the local club or shooting school?

Is there a gunfitter among the shop personnel? If not, arrangements must be made to try the gun and have it fitted at a shooting ground by their gunfitter. In the shop only an approximate gun fit by observation is possible. Accurate fitting can only be expected by actually shooting a gun in the fitter's presence on moving targets, and this may well take some months to achieve.

What guarantee or warranty is provided with the gun? Should alterations to the gun be required, can these be done by the vendor?

What will be the cost?

What after sales service is provided?

Assuming the gun eventually bought is correctly serviced and maintained, will the vendor buy it back, either for cash or against a grading up trade-in?

The English rules of proof must be considered and understood. All guns intended for use with nitro powder must bear valid proof marks at the time of sale, they must also be 'in proof'. That is, the barrels must not have been enlarged beyond a certain size after they have passed proof. These rules are for the protection of the customer and the trade.

There is, however, I believe, a weakness in English rules of proof. The internal diameter of 12 gauge shotgun barrels at a distance of 9 in. from the breech is specified. The barrel flats are stamped with either the figures of .719, .729, or .740; or with figures denoting metric measurements, immediately after they have been subject to and passed proof.

There is nothing specific laid down as to the maximum or minimum barrel wall thickness. The gun trade is well aware of this. Therefore in the best interests of their customers and themselves the more up-to-date gun shops use a barrel wall thickness gauge which also measures the concentricity of any guns they are buying or selling.

It is unfortunate that in the past there have been a few imported guns which, while legally in proof because of correct internal bore diameter, have barrels whose wall thickness varies. When gauged at 9 in. from the muzzles such barrels may be 35 thousandths of an inch thick on one side, whereas immediately opposite the thickness may be down to 12 thousandths of an inch. Such guns should not be bought. It is only fair to state that these guns are few and far between, but they do exist. The advice therefore must be to request the salesman to use his barrel wall gauge and visibly prove the wall thickness of any gun before purchase.

One further complication of English proof rules is that the English proof houses check the internal bore diameter by means of plug gauges before proof. Such plug gauges are naturally accurate but can be used only on the 'go – no go' principle. For instance, a barrel which accepts a .719 plug will be stamped after passing proof with the figures '.719'. Such guns can be and are legally sold by vendors who do not have a barrel wall gauge. Problems can afterwards arise if such a gun has its barrels dented. Although stamped as .719 the barrel may have as wide an internal diameter as .728.

To raise dents and polish internally is easily done by a skilled gunsmith. But the internal polishing will inevitably remove some metal which can very easily result in the barrel diameter being enlarged to .729 or more. A gun stamped '.719' to which this happens is then 'out of proof' and must be prepared and submitted for reproof at .729 before it can be legally sold, given away, lent or otherwise disposed of.

All this is understood by gun traders who will readily use their internal bore gauge to provide answers for the customer. Because of the foregoing a local gun shop of good reputation must be the novice's first choice when buying a gun.

Failing the existence of a suitable local shop there are large and excellent specialist shops. For those contemplating spending hundreds or even thousands of pounds a couple of hundred miles' journey could prove well worthwhile. Before purchase, guns can be tried and shot by appointment and answers to the previous questions obtained by the buyer.

Due to keen competition most new guns are competitively priced. The buyer can expect to get what he pays for – but not more.

Many reputable gun shops also sell guns by mail order. They will do all they can to provide a suitable gun, either new or secondhand, at a competitive price. They also provide an excellent after sales service.

There have been others who simply sell guns – full stop – with no after sales service. The prices asked for such guns are often very low, but subsequent repairs, stock alterations, etc., will require the gun to be taken to some other gun shop. These shops naturally prefer to look after the guns they have sold to their own customers first. Sometimes, because the mail order gun brought in for repair is not one they usually stock, they may refuse to repair or alter it. A similar problem can arise should the buyer decide to sell, the local gun shop refusing to purchase. Many guns sold by mail order firms are excellent value as purchased but problems of after sales service can cause difficulties.

Buying Secondhand Guns from the Trade

Secondhand guns in stock at reputable gun shops will have been stripped, adjusted and cleaned after purchase and before being offered for sale. Such guns are often good value for money and are usually guaranteed by the vendors, who will provide the same after sales service as they do for a new gun.

Prior to sale these guns can be shot and checked for gun fit. Also the vendors will gauge internal bore diameters and barrel wall thicknesses. In short, the buyer will be provided answers to the same questions as for a new gun.

Buying Secondhand Guns Privately

The old tag 'Let the buyer beware' is still only too true. The average layman taking up shooting cannot be expected to have sufficient knowledge or the required gauges to check the condition of any gun he is offered. In many cases the private vendor is equally uninformed. The wise buyer will arrange for the vendor to deposit the gun in question at his local gun shop. There they will gauge it, strip it down, check ribs and lumps for looseness, barrels for dents and bulges, black down the barrel on the action to check if 'off the face', test trigger pulls, check safety catches, ejectors and ejector timing, stock and fore-end for cracks, etc. They will also provide the buyer with their valuation of the gun, all of this costs time and money which has to be paid for.

Obviously there can be no after sales service expected when buying secondhand privately, nor, as a rule is there any warranty from the vendor.

The gun, if pronounced in suitable condition, can then be shot and checked for fit at a shooting school, any alterations having to be done by the local shop being paid for by the buyer.

The writer has examined many secondhand guns bought privately, unfortunately, nearly always after they have been bought. The greater proportion of such guns are in a sorry state, some even being out of proof. The English proof houses will and do take action against anyone selling an 'out of proof' gun. Even so, it is far better not to buy unless and until such guns have been properly vetted.

Buying by Auction

There are auction sales where an expert is employed who will gauge secondhand guns and readily provide answers to the buyers' questions. They cannot be expected to deal with gun fit though. For those who are prepared to take the chance on subsequent gun fit, a reasonably priced quality gun can often be purchased. After sales service is non-existent and again the buyer will have to go to a gun shop or shooting school for service repairs and fitting. In extreme cases guns so purchased may have to be restocked to provide the buyer with a reasonably fitted gun at a cost of some hundreds of pounds. The problems of resale also arise.

The Ethics of Shopping Around

Gun shop personnel who arrange to visit a shooting school or gun club with guns for trial and fit hope to effect a sale. There are many people who like to shop around, and this may prove to be good business and sound common sense. There are others who like to 'shoot-around'. These go from gun shop to gun shop, shooting maybe 50 targets and cartridges at each ground they visit while trying guns before buying. The gun trade is well used to this. To meet a prospective client and watch him shoot targets as above can be time consuming and expensive, costing between £30 and £40 per session. Therefore, most gun shop managers specify *before* they agree for a trial that while the prospective buyer is under *no* obligation to purchase any gun tried; he does have a definite obligation to pay a reasonable sum as agreed, to cover cost of labour, travel, clays and catridges, if no sale takes place.

A Final Warning

It is extremely easy for an instructor gun fitter to teach a novice with normal reactions and good health to break simple targets. Because of this the novice buyer and shooter will readily believe that the gun he is trying and shooting is ideal for his purpose and in his hands will prove to be a world-beating combination.

This is not so. Time is money to gun fitter and instructor. There will be little chance of a gun sale unless the novice achieves success with the gun being tried. Therefore, as many of the variables as possible must be eliminated. These variables are:

1   Inconsistent gun mounting and stance
2   Inaccurate reading of the target flight
3   Incorrect muzzle target picture
4   Inconsistent trigger pulling

The instructor will therefore premount the gun, which is loaded with a dummy cartridge or snap cap, correctly in the novice's shoulder pocket. The novice will have slightly more of his weight on his front foot, the toes of which should be pointing in the same direction as that taken by a simple straight going away and slightly rising target. The safety catch will be in the forward or ready to fire position.

To help the novice obtain the correct sight picture and trigger timing all the instructor then has to do is to put his right hand around the novice's left hand which is holding the gun barrels. The instructor's left hand will be lightly resting on the novice's shoulder. A few straight-away targets will be thrown, each time the instructor helping to point the gun barrels at the target. When the instructor believes the muzzle-target relationship is correct, he will tell the novice to pull the trigger.

Because of this exercise the novice will soon, usually within the space of ten targets thrown, obtain his own correct sight picture and also get used to the trigger pull. The instructor will then go through the same procedure except that he will allow the novice to point the premounted gun at another ten targets for example, each and every time pulling the trigger when the sight picture seems correct.

Because there is no muzzle blast or recoil the novice shooter should soon be pointing and pulling accurately. From his viewpoint immediately behind the novice the instructor will know if this is so. Until it is, the loading and firing of cartridges is a waste of time and money.

When the novice is acting as above, one cartridge at a time will be loaded in the gun. As before, the gun will be premounted with help from the instructor, the safety catch will be forward, the target will be thrown exactly on its previous trajectory and the novice will point and pull as before. By this programme of eliminating the variables success should be certain.

Now the work begins. Any good instructor can provide the novice with a sound basic technique in half a dozen lessons. By constantly dry practising his gun handling and mounting at home, and following this basic technique when shooting, the novice should in a few months become a safe and good shooter. If required, any final alterations to gun fit can then be done.

There are other shooters who are simply buying another gun. These may have shot for many years and can broadly be divided into two groups.

One group will have acquired a sound shooting technique either by trial and error, or instruction, or more usually by a combination of both. These people are a pleasure to be with. Their technique has eliminated most of the variables. All the instructor need do is to tell them where they are missing targets and they will then adjust their sight picture. The guns they buy will be suitable for their purpose and the subsequent performance of gun and shooter will be excellent.

The other group of shooters is known in the trade as 'straw clutchers'. They have usually shot for years, owned innumerable guns, hold many theories on how to shoot, and have no sound technique at all. Because of this their shooting is usually erratic in the extreme. Until they can be persuaded to take instruction and acquire the proper technique, one can do little with them. So much is this so that any gun they may buy is soon discarded as being unsuitable.

The fitter-instructor must candidly explain the problems arising from such an attitude. Only thus can these shooters be made to realize how small are the chances of a satisfactory gun purchase.

Suitable Clothing

Footwear

Clubs with permanent layouts for DTL, ABT, OT and Skeet mostly have concrete firing points and walkways. Almost any kind of light footwear can be worn, the rubber-soled training shoe with its non-slip sole being very popular.

The Sporting layouts at most clubs are of necessity spread out around a field or even in various bits of woodland. In summer the ground may be bone hard, surfaced with dry slippery grass. In winter it can be greasy, muddy, or even frozen solid. Smooth-soled footwear can be extremely dangerous on these surfaces, especially when the shooter is walking between firing points while carrying an assortment of guns and cartridges.

Waterproof boots or shoes with deeply cleated commando-type soles are therefore a sound choice. Clay shooting involves a lot of standing about, so socks should be worn which are loose and comfortable.

Trousers

Any comfortable pair will be suitable. In really cold or wet conditions some form of thermal underwear will make shooting less of a penance. If braces are worn, care must be taken that any metal adjuster is not positioned where the gun butt is placed in the shoulder pocket.

Depending on the weather, a vest, shirt, with or without a sweater will prove comfortable. Deep and bulky roll collars can impede gun mounting and should be avoided. Windcheater type of waterproof over-trousers and jacket are essential on really cold and wet days. The modern over-trousers with long zips up each leg make taking on and off easier. A hood on the jacket will also prove a boon, keeping out cold wind and rain.

The great majority of such wind and waterproof over-clothing is made of nylon or nylon-type material and can be expected to keep out the rain only for one season. After which they will be about as waterproof as a wicker basket.

Shooting Coat or Skeet Vest

There are many excellent garments available. Many shooters favour a vest and this should be large enough to fit over any and all clothing worn. Most modern cartridges have plastic cases and do not swell in wet pockets, therefore the vest can be worn over waterproofs on wet days.

There should be two large bellows pockets, each capable of holding 25 cartridges. The armholes must be cut large enough to allow freedom of movement without drag.

A collar is not required. Although in pre-war days one could obtain shooting coats with a small neat stand-up type of bandsman's collar, these are rarely seen today. A large collar with wide lapels is an unmitigated nuisance and will impede gun mounting.

The shoulder pad should cover the vest from shoulder top, right down to pocket top, it should also be wide enough to cover shoulder point. The surface should be wrinkle-free. A suede surface is often favoured by those whose gun butts have a plastic pad or very smooth wooden surface, whereas those whose guns have a rubber non-slip recoil pad favour a smooth leather surface. Only trial by the shooter can decide which surface suits him and his gun best. A back pocket is useful for holding things like score cards.

Shooting jackets should be on similar lines to vests. The jacket armhole should be roomy, some shooters even have underarm zips fitted to allow freer arm pivoting and movement.

Gloves

There are many excellent types of shooting gloves now available. The leather should be thin, supple, silk lined and with a cuff of warm material for winter wear. For summer the most favoured style is similar to driving gloves, with ventilated backs and no cuffs. Velcro wrist fastening helps to keep the gloves firmly in place.

Shooting Glasses

These are essential for the Sporting and Skeet disciplines. They should be shatterproof and have large lenses. There are many types available, almost every colour or tint. They should sit high on the face and nose, this will keep the top rim of the frames well above eye level.

For those who need prescription lenses a practical demonstration of the required 'high on the nose' type frame to the optician is well worthwhile. Having first obtained his permission, an empty gun in its case is taken along to the first consultation and gun mounting and eye position shown. The optician will then fully understand the type of frame wanted with its shatterproof lenses.

On really bright days some type of dark glasses can help, for clays are of many colours and light conditions vary. Many shooters now carry glasses with yellow, crimson, green, sand, grey, or photometric lenses, choosing the most suitable colour to suit clay colour and prevailing light conditions. Only by actually experimenting can the shooter decide which colour or tint suits him best.

Hearing Protection

This is very important. Most shooters of the writer's generation have impaired hearing caused by their shooting activities.

There are now available ear plugs of many kinds, also ear muffs, again of many types and weights. Muffs are regarded as offering the best protection. They should be light in weight and not so large that they impede gun mounting. The shooter is advised to try wearing various brands while mounting and shooting his gun, thus enabling him to buy the most suitable. Having done this he should print his name and CPSA number clearly on the outer case of each ear muff. This will prevent loss or owner confusion, which sometimes happens at large shoots.

Plugs can also be worn under the muffs but many shooters feel giddy when wearing them and they sometimes set up ear irritation. Anything inserted into the ear cavity should be kept as clean as possible so plugs should be regarded as personal property and never lent to another shooter.

Headwear

Modern shooters often wander about clay shoots bare-headed, which is a stupid practice. When shooting Sporting and Skeet disciplines there will always be the chance that on incoming targets, broken pieces will travel at high speed towards the shooter. For head and face protection the Americans and Continentals favour a shooting cap with a long peak, which can be obtained in either waterproof or lightweight material. Some have protective internal padding in the crown. These caps are popular and help to shield one's eyes from the sun or rain; however, water will run off the back and down one's neck in heavy rain.

The ordinary tweed cap finds favour with many and ear muffs are easily worn over either. The deerstalker is sometimes worn, with or without flaps, but is a nuisance when shooting driven targets which have to be taken overhead. As the head goes back, the back portion of the deerstalker catches in the collar and the hat falls off. Otherwise it is fine for stopping the rain running down one's neck.

Useful Equipment

Cartridge Belt

This is not often used by clay shooters. It is bulky around the waist, can hinder free gun mounting, and cause dragging of vest or jacket.

Cartridge Pouch

These are popular among Skeet shooters and are usually worn on a belt so that the pouch, which holds 25 cartridges, sits on the shooter's left hip, if he is a right-handed shot.

Cartridge Box

Much used by DTL shooters, this is a wooden or plastic cartridge box holding 50. This box should have a carrying handle, and hold the cartridges in five rows of ten. It should have a non-slip bottom, the reason for this being that at far too many DTL shoots, the stands provided for the shooters cartridges are bent, twisted and with sloping top surfaces. These boxes are a boon in windy weather. Those shooters

Above   Bogardus's patent glass-ball trap (1878).
Below left   American style for live pigeon shooting or glass ball (1878).
Below right   English style for live pigeon shooting or glass ball (1878).

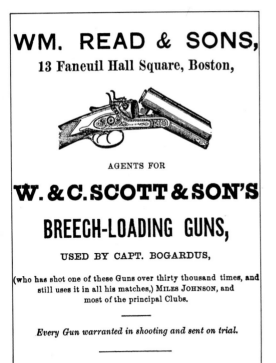
WINNING GUNS

IN THE

PRINCIPAL EVENTS

DURING THE

Summer Shooting Season of 1883

AT

HURLINGHAM

AND THE

GUN CLUB.

MAKER.	Number of Wins.	Money.	Added Prizes.
		£ s. d.	
Messrs. E. M. Reilly and Co.	82	3,162 10 0	16 Cups, value £505, and a Gun.
Messrs. J. Purdey and Son	55	2,446 0 0	9 Cups, value £925.
Messrs. J. Lang and Son ...	48	1,878 10 0	9 Cups, value £220.
Stephen Grant	40	1,371 15 0	4 Cups, value £140, and a Gun.
E. C. Hodges	34	1,233 15 0	8 Cups, value £290.
Messrs. Holland	8	352 0 0	3 Cups, value £105.
F. T. Baker	6	283 0 0	2 Cups, value £55.
Messrs. Adams and Co. ...	3	171 0 0	2 Cups, value £80.
Messrs. Henry (of Edinburgh)	1	140 0 0	1 Cup, value £50.
A. Lancaster	3	138 0 0	
Messrs. Woodward	2	131 0 0	2 Cups, value £40.
Green (of Cheltenham) ...	2	99 10 0	
Messrs. W. W. Greener ...	4	55 0 0	2 Cups, value £40.
Messrs. C. Lancaster and Co.	2	58 0 0	
H. Atkins	3	50 10 0	
Messrs. Boss and Co. ...	1	26 0 0	
Messrs. Cogswell and Harrison	2	20 0 0	

Far left W. & C. Scott & Sons breech loading gun used by Bogardus for live pigeon shooting and glass ball shooting.
Near left Winning guns, summer season at Hurlingham and The Gun Club in 1883.
Bottom left The Gun Club, Notting Hill (1883).
Right Early clay pigeon trap (1889). The pigeon or target has a tongue. The trap is a Ligowski.
Below Holland and Holland's shooting grounds (1896). The pattern plates and targets for testing the fit of a gun.

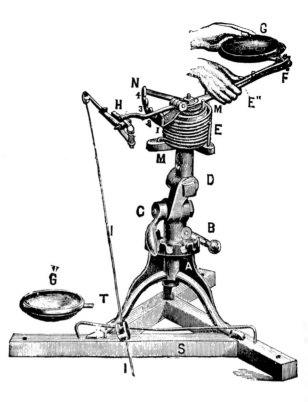

Above left Clay pigeons thrown to simulate driven partridge (1896).
Below left Killing clay pigeons at Holland and Holland (1896).
Above The Middlesex Gun Club (1902). A five man squad shooting clay pigeons at 18 yd rise.
Left Advertisement for Charles Lancaster's equipment (1924).

Above and below   The Blanton clay pigeon thrower (1982).

Above Targets: no. 1 is the zz, no. 2 is the plastic rabbit, no. 3 is an old type clay rabbit, no. 4 shows a modern heavier type of rabbit, no. 5 shows the battue, no. 6 the mini, no. 7 the midi and no. 8 the standard target.
Below Bowman-cocked trap and trapper.

Above   First lessons in
safe gun handling.
(*Holland and Holland*).
Left   Young ladies are just
as apt pupils.

who take their cartridges in the standard cardboard cartons will find as the cartons become nearly empty that they tend to blow off the stands. Other shooters in the squad will not be happy at this needless disruption of their rhythm. The cartridge box is useful to enable the shooter to know when he has shot his five targets from a firing point. The shooter who uses a different shot size for each barrel can easily select the proper cartridge.

A Cartridge Bag or Box for Sporting Shoots

A cartridge bag with a capacity of 100 or so is sometimes used. For shooters who use an assortment of shot sizes, the carrying of loose and mixed cartridges in such a bag can be a nuisance and cause distraction before stepping onto a firing point. The American type of leather box with its flap top will take 100 cartridges in its four cartons. Selection is easy and usually the box is simply placed on the cartridge stand. If no stand is available the shooter will place the correct number of cartridges in one pocket, plus a few spares in the other, before stepping onto the firing point.

There is a plastic box on the market which also holds four cartons of 25. These plastic boxes are light, waterproof, strong and handy.

All cartridge bags and boxes should have the shooter's name and CPSA number plainly printed on the outside in large letters.

Gun Cases

Much ingenuity and fine workmanship has been spent on gun case design and manufacture. There are still a few fine old leather and oak gun cases in use which were designed and supplied for a specific gun. Inside there was a compartment for barrels and fore-end, another for the stock and action, two holes in which nestled a pair of snap caps, and space under the barrels for a two-piece cleaning rod. A square hole held a nickel-plated oil bottle and a round hole held an ivory pill box which contained a spare pair of firing pins and springs. Another compartment held cloths and accessories for the cleaning rod and the whole case was lined with baize. There were eight brass corners to protect and strengthen the case, and three brass fasteners with locks to prevent it being opened by unauthorized persons. Two leather stirrup-type straps were also around the case, with a leather handle on the side. The owner's name or initials were usually stamped on the centre outside of the case. Containing the taken-down gun, the case was designed to balance nicely at its carrying handle.

These cases are rarely seen today, a new case as described would probably cost £300 to £400 or even more. The brass corners can cause severe damage to car upholstery and the whole case was both bulky and weighty. Cases were also available to carry a pair of guns and, although splendid in shape and design, were even more bulky and heavy, needing a strong man to carry them.

By the 1920s a gun case built on slimmer and lighter lines with leather protecting corners began to find favour. After the last war all kinds of lighter cases were designed. Made of fibreglass or plastic, most of these provide a fair amount of protection and can easily be accommodated in the boot of the modern car. Some cases have compartments, others have dimple foam rubber packing, others are supplied with foam rubber inserts, in which the shooter cuts out compartments to fit the components of the taken-down gun. Care must be taken to keep all gun cases dry; a damp gun put away in a dry case will develop rust in a few hours.

Block Leather Leg-of-Mutton Cases
These were much lighter than the oak and leather case and sometimes had a pouch stitched on the outside to take oil bottle and pull-through. They are rarely seen today, although there are similar leg-of-mutton cases made of fibreglass or some other synthetic material. Again they will cause rusting of the gun if damp. They are very difficult to dry because there is only one opening at the wide end of the case.

Soft Leather, Mail Canvas Leg-of-Mutton Cases
These come in many varieties. Some have a zip around both ends and along one side. These cases do not give as much protection as the previous ones, but if they get damp the inside can be opened out like a book and easily dried.

Full Length Sleeve Covers
Originally of leather with a single opening, these are now also available in thin plastic, mail canvas either lined or unlined, or thick plastic lined or unlined. The best type have a stiff protective collar built in at the small end to provide better protection for the barrel muzzles. Also a zip which goes full length up one side and across the wide end, allowing the sleeve cover to be opened out and dried.

The cheaper covers have an opening only at the wide end and once wet are very difficult to dry thoroughly. The problems of rusting are the same in any type of gun cover.

For comfort, sleeve covers used for carrying guns on a sporting layout should be fitted with a wide carrying sling.

A gun carried at the trail in a sleeve cover causes qualms among the knowledgeable. No one carries a closed gun at the trail without its sleeve cover, and the writer believes it is equally wrong to do so in a cover. Occasions have arisen when such guns have been found to be loaded; it is true they should *not* be, but it has happened all too frequently.

Cartridge Extractors
Modern cartridges rarely stick in the barrel chamber but when they do, some form of cartridge extractor is required. One can buy brass extractors in the shape of a finger ring fitted with three claws to grip the cartridge head. Unfortunately, on guns which have no primary mechanical extraction a sticking case will have the head stuck level with the

breech face. Therefore, these three claw cartridge extractors cannot be used.

A 2-oz fisherman's lead weight should be obtained. The soft lead can easily be hammered, changing its square tapered shape to that of a 2-in. length solid cylinder. The diameter of it must be small enough to allow it to pass easily through the tightest of choked barrels.

When an empty case does stick in the chamber the gun should have the other barrel unloaded, and the fore-end and barrels removed from the action. The lead weight should be dropped down the barrels from the muzzle end while the barrels are held vertical. This should easily produce enough force to push out the empty case.

A Pencil
Most referees are supplied with cheap ball-point pens. These can be temperamental in rainy conditions. The sporting target shooter can save himself and the rest of the squad much frustration by always carrying a pencil.

A Referee's Whistle
Sporting target rules specify targets thrown silent rise. This rule is often ignored and a whistle used on some firing points. A shooter may be called upon to referee at any time, in which case he may prefer to provide and use his own whistle.

A Shotgun Certificate
The police have the power to confiscate any gun in the possession of a shooter, who cannot, when requested, immediately produce a valid shotgun certificate. Therefore, shotgun certificates should always be carried.

Valid CPSA Membership Card
This card is issued annually to paid-up members and carries the members CPSA registered number. Its owner should keep it up to date with details of shoots attended and scores achieved. The owner's classification should also be shown.

The production of this card in the entries' tent will save the hard-working officials much time and will be appreciated greatly.

6 Safety, Stance, Style & Placing the Pellet Patterns on the Target

Safe Gun Handling

Having purchased a gun, preferably from a local gun shop by buying and trying as advised in Chapter 5, the novice should own a gun suitable for his chosen discipline which is stocked to provide an approximate fit.

It is essential that he should immediately become a paid-up member of the CPSA. Until it has received his application form and membership fee he will have *no valid third party insurance cover*. Once a member, he will receive all the booklets described in Chapter 1. He should also purchase from the Association the current rule book for his chosen discipline.

A visit to local clubs should result in joining the club with the most suitable facilities. If the gun was bought from a local gun shop the novice will have received some elementary instruction in safe gun handling. This instruction will usually have been in the sole company of a careful and safety-conscious shooting instructor or club coach. Before the novice rushes off with his new gun and shoots at a club in company he must consider and fully realize the following facts.

A shotgun was originally designed to kill. This it can still do if incorrectly handled, efficiently and messily reducing a human, bird or animal to a lifeless corpse in a moment of time. A surgeon friend did not overstate the case when he likened a carelessly handled loaded shotgun to a hand grenade or Mills bomb in its power to destroy.

Because of this a comprehensive course on safe gun handling is vital. This can be obtained from either a CPSA qualified club coach or a shooting school instructor. The CPSA's ten commandments must be studied, fully understood and followed implicitly. It is impossible here to cover all aspects of safe gun handling but the following facts should be remembered.

The Travelling Distance of Shot Pellets

In still air conditions when fired from a shotgun with the barrels inclined at the required angle to produce optimum range, 300 yd is regarded as the maximum distance for an English size 6 pellet. This is fine, but there have been cases where shot pellets have balled together and travelled even greater distances. Therefore extreme care should always be taken regarding shot fallout area.

Assembling and Taking Down a Shotgun
The vendor in the gun shop will certainly have demonstrated in careful detail how this is done. The novice must practise, always with an empty gun, until he can do this competently.

The Limitations of the Safety Catch
On the great majority of shotguns the safety catch simply locks the trigger, it does not hold the sears in the hammer or tumbler bents. The sears are only held therein by spring pressure. If a gun is dropped or bumped it is possible for one or both of the sears to be jarred out of their bents. If live cartridges are in the chamber(s) of such a gun they will be fired.

Because of this no gun is ever carried closed and loaded at a clay club, regardless of the position of the safety catch.

Loading a Gun
This is done only when on firing points and the gun barrels must even then always be kept pointing in a safe direction. The barrels must always be checked to make certain they contain no obstruction before a cartridge is put into the breech. The cartridges must be the correct gauge and of suitable length and load for a particular gun.

The insertion of a 20 bore cartridge into a 12 bore barrel chamber is possible. The 20 bore cartridge will drop down into the chamber and lodge at the chamber cone. To insert a 12 bore cartridge on top of the 20, and there is room, close the gun and fire it, will result at least in a shattered and blown up gun or even worse, in a maimed or dead human.

It is also possible to load a 28 bore cartridge into a 16 bore or even a 20 bore gun, such cartridges will usually travel far enough into the barrel chamber to allow a correct gauge cartridge to be inserted on top and the gun closed. When such a gun, so loaded, is fired the results will be equally horrendous.

The result of this instruction should ensure that the novice will act in a safe manner. He will know how and when to load his gun safely, and this only when on a firing point. He will never, ever, turn around or move from the firing point with a closed gun. At all other times his gun will be open and empty, or closed and empty in its sleeve cover. Guns in sleeve covers will *not* be carried at the trail.

If at any time in doubt about procedure at his club he can obtain information from the club safety officer, club coach, officials or other members. Rembering that at all times cpsa members are expected to act as their own safety officers.

Established club shooters, well-versed in safe gun handling, are the backbone of any club. They are always ready to help both club officials and other members. By their actions they set a good example while keeping a watchful eye on the less experienced. They well know that constant vigilance is required by all, at all times, to run a safe gun club.

Problems of Stance, Style and Placing the Pellet Patterns

Stance and Style
There have been thousands of words written on the so-called correct stance and style required for successful clay target shooting. Most of these have evolved over the last 100 years from those used in live bird shooting. Today there are almost as many stances and styles as there are target shooters.

In the 1880s Charles Lancaster advocated shooting off a stiff front leg with the heel of the backfoot lifted. World Live Pigeon Shooting Champion, J. Elliot, favoured a bent front leg and leant well forward. Champion Capt. Brewer stood erect, with both legs stiff. Other Champions stood very square to the firing point, lifting their right heel when swinging left, and their left heel when swinging right.

All the above positions have been successfully used in the past, furthermore, our modern champions still use them today.

In consultation with his coach the novice must evolve his own stance and style. A shooter's feet are simply his platform, upon which he should stand comfortably and well balanced. To begin with, the feet should be about 9 in. apart, with left foot about 9 in. forward of the right. The left toe should be pointing in the approximate direction of where he intends to break the target. Body weight should be slightly more on the front foot. The whole purpose being to adopt a stance which will allow him – when body, arms, and head are in a locked-up position, with gun butt in shoulder pocket – to move and swing as one unit, just like a gun turret. This move and swing should begin at the feet and ankles. Until this can be done consistently with confidence, shooting performance will be erratic and spasmodic.

By this method a suitable stance and style to suit a particular person can be evolved. It will have taken many hours of hard training to acquire but, eventually, like good gun mounting will become as natural as breathing.

Placing the Pellet Pattern on the Target
As with stance and style, the technique of placing the pellets on the target varies from champion to champion, sometimes even from target to target. It is further bedevilled by the fact that even the champions do not always do what they think they do.

Two observations from the past still hold true:

W. W. Greener:'There is no substitute for placing the pattern on the target'.

A. H. Bogardus:'No shot is big enough to stop a target without hitting it'.

The novice shooter has already had tuition in breaking simple targets, and also has some idea of muzzle target relationship. His next task after evolving his stance and style is to establish his own techniques for correct pellet placement. This is the essence of consistent and successful target breaking. Once such techniques have been acquired the shooter has always these to fall back upon whenever his shooting performance slumps.

The Need for Lead or Forward Allowance

Due to the time lag caused by the shooter willing himself to pull the trigger and the target being broken by the shot charge, the target may have travelled some 10 ft. This time lag is called sportman's time and will vary from shooter to shooter. Because of this sportman's time the successful breaking of a crossing target must have been preceded by the shooter pointing the gun at a point in space in front of the target when the trigger was pulled and the gun fired.

Countless shooters strenuously deny that they ever see or give such forward allowance. As one who has stood behind thousands of shooters I can assure these unbelievers that I have never seen a crossing target broken, unless the muzzles and gun were giving forward allowance. My views on this have been corroborated by other coaches.

Shooting is not a natural sport like running. The technique of good shooting can be acquired by coaching and training. Unless a novice has tunnel vision a coach can teach him to 'see lead' in a few minutes. For those who disagree, and there will be many, it is suggested they take their open and empty gun, close it, and point it at a clay target set upon a 4 ft post some 30 yd distant, while keeping the eye or eyes focussed on the target the muzzle point should be moved sideways some 10 ft. The shooter will still see the muzzles of the gun, as well as the target, therefore he will also see the gap between target and barrels. The art of seeing lead should always be cultivated. Once learnt, the shooter should be able to then call his shots, which will in turn help him to shoot better.

The behaviour of shot when fired must be understood and appreciated. After leaving the gun barrel, shot pellets travel in the shape of an ever lengthening and widening column. This width varies with the amount of barrel choking. At 30 yd from a half choke barrel the column diameter would be about 30 in. and the length may be 10 ft. Because of this shot string, any lead, however obtained, should always be over rather than underestimated. With the overestimate, there is always the chance of a target flying into some part of the string. With an underestimate of lead, the shooter has no mathematical chance of breaking a crossing target, all the shot charge will pass behind it.

In terms of time and motion the CPSA/C. Wilson coaching 'method' of gun mounting while keeping the muzzles on the target, then pulling out in front while still swinging, has much to commend it. Any shooter who is taught the above, and who by constant practice can smash simple single targets consistently, will have acquired a sound basic technique. Upon this he can then build and subsequently improve his performance.

Where the target is thrown as a single and the shooter has time, the method works well. On some targets, like Trench, it is not possible to put the muzzles immediately on the target – such targets have to be caught up. With doubles thrown in different directions, the second target has also to be caught up. Therefore a short description and understanding of other successful techniques must be given.

The Smoke Trail Technique

Here the muzzles are placed behind the target on its imaginary smoke Trail, the barrels are swung 'through' the target without check. There are then variations on the timing of the trigger pulling, some shooters pulling as they go through the target, relying on the fact that they must have been and still are swinging faster than the target. If they were not, they could not have caught and passed it.

Other shooters wait until they see some daylight between barrels and target, pulling when they see what they believe to be the correct amount.

Others see what they believe to be the correct amount of daylight and continue their swing with a maintained lead or amount of daylight, matching their muzzle swing to the speed of the target.

The Point-out or Cut Them off Technique

Here the eye picks up the target line. The muzzles are placed and kept on this target line, but in front of the target. The distance in front will vary according to the speed and direction of the target. This lead or forward allowance will be maintained throughout gun mounting, and during the time gun and shooter are moving as one unit in the locked-up position. The trigger is finally pulled without check of swing.

Any good coach will readily demonstrate any of these techniques. Until the novice has been taught to use such techniques successfully his full potential as a shooter cannot be realized.

The top class shooter, while usually favouring one of the foregoing techniques, will have acquired the experience and expertise to switch to another, when target speeds and trajectories demand it.

7 How to Shoot the Various Disciplines

There are many who seem to have a haphazard approach to clay target shooting. Having acquired the correct equipment of suitable gun and cartridges for the discipline of their choice, plus a short and elementary course of instruction in gun handling and safety, they believe that all that is required to become a champion is to shoot cartridges. They proceed to shoot full round after full round in pursuit of perfection. Because of this hurry they never learn the basics, and good results are rarely achieved.

For all disciplines a planned sequence of training with a coach will more quickly produce the best and most lasting success. The problems of stance, style, and lead have previously been considered. Also the importance of acquiring and understanding a suitable technique and how this may vary from person to person.

The Down the Line Discipline

The novice should first study and understand the DTL rule book.

All DTL traps should be set in still air to throw regulation targets before being used in a registered competition. (See fig. 1, page 5.)

To do this, three marker pegs are placed at c2, c3, and c4. The referee stands on firing point 3 (FP3) and the trap is adjusted until the straight-away target passes through the height hoop set 10 yd in front of the trap and drops on marker c3. The same procedure is followed to set the straight-away from FP1, the trap being swung to the right until this straight-away target drops on c4. The reverse is then done from FP5, the straight-away as viewed from here dropping on c2.

After being passed by the chief referee and jury the trap will then be allowed to oscillate, to throw targets of unpredictable angles between the points B – c2 and c4. The target will travel 52 yd.

Before the novice attempts to shoot such unpredictable targets he should attend his club on a practice night. The club coach will first set the DTL trap to throw and keep throwing the straight-away target from FP3. This is very easy to do on modern DTL traps like the Danlac. The Western White Flyers, and most other traps can easily be modified.

Under instruction from the coach the novice must first learn to shoot this straight-away from FP3. He should, as always, first begin by using a snap cap in the barrel chamber.

DTL is one of the disciplines where the gun is premounted before calling for the target. To do this correctly the gun should be pointed up into the sky at a place slightly higher than the target's highest trajectory. The gun is then placed with comb up into the cheek, pulled back into the shoulder, the body is then bent slightly forward from the waist, and the gun muzzles held pointing just over the top centre of the trap house roof.

The eye or eyes should be carefully focussed at a point about 5 yd in front and over the top centre of the trap house. When the target is called for and thrown, it will be first seen as a blurred streak. As soon as the trajectory is clearly established the shooter will straighten his body, bringing the gun muzzles up to a place immediately under the target. Most coaches describe this correct sight picture as having 'the target sitting on the front sight'. The trigger is pulled as this sight picture is established. There must be no lifting of head or stopping of gun and body movement.

By observation, an experienced coach standing immediately behind his pupil will know when he hears the click of the hammer falling, whether the gun point and timing of trigger pull is correct. Until he is satisfied this is so, there is little point in using live cartridges. Once he is satisfied that the barrel point-target relationship and timing of trigger pull is correct, he will allow the novice to load one cartridge only. The procedure, except for the substitution of the live cartridge for the snap cap, will be the same as before.

Successful shooting at this straight-away should be achieved within, at most, ten shots.

Once this technique of accurate straight-away target shooting has been performed successfully, with full understanding, some movement of the pupil from FP3 can commence. All other shooting of regulation targets thrown on unpredictable trajectories are but a variation on the original theme of the straight-away target.

Having mastered the straight-away, and with the trap still set to throw the same targets, the pupil should continue with his controlled and progressive approach.

He will move sideways off FP3. The distance he moves may only be a couple of feet, or it may be the full 9 ft distance to FP2. This movement will be at the discretion of the coach. After each sideways movement the pupil will shoot at the targets until he achieves success. Each miss being analysed by the coach and the suggested remedy applied. Eventually the pupil should be able to break these targets when shooting from FP1. He will then reverse his movements, back to FP2 and continuing through FP3 –4 and ending on FP5. By doing this the pupil should acquire both knowledge and confidence in the breaking of these fixed targets from all five firing points.

The trap is now set to throw straight-aways from FP5. The pupil should have no difficulty with this target. When success is achieved, he will move sideways a few feet at a time, learning the different sight picture required, until eventually he has arrived back at FP1, by which time he will be shooting the straight-away from FP5 as a full left-hander.

The procedure is now reversed, the trap being set to throw a straight-away from FP1. Once more the pupil will begin shooting this straight-away, only moving sideways when he is consistently breaking targets. He will eventually arrive at FP5, where the straight-away from FP1 is seen and shot as a full right-hander.

This system of training should instil in the pupil the know-how for breaking any DTL target.

During all this time the pupil will have been mounting his gun with the muzzles held on the centre of the trap house roof. A method still successfully used by many present-day champions. This is called the low hold centre point technique.

There are two other techniques of varying gun points which can now be considered.

a   The low hold five position gun point.

b   The high hold five position gun point.

Shooters, who because of left eye dominance shoot with this eye closed, should always use the low centre hold or the (a) low hold five position gun point. Those who have right eye dominance can use any of the three holds with success.

The Five Position Low House Hold

This is very popular. The technique being that on FP1, the gun point is on the left hand corner of the trap house. For most people the full left-hander is a difficult target to break; by adopting this gun point the target angle can easily be read and the gun and body movement reduced.

We have seen that the full angle to the right from FP1 is really a straight-away, and therefore needs little movement of gun and shooter.

On FP2 the gun point is midway between the left hand corner of the trap house roof and the centre.

On FP3 the gun point is centre of the trap house.

On FP4 it is midway between centre and right hand trap house corner.

On FP5 the right hand corner.

By using this series of low gun point holds, the amount of gun movement is reduced on the angle targets.

The Five Position High House Hold

Technique (b) or the high hold is very popular with those who have right eye dominance and shoot with both eyes open. They take the same gun points and holds as for (a), except that they hold much higher and above the trap house roof. Having taken these high holds they focus their eyes down and around the gun barrel(s). Their left eye should be looking out front of the trap house and their right eye apparently seeing through the barrel.

When the target is thrown their left eye establishes the trajectory and the gun muzzles will be moved across to come onto the leading edge of the target. This high hold is by far the quickest method of breaking targets when practised by an expert.

The reason why a one-eyed shooter cannot use this method is simple. Because one eye is closed, any straight-away which comes out under the high held barrel will not be seen immediately. This will allow it to travel a considerable distance before it is seen, and its trajectory read, the gun point corrected and the shot taken.

By the foregoing method of progressive training, the novice/pupil should have a full understanding of target trajectories, gun points and sight pictures.

The trap can now be set to throw regulation targets at unpredictable angles. Because of his previous training the shooter should soon be able to produce consistent and respectable scores and, as far as breaking targets is concerned, ready for competition shooting.

A careful study of squad behaviour is advised. The new competitor is usually told to 'Try to get in a good squad'. This is fine, but until he understands what makes a good squad, he will find it difficult to get into one, and even more to retain his place, especially if he does not conform.

Squad Order of Firing

To get into a good and established squad the new shooter must be ready to begin shooting on whichever firing point he is offered. This will make him the more readily accepted by the rest of the squad.

Even top shooters in good squads have their idiosyncrasies, having for years always begun as, say, no. 2 in a squad, they firmly believe that for them this is the only way to shoot good scores. Because of this belief, it usually is so. Far better to begin happily on any firing point offered and avoid acquiring such superstitious beliefs.

It is a fact that 100 straights have been shot by shooters beginning on any of the five firing points. Therefore accept any firing point offered, for all stations and their targets will pose problems at some time or another.

'The Good Squad'

The squad leader is usually a mature competitor with wide experience, he and the rest of the squad trusting each other implicitly.

All the squad members will be stood ready and waiting, complete with everything they require to shoot their next stage by such time as the leader of the preceding squad begins to shoot the first of his last five targets on FP5.

The reasons for this are many. The new squad then has a chance to see how the targets fly, and whether there is any variation due to wind for instance. Also the squad members have a chance to settle down before they walk onto their firing points.

Line Behaviour

The members of the squad try and take their rhythm from no. 1 or the squad leader. Even so, all have their natural speed for loading and closing their gun, mounting same and calling for their target. They each try and maintain this timing and rhythm all through the stage.

No one will move or close his gun until his left hand neighbour has shot, brought the gun down and opened it. All call for their targets in a clear voice. None claim for imaginary chips off unbroken targets. No one moves from his firing point until the referee calls 'Change'. The squad leader will not call for the first target after 'Change' until the referee calls 'Line ready'. Talking among the squad is taboo until the referee says 'Unload and stand down'.

The new shooter must fully understand all the foregoing; if he does, and then when in a good squad, conforms, he will find life much easier and his scores will improve.

It is inevitable that on some occasions a new shooter will be somewhat overawed on joining such a squad. Because of this it will be easy for him to 'go to pieces'. This is nothing new and will have already happened in the past to other members of the squad.

The new shooter can only fall back on his proven technique, shooting his own targets one at a time, and accept that such traumatic experiences happen to all.

He should endeavour to keep going through the full competition. Then afterwards it must be 'back to the drawing board' with his coach to find the fault and practise the remedy. All his experiments should be done during practice or training. To go into a competition with any unsorted problems is asking for trouble.

He should tune out the whole world. There is someone to throw the targets, call kill or lost, and keep the score. All *he* has to do is shoot his own targets, one at a time, with full concentration.

Behaviour Between Stages

Shooters who are going well do not normally wish to discuss their scores. Those who are shooting badly prefer to suffer in silence.

The Score Board

A study of the score board will not help. Working out the possible scores and permutations of one's rivals and oneself is futile. As long as the new shooter keeps breaking targets no one can beat him. No matter whether his rival is a champion many times over, he, too, has to keep breaking targets to win. The new shooter has nothing to lose, although hard to get to the top, it is easier to do this than to stay there. There is only one place to go from the top, and that is down. This is as inevitable as night following day, and applies to any clay shooting discipline, for no one beats his particular discipline for ever.

DTL *Ties and Tie Shooting*

All ties shall, whenever possible, be shot off and in such a manner as the management deems best fitted to preserve the equity of the competition. It is desirable that ties in competitions of 50 or more targets should be shot off in 25-bird stages.

If the management decides, however, that the ties shall be shot off 'miss and out', the method of procedure is as follows.

All those in the tie shall shoot from no. 3 firing point, in the order in which they finished the competition, at a single target. The next target shall be shot from no. 4 firing point and the following targets from nos 5, 1, and 2 firing points, respectively, and so on until a decision is reached. Any competitor who misses a target is at once out of the competition, unless it happens that all the remaining competitors miss a target on the same firing point', in which case they shall continue the competition as though all had broken their targets.

Winning or Losing

The following notes are applicable to all the disciplines in this chapter. Only the rules of procedure for the resolving of ties varies.

As soon as a shooter has shot his final stage in a shoot he should check his total score to see if he is high gun, somewhere or other in the money, has lost, or is likely to be involved in a shoot-off or tie shoot.

If he is involved he should realize that it is his responsibility to be at the selected layout whenever required. In addition to his gun and normal shooting gear, he should have more than sufficient cartridges of his favourite brand. Many shoot-offs have been lost because a contender took only enough cartridges for the one round, subsequently finding at the end of that round that the tie is still unbroken. Then to have to rush off to the car to pick up more cartridges can easily result in broken concentration, unbroken targets, and second place or worse.

One need not go as far as the American Champion who was supposed to go to the shoot-off layout with 500 cartridges, his method of showing the opposition *his* confidence in himself, and *his* determination to keep breaking targets until he won.

Shooting Order in Shoot-off Tactics

Sometimes the organizers require that those in the tie shoot shall shoot off in the order in which they finished the competition. It is more usual to settle the order by tossing a coin, the winner of the toss being allowed to decide whether he wishes to shoot first or not. Most experienced shooters like to shoot first, the idea being that there is more pressure put on the following shooter. This is especially so if no. 1 keeps on breaking his targets, no. 2 then having to break his, just to keep tying.

Tie Shoot Behaviour

Most shooters behave impeccably, but there are a few who do not and these people will stop at nothing to win if allowed. Moving when they should not, firing very late second barrels at clay fragments, but only at rare intervals. The idea being that the opponent begins to wonder 'Will he, or won't he?', also eject their empties, or even if possible, blow smoke from their barrels across the opposition. In fact, anything to gain an unfair advantage. The wide-awake referee and jury man will quietly and firmly stop such behaviour.

Two examples of this behaviour come to mind. Both happened many years before the war and those concerned are long dead. One gentleman was firing extremely late second barrels at fragments, but only about every fifth target; eventually the referee called 'second barrel kill'. Immediately the shooter claimed he had killed the target with his first shot. The referee asked him, 'Why fire again so late, if you knew you hit it with your first barrel?' The other incident was when a shooter 'accidentally' blew a hole in the ground for the second time in a 25-bird tie shoot just as his opponent was calling for his target. The referee immediately took the gun, carefully examined it, found the trigger pulls normal, and disqualified the shooter from not only the tie shoot but the entire competition. His ruling – 'Unsafe and careless gun handling'.

At the end of a shoot-off, whatever the result, it is customary to shake hands with one's opponents, trying not to look too pleased or disappointed with the result.

The Prize Giving
Even if one is not in the money, one should try to stay for the prize giving; all the winners, especially the colts and ladies, deserve their meed of applause.

Should one be fortunate enough to be in the money, it is good manners to first remove one's head gear before collecting a prize.

Double Rise Shooting

This discipline has never been well supported. The old type of DTL Black Diamond trap was easy to set up to throw doubles. Some modern automatic traps cannot be used at all for doubles. Double rise is also not popular with trappers, for even an experienced trapper can lose the skin off his fingers with a fast squad.

Targets are thrown as true doubles, to DTL distances and elevations. The left hand target is set to fly as a straight-away from firing point 5, the right hand target being set as a straight-away from firing point 1.

Stance, gun points, training, all this is similar to that for DTL.

Selecting which Target to Take First
As always wind has a bearing on this. A cross wind will, of course, cause one target to fly higher than the other. Most shooters take the lower target first in such conditions.

Normal Weather and Targets
One should decide which target to take first. If the left-hander from FP1, this leaves the second target as a straight-away. The same can be done on FP2. On FP3 both targets are, or should be, angling equally, therefore

the shooter can take either first. On FP4 and 5, those who take the angle target first will take the right-hander first, leaving the other as more or less a straight-away. Other shooters prefer to shoot the straight-away first. Only by training with a competent coach can a shooter decide which suits him best.

Targets should be taken as quickly as possible. If not, the second target will probably be dropping and also curling, making it more difficult to shoot with one's normal trap gun.

Both targets must be shot at to score. To shoot again at the first or same missed target will result in the referee declaring, 'pair lost'.

Squad Behaviour

Similar to that for DTL. But because the targets are thrown on fixed trajectories, it is worthwhile until one has experience, to try and avoid the position of squad leader if possible. The reason being that every time the squad changes from one firing point to another, the squad leader will not see a pair of targets thrown before he has to shoot them. The rest of the squad has this advantage.

Double Rise Ties and Tie Shooting

Ties in Double Rise events are usually shot off at either five pairs per competitor, one pair from each firing point, or at ten pairs per competitor, two pairs from each firing point. If, however, it is decided to shoot off the tie 'miss and out', the procedure is the same as for DTL, except that a pair of targets will be shot at from the several firing points instead of one target, the tie shoot being continued until a decision is reached.

English Skeet

The advice given in the first two paragraphs of this chapter apply equally to English Skeet, and all other disciplines.

It is assumed that the novice has acquired a suitable gun and cartridges, and has had an elementary course in safe gun handling. He will have obtained the current and appropriate rule book and perused it until he understands it.

Spectacles and Head Gear

A glance at the front and sides of any Skeet house will show the scars of being struck by bits of broken targets. These target fragments can cut human flesh to the bone, or destroy precious eyesight in an instant. Therefore, shatterproof spectacles and some form of cap with a good peak is mandatory. Furthermore, pellets can ricochet when they strike clay targets, and can blind a shooter, referee or button presser. The margin of error, especially on Stations 1 and 7, is minimal.

A pair of ear muffs, plus a comfortable Skeet vest or jacket is also required.

Above Farey fully automatic self-loading trap.
Below Acoustic release microphones, control box with bank of five switches. The operator has in his left hand a master electric release switch on a wander lead.

Above Bowman manual traps in a Universal five trap layout. Traps may be released manually, by electric switch or by acoustics. Note the aiming mark on the traphouse roof.

Left Mobile crane with trap house on jib. Contains an automatic Danlac ball trap, 300 target turret, with three button switch on a 100 yd wander lead allowing the vertical and horizontal target trajectories to be altered at will. Target release up to 1 per second.

Below The 30 ft tower at Remington Farms, USA. There is an automatic ball trap inside. Targets released by switch on wander lead. Five firing points in a 25 yd half circle around the trap house. Competition called 'Aw Shucks'.
Right A 30 ft tower with two Farey Levermatic traps. The trapper is screened from the shooter by trees. Targets released manually by trapper on signal by buzzer.

A trap fixed on the platform of a fork lift truck. The shooter is caged, the targets being thrown away from him over his head.

Above This trap is cocked by pulling the arm back and around 'clockwise' until it is 'over centre'. It is not held cocked mechanically and may be jarred off. Most trappers cock the trap with their right hand, holding it cocked until they have placed the target on the arm with their left hand. All traps are potential hazards.

Below To release, the trapper, who is well clear of the trap arm and target, simply pushes the arm back over centre.

Top left This trap cocks to a positive stop, it is released by means of a lever. The trapper is placing the second target further up the trap arm, whilst keeping his left hand well above the trap arm. This target spacing will throw wider doubles, which are shown being thrown on the next page.

Centre left Specially posed to show the unforgivable sin. A cocked, loaded, and unattended trap is a menace to anyone in its vicinity.

Bottom left Targets set exactly above one another to throw close doubles. The target stops are movable in their slots to allow variation of target flight.

Right The targets being thrown as wider doubles

The close trajectory of the targets in flight when they are placed above one another as in previous bottom left picture.

Skeet Layouts
There are two trap houses, one called high house or (A), the other called low house or (B). Each house contains a trap set to throw its targets in still air conditions, on fixed and known trajectories. (See fig. 4, page 7). The variation in the angles of the targets when shot is due to the shooter moving from Station 1 through 2,3,4,5,6 and to 7 on the Skeet layout. Station 7 is at the front side of the low house. There is a high house single followed by a low house single shot at each of the seven stations.

In addition there will be simultaneous doubles thrown from Stations 1 and 2, with the high house target taken or shot first. A double on Station 4 can be shot in either order, the shooter simply nominating which target he intends to shoot first. Doubles are also thrown from Stations 6 and 7, here the low house target is shot first. All this adds up to 24 targets. The other target is termed the optional, it is a repeat of the first target missed, or if all targets have been broken the optional or 25th target is then taken as low 7 or high 1 from Station 7.

A planned or disciplined approach is advocated. It is usual to commence training with the low house single taken from Station 1. All low house singles taken from any station, from 1 through to 7, being but a variation of this Station 1 low house target.

The converse is true, beginning on Station 7, the high house target is shot as a single. Again all high house targets, taken from 7 through to 1, are but variations on this target.

Foot Position and Stance
This is a personal matter. Straights have been shot by those who shoot with a stiff front leg, a bent front leg, the double knees crouch, etc. It is possible to obtain numerous diagrams, showing the advised foot positions for each target, from every station.

However, each novice, in conjunction with his coach, should arrive at what is to him, a comfortable position. As a start all shooters should point the toe of their front foot approximately at the point where any target will be when they break it. All targets must be broken before they have passed the other trap house.

Beginning on Station 1 the pupil will therefore point his front foot as above, if his gun mounting is inefficient the coach will carefully help him to premount his gun correctly in the shoulder pocket. The gun will be loaded with a snap cap. The gun barrel should be in a straight line over his front foot and point at the place in the sky where the target is to be broken.

The locked-up gun and shooter will then wind back on the known trajectory of the low house target. It is usual to wind back to a distance some two-thirds back towards the low house. When the target is thrown the pupil should swing the muzzles up and on to this incoming target, he should 'lock on to the target' then pull out in front 'seeing some daylight' and pull the trigger without check of swing.

Any competent coach will know from experience the correct sight picture required at the time the trigger is pulled. There is no need to fire cartridges and see shot, in fact, muzzle blast and recoil make it much more difficult for the pupil to acquire the correct muzzle target picture unless and until he has carried out the above dry firing technique.

Sometimes it is difficult for a coach to convey in words to his pupil the sight picture required. In this case, the coach will place his left hand on the pupil's shoulder, his right hand on the barrels, and actually help the pupil keep his swing going until this correct sight picture is acquired.

There are some coaches who, because of their lack of height, find this method of demonstrating the correct sight picture difficult, if not impossible, to do. They cannot stand close behind the pupil and see over his shoulder. The alternative for them is to take the place of the pupil, and talk themselves through mounting the gun, wind back and when the target appears, talk themselves through the technique of muzzles on target, pull out in front and fire. Because the coach is not tall, almost any pupil can see over his shoulder and obtain the correct sight picture.

There is another method practised by an American all time 'great' shooter and coach, Grant Ilseng. He lets the gun stock lie over his fore-arm and, while shooting almost from the hip, demonstrates the target muzzle sight picture required to his pupil.

Until a pupil has experience, it is usually a waste of time trying to explain the lead required in feet or inches. Even though this has been established many times for all targets by the cartridge makers. What one pupil sees as a 2 ft lead, another may see as 2 in. or maybe a 6 ft lead.

The knowledge required to break the low house single incomers from Station 1 should soon be acquired. The pupil will then be moved from 1 towards Station 2. The target trajectory will then be slightly more crossing the pupil, he will have to see more daylight between target and muzzles as he pulls the trigger.

As he learns to read the target, see the correct sight picture, and successfully break targets, the coach will move him a few feet at a time towards the next station. In time, and this may take a couple of hours or even days, the pupil should arrive at Station 7, having got the knowledge and expertise required for breaking low house singles from Station 1 through to Station 7.

Problems Arising
Inevitably there will have been problems on the way from Stations 1 to 7. At any time a pupil can suddenly 'lose' his timing and sight picture. If he is allowed to continue shooting and missing that particular target, he will quickly lose his confidence and acquire an almighty 'hoodoo' about that target and station which may take years to eradicate.

The coach well knows this problem. As soon as the 'trouble' appears he will immediately move the pupil from the problem station and back towards high house where success was being achieved. Timing and confidence should soon be restored, and only then will the pupil once again be moved a few feet at a time towards the problem station, and eventually finish at the low house Station 7.

High House Singles

The pupil now begins to learn the sight picture for high house singles. Beginning on Station 7, with the high house as an incomer, he will travel back around and through the stations until he arrives at Station 1.

The Ideal Spot at which to Break Targets

If only single targets were shot, it would be easy to specify the ideal spot for each target. There are, however, five pairs of doubles to consider. There are two schools of thought on how to shoot doubles. There are those shooters who take their incoming singles on Stations 1, 2, 6 and 7 early, often before the crossing point. Inevitably, when taking these targets as the second target of their doubles, they cannot take them so early, therefore they have to learn another sight picture and take them well after the crossing point.

Shooters of the second school of thought let the single targets come well in, shooting them in the same place as the second target of their doubles. By doing this they have to learn only the one sight picture at each station for incomers, whether taken as singles or as the second target of doubles.

Station 4 Doubles

Many shooters find this the most difficult double, with the second target being the most easily missed. The shooter can choose to shoot either target first. Some shooters always take the high house target first, others the low house target. The thinking expert, however, will carefully observe both targets. If there is a cross wind, it will cause one target to beat down, the other, driving into the wind, will lift and hang high in the air. In these conditions the expert will take the beating down target first.

In conditions of poor light, the high house target can usually be seen more quickly against the sky, the low target often being difficult to pick up until it has risen into view in the sky at about the crossing peg. Therefore the high house target will be taken first when the light is poor.

The coach will explain all the foregoing problems to his pupil before doubles are attempted. When the pupil has attained a reasonable level of competence in safe gun handling and the breaking of Skeet targets, he may consider shooting competition.

There are as many taboos and superstitions in shooting competition Skeet as in any other discipline. As always, try and get in a good squad, and then be prepared to conform. The new shooter should accept any position offered in a 'good squad'. The hardest position to shoot being no. 1 as squad leader.

Squad Behaviour

The squad leader will begin by standing on Station 1, he will have the rest of his squad members standing close by in their firing order. The button presser will then show targets as follows. High 1, low 1, and the Station 1 double. If there is to be any query about target trajectories, this is now the time for it.

Practice Targets

Two practice targets per competitor may be allowed. If so, it is advised that both targets be taken as high 1 singles. This at least should enable one to break the first target in the competition with little trouble.

At each station the squad will stand quietly, in line across on Stations 1 and 7, and in line astern on the other five stations. All the new man has to remember is the name and the face of the man he is following in the squad. It is best to take at the least 28 cartridges. In theory one uses only 25 per round. In competition there are such things as no birds, irregular doubles, etc., which may result in shooting another two or three cartridges. After shooting each in turn on a particular station, no member will move to the next station until all the squad members have shot. The squad then moves as one unit. Except for calling for targets or legitimate queries to the referee, talking is taboo. When the squad has finished shooting the round, it is the duty of each member to check his own score, find out when and at which layout the next round is to be shot, then be ready and waiting at that layout a few minutes before the previous squad finishes.

Ties and Tie Shooting

If two or more shooters obtain equal scores, precedence for the first three places in championships are decided by tie shooting in 25-bird rounds, until a difference in scores occurs.

Poor Performance

As always, when taking up a new discipline the switch from training sessions to competition shooting can cause problems. Targets which were easy to break in practice suddenly become very difficult, timing becomes ragged and confidence evaporates.

At all times the new shooter must avoid inquests during the round. Afterwards he should make a note of his problem targets missed during the round. As soon as possible he should have a training session with his coach and relearn how to break these targets.

He should also take heart from the remarks attributed to a famous American Skeet Champion, whose answer to the query, 'Which was *your* particular problem target?' was, briefly, 'Each and all of them, at some time or other'.

The writer also well remembers when D. D. Dodds, one of our top Skeet shots, was asked, 'How did *you* shoot a 100 straight at Skeet?', replied, with truth, 'With great difficulty'.

Every target has to be shot with full concentration, one at a time. Good scores come only with and through hard work and much training.

American Skeet

Although not often shot in Britain, there are a few Rod and Gun Clubs at some of the American air bases here.

There is little difference between American and English Skeet as far as target speeds, trajectories and distances thrown. The targets must be broken before they pass the opposite house, and gun position is optional. The main difference is that Station 4 doubles are not shot, there is a Station 8 situated midway between the two houses, and a single incomer is shot here from each house. The targets have to be broken before they pass the crossing mark.

Those who are fortunate enough to have access to these Rod and Gun Skeet layouts should try their Skeet discipline. They will receive a warm and friendly welcome. The targets will be regulation and the refereeing standards high. There will be experienced coaches ready and willing to help new members. The training programme advised for English Skeet is also suitable for American, there only being the two Station 8 targets extra to shoot.

The majority of American shooters favour the gun up position when calling for their targets. This does reduce the variables and produces better scores, and is proved by the wonderful long runs shot in the United States. These long runs are not the result of luck, but of sound technique, coupled to much hard work.

The correct NSSA Skeet rule book, surely the most comprehensive ever produced, should be acquired and understood. These rules are totally applied, any attempt at sand-bagging is given short shrift, and anyone found fiddling his scores is banned for life.

The remarks about shooting in a good squad hold just as true for this Skeet. In fact, it is my belief and experience that the American squads have a higher standard of behaviour than ours, and this results in their producing better scores.

Ties and Tie Shooting
American shooters have become so good that recently some of their tie shoots have gone to 24 rounds before a result has been obtained. Therefore a new shoot-off with doubles at all Stations from 1 to 7 is being tried. This is popular, and now competitions are being put on for shooting a brand of Skeet called Doubles at All Stations, as an alternative to the present eight Station Skeet.

ISU Skeet

This is one of the Olympic Shooting Disciplines and very difficult.

The targets travel faster and further. There is a built-in delay of up to three seconds between the shooter's call and the release of the target or targets. Gun position on calling for the target is 'down' and rigidly defined, no gun movement being allowed until the target appears.

A round consists of 25 targets, thrown as per the rule book. Rumour has it that changes in the number/s of singles and doubles thrown is again being considered. Therefore, an up-to-date rule book should be obtained and understood.

There are many different systems of training for ISU Skeet, each country having and using its own techniques. One foreigner, an ex-world champion, is reputed to have shot more than 5000 cartridges, not at targets, but simply to teach his muscles and mind perfect trigger pulling and timing.

One of our British champions, almost certainly in the world top ten ISU Skeet shots, is also a coach of wide experience. He first teaches his pupils a technique of coming from behind the target, pulling through and firing as soon as the sight picture is correct. His own technique, however, is to come up in front of his targets and shoot a maintained lead wherever possible.

Whatever technique is prescribed by a coach, there will be much hard work on the part of the pupil before good scores are achieved. The following progressive training, based on that for English or American Skeet, has proved its value over the years.

To begin, the targets will be thrown full distance. The delay timer will be switched off. The gun will be premounted. The same training scheme as advised for English Skeet will be followed, i.e. all low house singles, all high house singles. Then doubles where applicable.

There is only then the shooting of Station 8 to be learnt. To do this the pupil will commence on Station 1, call for the low house target and shoot it. He will move in towards the low house until he arrives on Station 8, the place from which he will eventually have to shoot this target. After doing this successfully, the pupil will begin on Station 7, calling for the high house target. Again, as he succeeds, he will move in until he is shooting and breaking this target from Station 8.

In this way he will have obtained the correct sight pictures for all 25 targets. He will then begin all over again with a single incomer on Station 1, this time he will have the gun in the down position. When, again, he has learnt to shoot successfully all his targets, he can have the delay switched on, and go through the whole training process of singles, doubles, etc. Each problem being diagnosed as it happens by the coach, and the remedy supplied and applied.

The above training programme may seem lengthy and laborious, which it is, but such a programme will produce the quickest and most lasting results.

Only then should competition shooting be attempted. Once again the advice is to get into a good squad and conform, in the same way as when in an English or American Skeet squad.

Problems due to Loss of Form during a Competition Shoot
The advice for English Skeet, namely to have more coaching afterwards applies also to American and ISU Skeet. The problem of what to do for the remainder of a competition is still to be considered. The faults and remedies now suggested apply equally to all Skeet disciplines.

The shooter himself must have a positive approach. The rest of the squad members each have their problems and wish to be left alone. A Skeet layout can be a very lonely place at such times.

The manner in which targets are being broken should always be watched carefully. Little chips off leading or trailing edges of targets should indicate whether the leads are on the long or short side. The first target dropped should cause the shooter to consider his mental check list.

Was the head lifted, causing the target to be missed over the top?

Was there a check of swing and/or follow through, causing the target to be missed behind?

Was the target ridden too far in an attempt to make sure of a kill, resulting in a miss behind?

Were the muzzles swung on the target trajectory?

If by use of this check list the shooter is confident that he is truly on the line of the target, with cheek tight to comb and no check of swing, logically, the targets can only be missed either behind or in front.

The positive approach now continues, on the next target the sight picture is opened up. To repeat simply everything the same as for the missed target is stupid, resulting in punching another hole in the sky, and another missed target. However, supposing having opened up his picture the target still travels on unscathed, what then? Strangely enough this often happens with those who are suddenly or rapidly becoming first class shots. They have been instructed to 'open up their picture' and keep the leads on the long side. This has worked well, now all has fallen apart, and the shooter 'doesn't know where he is missing'. There can be only one place left for the pellet pattern and that is in front of the target.

By constant training, plus dry gun mounting, the speed and accuracy of swing has been improved, therefore the target can now be easily missed in front. The remedy is to keep the speed of swing the same and cut down the sight picture.

The Experts
Missing targets in front can also occur among the experts, especially in ISU Skeet, top shooters by dint of long practice 'get in the groove'. They set themselves up for the target, which in flight produces an almost subconscious and automatic reaction. If the target is on its proper trajectory (or in the groove) all is well, but if the wind has altered trajectories or speed, the shooter can easily miss. However, the top shots know this and if it happens, they apply the appropriate remedy of really reading the targets and modify how they shoot the rest of their targets in that round.

Once any shooter finishes his competition he should note his problem targets in his diary. Then with the subsequent help of his coach, he can ascertain the how and the why of the fault, and by training apply the correct remedy.

Ties and Tie Shooting
If two or more shooters obtain equal scores, precedence for the first three places is decided by tie shoot-off in rounds of 25 targets, up to a maximum of three tie breaking series. If after the three series the tie is not broken the competitors will be classified equal.

English Sporting

There have been many changes in the rules specifying the types of targets allowed. Originally standard targets and rabbit targets were specified. Then the rabbit target became difficult to obtain and only the standard was allowed.

A variety of targets from minis, midis, battue, standard and rabbits began to be manufactured for use in FITASC Sporting. To make English Sporting more attractive, the CPSA Executive amended English Sporting rules, to allow all these targets to be used. This move was welcomed by FITASC shooters, giving them the chance to shoot FITASC type targets in English Sporting. It is said that consideration is once again being given to banning all except standard DTL or Skeet type targets for English Sporting, but one hopes that such a retrograde step is not taken.

As with other disciplines it is assumed the newcomer to Sporting has acquired a suitable gun(s) of approximate fit, received elementary lessons in safe gun handling and some experience in shooting simple targets.

In Chapter 3 we saw that Sporting targets can be thrown in any safe direction. Years ago the live bird shooter's criticism of Sporting clay layouts was that such targets were too easy and that all one did was to wait until they slowed down. With modern targets leaving trap arms at nearly 100 mph, this objection is no longer true.

The practice of naming various firing points after game birds, wildfowl, vermin or beasts is becoming less popular, the reason being the vast difference between the target speed and that of live bird or beast.

A planned progression of training is again advocated. Types of targets can be roughly divided into four groups.

1   The going-away
2   The incomer
3   The right to left crosser
4   The left to right crosser

Once the correct technique is learnt for shooting these groups, all other Sporting targets are but variations.

1   The Going-Away Target

This should be the first one to be attempted, and should be taken as straight-aways at a fixed elevation. All going-away targets place a premium on accurate gun mounting and pointing. Any error by the shooter in these at 20 yd will be progressively greater at 40 yd, it being a well known fact that two diverging lines of travel for targets and pellets will not meet. Once this straight-away is mastered the elevations can be varied, after which the target angles, right or left, can be introduced. Finally, the pupil will be moved sideways, left or right from his original firing point, and in this manner acquire the correct sight picture for all going-away targets.

Those clubs which are fortunate enough to have a Danlac ABT layout, with the three button switch allowing any going-away target to be thrown and repeated time after time, could well use it for Sporting target training. The shooter should stand close to the back of the ABT trap house with his gun in the down position.

2   The Incomer

These targets can be high or low, also be angled left or right. In the writer's opinion all such low targets should be banned. No matter how effective any caging of the shooter may be, there is always the chance of a gun being swung around or dropped. To shoot really low targets also results in a shower of clay fragments dropping around and behind the competitor, referee, waiting competitors and any audience. However, at the present time such targets are thrown and must be shot. Shatterproof spectacles, hearing protection and head wear are essential.

Once again training begins with the straight incomer, and carries on through all variations in trajectories, heights and angles, until the sight pictures are well understood.

3   The Right to Left Crosser

Training begins with a full right-angled crosser, and again goes through all the variations. The problems of wrong master eye can cause missing of such targets in front. When doubles are eventually thrown, the rear target should be shot first, with the gun swung without check to then take the front target with the second shot.

4   The Left to Right Crosser

This requires the same training sequence, except that the target(s) are travelling in the opposite direction. Any left master eye dominance will result in missing behind the target.

How to Become Proficient

The newcomer now has a choice of three courses of action in learning how to shoot Sporting targets, either

a   The shooting school

b   The CPSA affiliated club which has a good Sporting layout, plus the services of a CPSA qualified coach.

c   Simply to visit any club to shoot Sporting targets either as practice or competition.

The shooting school (a) will initially be the most expensive, especially during the first few weeks. But in the long run will not only prove to be money well spent but will quickly produce safe, good class shooters.

Good shooting schools who specialize in Sporting target shooting will usually have many traps fixed at ground level, behind screens, and in both low and high towers. At one shooting school in Hampshire there are some 80 traps.

Pupils attending these schools and taking a course of lessons will be given individual attention. The coach will produce targets in any one of the four groups, which become progressively more difficult as the pupil's skill improves. Even more important, the pupil will be given a concise and reasoned explanation of the how and why the target was missed, and the remedy explained. The pupil can then apply the remedy and prove to himself that the diagnosis was correct. In addition the pupil will be expected and encouraged to think for himself, to 'call his own shots'. By this means the pupil will soon be able to diagnose and prescribe for himself, and the result will be a thinking, safe, and efficient shooter.

No shooting school coach worth the name is ever interested in producing a zombie-like shooter who has been programmed to shoot all his targets mechanically. These zombies fall apart when attempting to shoot competitions without their coach being present.

Another benefit arising from being taught at a good school is that when problems arise, and they will, the shooter can return to his friend and coach for a refresher.

With regard to (b), if the club is a good one and the CPSA qualified coach is one who has specialized in Sporting targets, good results can be achieved. There are 200 or more CPSA coaches at the present and some of them could make a living at full-time coaching. Inevitably there are others, who maybe due to the limitations of their club's Sporting layout, or a combination of too many members and too few facilities, do not have enough experience. These coaches can and do provide the elementary basics; however, if a shooter wishes to progress he must go to a more experienced CPSA coach at another club. If within his area there is no such coach or club available, he, too, must visit the professional shooting school in order to progress.

As to (c) this is fine for the clay target and cartridge manufacturers. It is worth repeating that shooting is not a natural sport. In the writer's opinion there is no such thing as a natural shot. True, there are many who, having good co-ordination and concentration, are quickly taught, or less quickly, by much trial and error, themselves become good shots.

The new shooter to English Sporting, who simply shoots practice and competition to the depths of his pocket, will do just that. With no established technique on which to base his efforts, plus the fact that all the other club members will kindly and freely proffer advice, his path to success will be hard and long. There are some club members who, although not qualified coaches, are fully competent, whereas many others, although kindly and well meaning, are not. Because of these facts the new shooter will inevitably become a victim of the confusion caused by over coaching and any progress he makes will be slow and erratic. Eventually he will do one of three things,

Shoot just for fun.

Give up shooting in disgust.

Take a course of lessons with a professional.

Squads in Shooting Competitions
This varies from club to club. If squadding is practised, as always, get in a good squad and conform. Remember squad order, the name and the face of the man preceding. Take plenty of cartridges onto the firing point and keep quiet when standing behind.

If squadding is not practised, and the shooter is allowed to shoot around the layout at will, it is worthwhile trying to go around with one or two trusted friends.

The course should normally be shot straight round, beginning at firing point no. 1 and taking each point in numerical order until all have been shot.

'Walking the Course' before Shooting
Fine for those who like exercise, but any competent shooter should be able, by watching the competitor in front of him, to read the targets and decide the best combination of gun and cartridge required for any particular firing point. The exception to this can be when the targets on some firing points are thrown into or across the sun. It then makes sense to shoot these, if possible, when the sun is not a hazard.

It is usual to show a target(s) to a competitor, if, when he arrives at a firing point there is no one shooting. If there is some one shooting, there is really no justification for the request to 'see a target'. Such a request should not be made, for it will generally be refused.

Firing Point Behaviour
The competitor must set his own pace and rhythm. He will have more than enough cartridges with him for that firing point, it being usual to put the correct number required in one pocket to obviate counting. When the pocket is empty all the targets should have been shot. A few spare cartridges should be in another pocket in case of no targets etc. The safety catch should be checked every time one steps onto a firing point. This practice is essential, especially if someone else has previously been handling the gun.

Calling for the Target
Targets are supposed to be thrown silent rise, with a delay of up to three seconds. Where this is so, the shooter should call in a clear voice. The referee will be wearing ear protectors, and he is usually placed behind the shooter. He has a hard enough job, without having to strain his ears to hear the whisperers. As the target(s) are shot, the referee will call 'kill' or 'lost' each time. A shooter who disagrees with this verdict should quietly protest at once. It should be realized by the shooter that trapping manually is a hard and boring task. When doubles are thrown from the same trap, time must be allowed by the shooter between calls. Those shooters who load and call quickly will harass the trapper, the result being badly spaced doubles, thus the fault is of the shooter's own making.

When all the targets have been shot, he should open his gun, take out the cartridges, if any, and then and then only, turn around. He should take his score card from the referee, check the score and if wrong, query it. Then thank the referee and walk quietly away.

Ties and Tie Shooting

Ties for first place will be decided as follows. The stand will be drawn out from a hat and the tied shooters will shoot on this stand, miss and out.

FITASC Sporting

This is the toughest type of Sporting. Although the targets thrown are similar to English, the fact that only one gun is allowed, plus a heavier load cartridge, 1¼ oz, does make a vast difference.

There is no chance of standing and watching targets while previous squads shoot. On each firing point a squad is shown the sequence of target(s) thrown, after which it is 'straight in' for the shooter. All of which places a premium on his ability to remember where to look for the target and 'read it'.

There is the problem of extra cost with FITASC. This is unavoidable due to the extra expense of more traps and trappers. A two day weekend shoot can easily cost a competitor £150.

The new shooter should obtain a copy and understand the FITASC rules. An apprenticeship of two years' shooting English Sporting is advised. Those who cannot make the grade at English Sporting are unlikely to progress very far at FITASC.

The same progressive training programme as for English is suggested. A few years ago it was difficult to find suitable clubs, or even schools, who were able to throw FITASC type targets in sufficient variety. Today there are a few clubs and schools providing splendid training facilities. Some have professional coaches who have themselves shot FITASC and know well both problems and answers.

Squads and Squadding

Squads and the order of shooting is done by draw. The advice given for English, regarding fire point and squad behaviour, applies equally to FITASC.

Ties and Tie Shooting

If two or more shooters score the same results in a championship the shoot-off for the first three places will occur in new rounds of 25 birds until a difference shows up.

FITASC Sporting is one of the toughest disciplines and it is also one of the most rewarding. Happily, it is also one of the disciplines where our shooters do well, male, female, and veterans having won Gold Medals at British, European and World Championship levels.

Olympic Trap or Trench

This, as the name implies, in an Olympic discipline. The ot layout consists of a trap pit with the upper surface of the roof on the same level as the five shooting stations. The trap pit should have an internal length of approximately 20 m. There are 15 traps, divided into five groups of three. The distances between traps in a group must be equal, from 1.0 to 1.10 m. Distances between the centre traps in the group is normally 3 to 3.30 m. (See fig. 5, page 7.) Each trap should be provided with seals for the adjustments for elevation, angle, and also for mainspring tension. Hand-loaded traps must have two stops to prevent accidental or deliberate movement of the target on the throwing arm, thereby changing the preset directions of the target. Targets will travel 70 to 80 m.

Trap release shall be electric manual or electric microphone. The latter must be provided with an automatic delay of 0.1 to 0.2 seconds. The release devices must guarantee equal distribution of targets to each shooter in a round of 25 targets. This must be ten targets to the right, ten targets to the left, and five targets to the centre. To do this each group of three traps must throw targets as follows.

Two targets from the left side trap, two from the right side trap, and one from the centre trap in each group as the shooters progress. After each five targets have been released and shot from shooting Stations 1 through to 5, the selector index must be advanced one stop.

The Shooting Stations

These five stations will be situated on a straight line at a distance of 15 m to the rear of the front edge of the trap pit. Each station should be marked with a square, 1×1 m, and centred on a line with the middle trap in each group. A sixth or waiting position, will be placed 2 m to the rear, and slightly left of Station 1, for shooter no. 6 in the squad to wait on. All six positions will have a table on which to place extra cartridges etc.

There should be a path 3 to 4 m behind the shooting stations which must be used by shooters moving from Station 5 to Station 1.

Targets, Distances and Elevations

At the present time there are nine tables or schemes in the rules to enable the traps to be set. Once the 15 traps have been set by the use of an angleometer, also height and distance markers, they must be approved by the jury and sealed. One trial target will be thrown from each trap in sequence. These targets may be observed by the shooters.

All competitors, coaches, team officials, etc., are prohibited from entering the trap pits after the jury has examined and approved the trap settings.

Training Procedure

It is assumed that the novice has a copy of the correct rules, and understands their meaning. Also, that he has an appropriate gun of approximate fit, and has received elementary lessons in safe gun handling and the shooting of simple targets. For OT shooting this is not really good enough. The OT shooter should have served at least a two-year apprenticeship in DTL shooting. Those who have either failed in DTL or worse, have never shot the discipline, will inevitably have a traumatic experience when attempting to shoot OT.

It is commonplace for even first class shooters of DTL with AA classification to find problems on OT at first. Their scores of 24 and 25, achieved on DTL, will plummet to 10 or 15, sometimes even five per round. It must be understood that not only are the OT targets thrown faster and farther, but the distances thrown vary between target and target from one trap to another.

Regardless of any previous DTL experience, intending OT shooters must still follow a planned and progressive training programme.

It is usual to attempt first the straight forward target thrown from the centre trap of each of the five groups. Although each trap is set to keep throwing its single targets, each on the same trajectory and generally straight forward, there can be a maximum variation of 15° to left or right. Therefore the centre trap from Station 1 group may throw its straight forward 15° right, on Station 2 group, the centre trap may throw 15° left. The elevations of such targets can be set to be of a height of 1 m up to 4 m at a distance of 10 m from the trap.

Stance

Only by trial and error can the new shooter and his coach arrive at a correct and comfortable stance. One has, however, to begin some-where, it is customary to stand on any of the five shooting stations, and point the front foot at the centre mark on the trap house roof for that station. In the fullness of time the pupil will, as always, evolve a suitable stance. By pointing centre as above, the pupil should be able to swing gun, body, as a locked-up unit far enough to right or left to break any or all the targets thrown.

Gun Mounting

The head should be fairly erect and slightly turned to the left. The gun will be mounted by placing the stock comb up into the cheek and then pulling the butt back into the shoulder pocket. If the head is not moved during mounting, the fault of stock crawling should be eradicated. (See illustrations between pages 102 and 103.) Stock crawling is an all too common fault, and is caused by placing the gun butt too low in the shoulder pocket and then bringing the head down and the cheek forward onto the stock comb. This fault causes tension in neck muscles, the shooter's eyes are also swivelled upwards to look through his eyebrows, which causes tension of the eye ball muscles.

In the course of a competition shoot this muscular tension causes headaches, eye strain, and encourages head lifting, which in turn introduces variables in pattern placing.

There are shooters who have this faulty mounting technique and who also stock crawl, despite this, they can and do produce winning scores. This is due to sheer concentration and hours and hours of hard training. The new shooter will be encouraged by his coach not to emulate such faults.

Gun Point

It is essential, due to the high speed and wide angles of targets, that the gun point is on or about the centre aiming mark on the Trench house roof. Only the experience gained from long training should cause a shooter to alter such a low point.

The Correct Use of the Eye(s)

The target trajectory must be established as soon as possible. If a shooter's eyes are focussed on, say, the centre aiming mark before calling for the target it will first appear as a blur, and the eye focus will have to be changed in an endeavour to see it more clearly. The better technique is to look out and over the gun point, focussing the eye or eyes at a point about 10 to 12 yd in front of the centre mark. When the target then appears as a blur it will come into focus at the 10 to 12 yd mark, by which time the blur will have been transferred into a well and clearly defined target trajectory, enabling the gun, muzzles and body to be locked into and swing up, into, and with the target.

The pupil should take up his position on Station 1. He will shoot at only the straight forward target which is thrown from the centre of the three traps. The coach will show him this straight forward target to establish the target trajectory. Even if the pupil is an expert DTL shooter, this is still worthwhile. The pupil will be helped to 'set himself up' with gun loaded with snap cap, mounted correctly, and eyes focussed out in front of the centre or aiming mark on the trap house roof. The pupil should call for his own target, read its line, swing up into and through its flight line, pulling the trigger when he thinks the sight picture is correct. The coach will know whether the gun point was out in front of the target far enough when the trigger was pulled. The absence of muzzle blast and recoil will enable the pupil to more quickly acquire this sight picture. Once established, single live cartridges may be used. Trying to shoot a round of 25 Trench targets without preliminary tuition is an expensive way of producing loud bangs to no useful purpose.

When the pupil has been taught the correct technique for this target on Station 1, he can be allowed to train while using two cartridges. During this training time, the coach will be carefully watching for the most common faults. Stock crawling, calling for the target before the eyes are properly focussed, head lifting (bird watching), and/or check of swing.

Having mastered the target on Station 1, the next target to be shot at will be the straight forward from Station 2. Then Stations 3, 4 and 5.

By this time the pupil should be getting used to the speed of the targets. He can then begin on Station 1, and taking the right-hander, once again train on this until success is achieved. The sequence then will be, Stations 2, 3, 4 and 5, shooting all the right-handers. Then he should go back to Station 1, and take all the left-handers through to Station 5. The coach will be explaining at all times, diagnosing faults and prescribing remedies.

This period of training can take weeks, but experience has proved this to be the most efficient method of taking up the OT discipline.

When proficiency has been achieved on the 15 different targets thrown on a layout using a specific scheme, the pupil can be allowed to try training, either solo or in a squad. The targets will be thrown as for competition, therefore which target on what trajectory due to come next will not be known, making it even more difficult for the pupil to catch up, pull out and break.

Here the services of a good coach are invaluable, by dint of observation and even exhortation, the pupil should eventually achieve his own level of competence, and have some idea of the problems involved plus the answers. Then, and only then, should he think about shooting competitions.

The Good Squad

As usual there are taboos and etiquette of squad behaviour to be observed. Most of which are based on good manners and common sense.

In big competitions the squadding is done by draw, and the shooter takes the place he is allocated. If the shooter wishes, he may watch the target sequence being shown to the jury before the shoot commences. Regardless of squad hustlers, loud hailers etc., it is the shooter's own and sole responsibility to be on the correct layout at the proper time, and ready with all his equipment and cartridges when the referee calls his name. If he is not, he can be zeroed or fined three targets for that round.

Squad Behaviour During Shooting

Most of the international shooters wear blinkers to cut out distractions and help concentration. The rules for when to close the gun, the time allowed after the preceding shooter has fired, and when to move to the next peg, must be fully understood and obeyed.

In the writer's opinion, most OT shooters are loners. They tune out everything, wanting only to kill all their own 25 targets without hindrance, obstruction or distraction. Those who transgress will soon be jumped on by referee and jury, which will have an adverse effect on their own scores.

Loss of Performance During a Shoot

What has been written previously on this for other disciplines holds true for OT and the suggested remedies also apply. Use one's mental fault check list and keep trying. Cut out all variables, avoid what most OT shooters do in trouble, i.e. getting slower and slower in calling for the

Top right and left   This gun is empty, safe and seen to be safe.
Bottom right and left   A menace to any living thing within 300 yd.

Top left   There is a closed gun in this sleeve cover. Although in theory the gun should be empty, it is human to err. No closed gun should be carried in this manner.

Top right   The safe way to carry a closed gun in its sleeve cover.

Bottom left   Although specially posed by myself with a known empty gun, this photo still totally scares me. Besides breaking the CPSA rules, it is utterly stupid and highly dangerous.

Bottom right   Another specially posed photo with a known empty gun, just as stupid and dangerous.

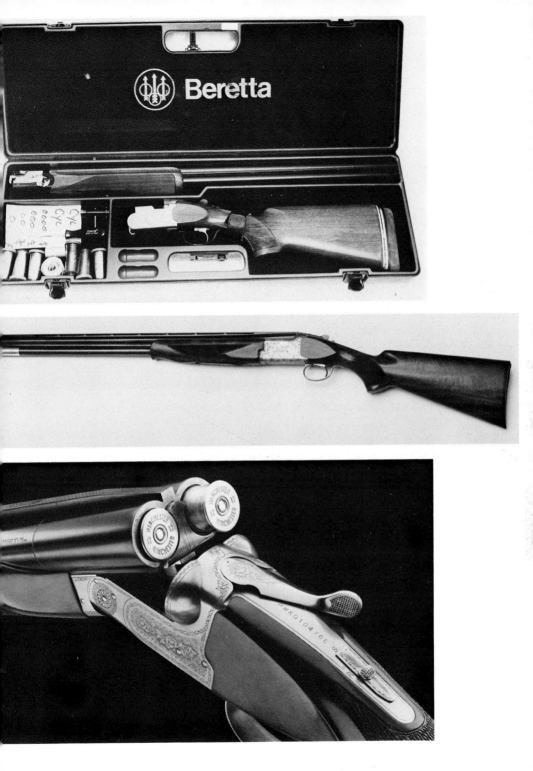

Top   The all-purpose gun. In fitted case with screw-in choke tubes and interchangeable Skeet, Sporting or trap type stocks. Guns designed to this concept are available from many makers.

Centre   The Browning Citori, available with screw-in chockes and fitted case.

Bottom   For side-by-side enthusiasts. The Winchester 23 XTR with screw-in chokes and fitted case.

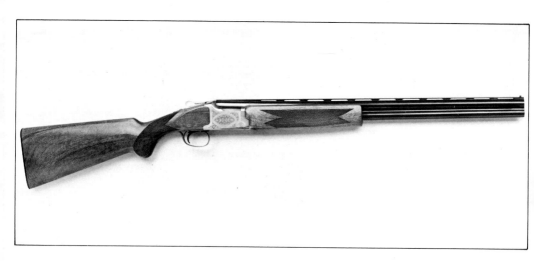

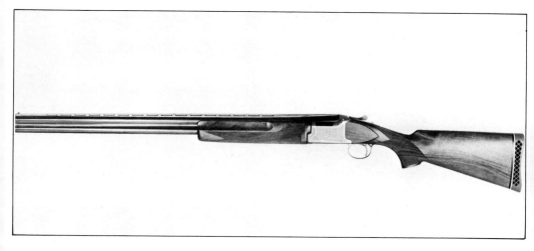

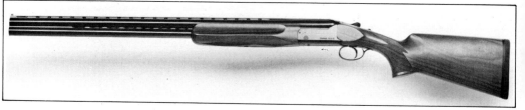

Top Parker Hale over and under double-barrelled hammerless ejector boxlock 12 bore gun. Fitted with half pistol grip, single selective trigger, ventilated rib, sporting type fore-end. (*Parker Hale*).

Centre Parker Hale over and under double-barrelled hammerless ejector boxlock 12 bore trap gun. Fitted with ventilated recoil pad, full pistol grip stock, single selective trigger, beavertail fore-end, ventilated rib.

Bottom Perazzi MX3, available with screw-in chokes interchangeable stocks and fitted case.

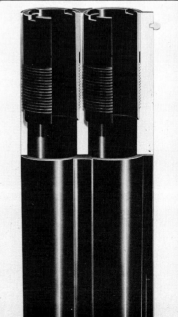

Top The Benelli, a modern semi-automatic, again with screw-in chokes. Plus a small selection of the many makes of cartridge available at present.
Centre The Winchester Disperante or Spreader Cartridge. Designed to produce improved cylindrical patterns from tightly choked barrels.
Bottom Sectioned Browning choke tube.

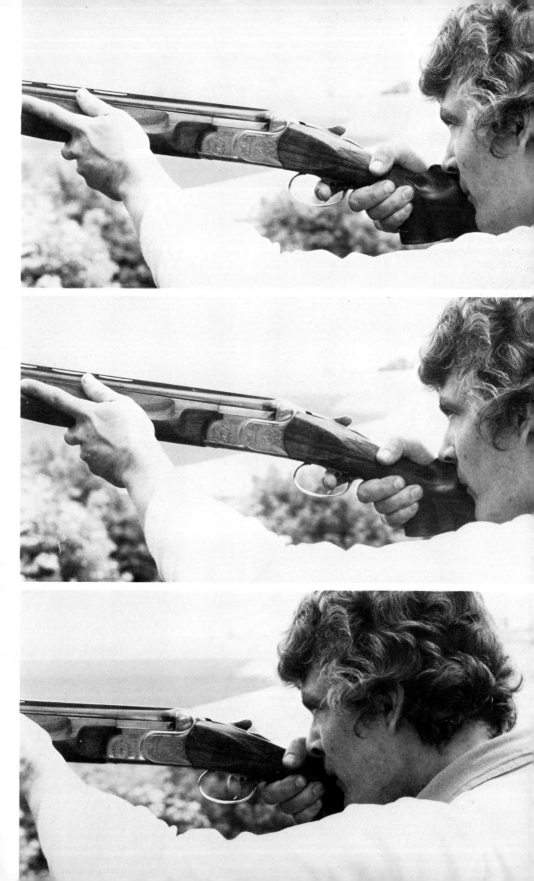

Top left   Trigger finger so placed to locate the trigger exactly on the first joint. Note the correct gap between nose and the second, third, and fourth fingers. See also the position of the front hand, a light hold with the forefinger and thumb lying alongside the barrels.

Centre left   The holds of both hands are the same, as is the position of the trigger finger. The shooter has begun to 'stock crawl'. Note the lessened gap between nose and fingers.

Bottom left   Even more 'stock crawling'. The close proximity of nose and fingers may prove painful.

Top   Some shooters prefer to use the pad of their trigger finger. Because this pad is fleshy there will be slightly more 'give' when the trigger is pulled.

Bottom   Front hand position normal, some 'stock crawling', the tip of the finger is being used to pull the trigger. This usage of the tip can sometimes result in pressure being placed on the side of the trigger instead of being applied straight backwards. Can cause seemingly variable pressures.

Top Again the tip of the finger is being used – not advised.

Centre Here the finger is placed so far through that the second pad is being used. This can sometimes cause bruising of the side of the second finger by the trigger guard.

Right The pad of the first finger is being used to pull the trigger, although there is more 'give' when using the pad. This shooter prefers to shoot in this way and his performance leaves nothing to be desired.

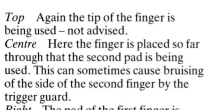

target and shooting it. Once the shoot is over, try to remember the problem targets, then in the company of one's coach, visit an OT layout and find the answers.

Ties and Tie Shooting
If two or more shooters obtain equal scores, precedence for the first three places in the competition is decided by shoot-off in rounds of 25 targets up to a maximum of three tie-breaking series. If after the three series the tie is not broken, the competitors will be classified equal.

Universal or Five Trap Trench

This is a similar discipline to Olympic Trench. There are, however, five traps spaced 1 m apart, set in a pit or trench. All traps are set to throw single targets at fixed and different trajectories. The targets must travel 75 m. The first two traps, nos 1 and 2, reading from the left, will throw angled targets to the right. The centre or no. 3 trap, will throw the straight forward target and must not deviate more than 20° left or right of the median line. Traps 4 and 5 will throw angled targets to the left.

The five shooting stations are set 15 m rear ward of the trench, they are numbered from the left, 1, 2, 3, 4 and 5 and are spaced 2.5 m apart. (See fig. 10, page 9.)

The shooters move from station to station as for OT. The shooter on call for his target may have a target thrown from any of the five traps. In a round of 25 targets, he should receive ten left-handers, ten right-handers, and five straight forward targets. So should the rest of the squad. The order of throwing will be unknown. During big competitions the target trajectories and angles are changed every evening and then the traps are sealed. All the problems of guns, ammunition, etc., are similar to those for OT. A careful study of an up-to-date UT rule book is essential.

Training
Because traps 1 and 2 are set to throw right-handed targets, trap 3 to throw the straight forward, and traps 4 and 5 to throw the left-hander, a progressive system of training can be followed.

The target release system must be fixed to allow targets from any single trap to be thrown at will and repeated as required. The pupil will commence with the straight forward target from trap 3, on Station 3. His stance, gun mounting and eye focussing, will be similar to that for OT. He should use a snap cap until his coach is satisfied the target line is being read, gun muzzles swung up, into and through the target without check. Live ammunition can then be used.

When this target from the middle trap can be successfully broken from Station 3, the pupil can progress back to Station 2, to Station 1, then forward from 1 through 2, 3, 4 and 5, all the time taking the target from trap 3.

The pupil can then begin on Station 1, the coach will throw the right-handed angled target from no. 1 trap, the pupil should progress from Station 1 through 2, 3, 4 and 5, still taking the right-hander from no. 1 trap. The next step is to begin again on Station 1 and taking the right-hander from trap 2, again work right across through all stations to 5.

Then back again to Station 1, taking the left-hander from trap 4 right through to Station 5.

Finally back to Station 1, taking the left-hander from trap 5 right through to Station 5.

This system of training should provide the pupil with an approximate sight picture for all five targets. Even when the traps on a Universal Trench layout are altered the basic technique will be similar.

After following the above training course, and being passed as competent by his coach, the pupil can consider competition shooting.

Squads, Squad Behaviour, Loss of Form, etc.
The advice given for Olympic Trench applies equally well to Universal Trench.

Ties and Tie Shooting
If two or more shooters obtain the same score in a competition, precedence for the first three places will be decided by tie shooting in 25-bird stages until a difference in the scores occurs.

Automatic Ball Trap

This is in many ways a similar discipline to Olympic Trench. The single trap used is set in a pit, the roof of which is level with the ground and on the same elevation as the surfaces of the five shooting stations.

These five stations shall be arranged in an arc, measured and drawn 15 m to the rear of the trap house. Station no. 3 is centred on an imaginary line drawn through the centre of the trap house and at right angles to its front. The stations are 3 m apart.

The trap is a single multi-oscillating (vertical and horizontal direction) mechanical or electrically operated trap, either manually or automatically loaded. Targets may be released manually, electrically or microphone electrically. The trap is so constructed that it will throw at random and with continuously changing angles and elevations an unbroken target within the vertical and horizontal limits stated in these rules. (See figs 6 to 9, pages 8–9.)

Target Distances, Angles and Elevation
The trap shall be adjusted so that in calm weather the targets will travel 75 m (+ or −5 m) over level ground. The height of the target above the level of the trap house roof and 10 m forward of the trap, shall be at least 1 m and not higher than 4 m.

The targets will be thrown within an area of not less than 30° or more than 45°, right and left of the imaginary centre line drawn through the centre of the trap house and Station 3. The horizontal angles are to be measured from the front edge of the trap house.

The shooters move from station to station as for OT. The shooter on calling for his target may have a target thrown anywhere within the above prescribed angles, heights and distances. At the present time it is possible, although unlikely, for a shooter to get a preponderance of similar targets, and for this reason ABT may never become an Olympic discipline. In the writer's opinion should clay target machines and their operation ever come under the control of the 'man from the Ministry', all manually operated traps, as in use at present, will be banned. The automatically loaded traps which do not require a trapper to place each target individually upon an oscillating trap arm, will then become mandatory.

In this age of electronics it is possible to programme an automatically loaded ball trap to throw a series of randomized targets so that each shooter is thrown in a round of 25 targets the following: ten left-handers, ten right-handers, and five going away. When this comes to pass, the discipline of ABT will have arrived, and the writer believes will then quickly take the place of OT.

Training

A similar training programme as previously laid down for OT can be used, with the following important differences. It is essential that whatever trap is used for training purposes, it must be capable of being set to throw and keep on throwing a series of targets all travelling on the same trajectories. At the present time the Danlac is an ideal trap for this purpose. These traps are fitted with a three button switch on the end of a long wander lead. With the first button on the switch, one can vary and then hold a specific angle for targets thrown, the second button controls and holds the targets elevation, the third button releases the target.

Training is simple on these traps. The shooter commences on Station 3. The trap will be set to throw a low elevation straight-away target. The shooter will premount his gun as for Station 3 OT and focus his eyes out over and around the barrels to a point 10 m in front of the trap house roof. Once he has become proficient on such a target he can move progressively left across to Station 1, then right back from 1 through 2, 3, 4 and to 5.

The trap is then set to throw the straight-away from Station 3, but at the middle elevation. Again the shooter commences on Station 3 and moves left as success is achieved across to 1. Then back through 2, 3, 4 and to 5.

The trap is then set to throw straight-aways from 3 at maximum elevation, the shooter using the same procedure, going from 3 through to 2 and then 1, then back from 1 through 2, 3, 4 and to 5.

All this will take many hours and many cartridges, it will also cost much money. Even so, if an experienced coach is in attendance success should be assured.

Having shot and become proficient at the straight-away at all elevations from all five stations, the same procedure of training is followed for the full left-hander at its lowest elevation, its mid elevation and its maximum elevation. The trap is finally set to throw the full low right-hander, then the mid elevation, and finally the maximum elevation targets. Once more the full sequence of training beginning on Station 3 is done.

Automatic Ball Trap is one of the most demanding disciplines and unless a training programme as above is followed, any success achieved must be slow, uncertain and costly.

Once a pupil has completed a full training course and has been passed as competent by his coach, he can consider competition shooting.

Squads, squad behaviour, loss of form, etc. for all these the advice given for OT applies equally well, and should be carefully followed.

Ties and Tie Shooting

If two or more shooters obtain equal scores, precedence for the first three places are decided by tie shoot-off in rounds of 25 targets, until a difference in the scores occurs.

8 The Referee

The referee, referred to in some rule books as the umpire, should be a person of wide experience in clay target shooting, especially in the discipline in which he is officiating. He should have a full understanding of the appropriate rules and their interpretation. Also a thorough knowledge of shotguns and their safe handling. Although a similar knowledge of human nature is not specified in any of the rule books, it is essential for any referee.

In any discipline before competition shooting begins, it is the prerogative of a prudent referee to check with the appointed jury that the targets to be thrown are regulation.

As each squad arrives on a layout, the referee will check that all members of that squad are present and know their order of firing. Any absent members' names will be clearly called three times in one minute by the referee. Members who are then still not present may be adjudged to be *absent* by the referee, who will then take appropriate action as laid down by the rules. This action varies in different disciplines.

It cannot be too strongly stressed that it is the duty of a shooter to be ready on any specific layout with gun and sufficient ammunition. Even when a squad hustler is employed, the onus is still on the shooter. Late or non-attendance can result in a fine of up to three targets in a round and/or eventual disqualification from the competition.

Once a referee has a squad assembled, his main function is to ensure that the equity of a competition is preserved and that all shotguns are handled safely. Moreover, to make immediate decisions regarding dead, lost, or irregular targets, which he should do by calling in a clear voice and/or with a distinct signal.

He must also be able to rule whether a gun has a malfunction, allowable or not. He should well understand that he is not there to harass the shooter.

The past two decades have seen a rapid growth in the sport. Inevitably many new shooters have little knowledge of the rules or what constitutes safe behaviour. The CPSA Executive have been rightly concerned about this and through their Coaching Committee run courses and examinations for would-be referees. It is to be hoped that this will further develop until all shoots, of whatever discipline, will be controlled by CPSA fully qualified and paid referees.

The duties of a referee vary between the disciplines, as follows.

DTL

The rules state that a 'puller shall release the target on call from the shooter. The referee shall announce the result and it shall be recorded on a score sheet'. So much for the rules. At most shoots the duties of referee and puller are now performed by one person, assisted by a scorer.

The rules also state that a bell shall be rung when the required five targets have been shot at each position from 1 to 5. A bell is rarely used today. Instead the scorer calls 'change' in a loud voice as soon as shooter no. 5 has shot his fifth target on a position. When this happens, all the shooters move to their right, except for the shooter on position 5. He will take any cartridges out of his open gun, and walk quietly back behind the squad to position 1. When all the members of the squad have moved and are settled on their new position, the referee will call 'line ready'. Then the squad leader will load and close his gun and call for his next target.

The referee will not allow any shooter movement, except on the call of change, or conversation, except for protests from the shooter. These he should attempt to resolve immediately.

All shooters should have sufficient ammunition for a full round. It is not generally realized that shooters can be fined or zeroed one target if they run out of ammunition during a round.

Pulling and Button Pressing
The words 'puller' and 'pulling' are derived from the fact that with the old Black Diamond traps used for DTL there was indeed a puller. He stood behind Station 3, and by pushing and pulling on a long lever, cocked the trap and released it.

In modern times most traps are cocked hydraulically or electrically, the targets being released electrically or acoustically. Whichever method is used, it is possible for the shooter to get slow or fast pulls. This can cause much annoyance between the puller or button presser and the members of the squad shooting. Also, most acoustic releases are fitted with a built-in delay, variable from 0.1 to 0.2 seconds. Therefore it is not unknown that targets on one layout are being released at a slower or faster delay than the targets thrown on an adjoining layout. Such a variation in timing is wrong. A good chief referee will make certain that all layouts at a particular ground have their acoustics carefully adjusted to provide exactly the same delay.

The Problems of Manual Release
At small shoots with only one layout operating, it is reasonably easy for the targets to be thrown immediately on the shooter's call. However, at larger shoots where the layouts are close together, a call from an adjoining layout can cause confusion. The puller will be keyed up, hearing and mistaking the call, and can throw the target. If the puller is really on the ball he will quickly call 'No bird'. Once he has done this,

regardless of whether the target is shot at, missed or killed, such a target is no longer part of a competition. Therefore, no result is scored and a fresh target must be thrown.

The same thing can happen if a slow pull is given, the referee should at once call 'No bird'. Problems can arise if a slow pull is given and the shooter fires before 'No bird' is called. It can be further complicated by the fact that shooters who are really keyed up and given a slow pull will sometimes be unable to stop themselves firing at least one shot at such a target. An experienced referee will know if he did give a slow or fast pull, and if he did he will usually allow another target, even if a single shot had been fired. If a shooter fires two shots, this action is deemed by the referee to prove acceptance of the target and the result must be scored.

Any shooter being given a slow or fast pull has the right to refuse the target. Again the puller/referee knows in his own mind whether the pull was fast or slow and should then judge accordingly.

Broken Targets
Broken targets, regardless of whether shot at or not, or whether 'No bird' is called or not, should not be scored and a fresh target must be thrown.

Irregular Targets
At the commencement of a stage or round of a registered shoot it is customary for the referee to 'show' the squad a target. Sometimes each member of a squad will be allowed to shoot one practice target from his first firing point. If any squad member believes the target shown, or the practice targets are not regulation, then is the time to protest to the referee.

Once traps in good condition have been correctly set up, irregular targets should be rare indeed. However, a shooter can refuse at any time in a competition to shoot at what he believes to be an irregular target. If the referee agrees, the shooter will be thrown another target. Should the referee disagree, the refused target will be scored as lost. Should a shooter fire one or two shots at an irregular target, he is deemed to have accepted it, and the referee, unless he had already ruled 'No bird', can insist on the result being scored.

Balk
Another tough problem. A piece of paper blowing across the ground in front of the shooters, empty cartons being thrown out of the trap house, someone talking loudly close behind the squad, stray dogs, children and so on – all these can cause distraction to the shooter. If such occur just as the shooter fires, the referee may, if he so decides, rule a balk. However, if they occur before the shooter calls for his target, and he subsequently fires, it is usual for the referee to rule that by calling and firing, the shooter has accepted the target, and the result will be scored.

Kill or Lost

Only the referee can decide this. In the case of a jury or club committee deciding a referee is incompetent and making wrong decisions regarding kills or losses, he can subsequently be removed. However, he cannot be overruled and his previous decisions must stand.

Jury Appeals

The jury has the right to overrule the referee on a point of law. A shooter who disagrees with a referee's ruling on a point of law should immediately raise his hand and quietly protest to the referee. The referee will note the protest, and if there is a jury present it can immediately give a ruling. If no jury is present, the disagreeing shooter can at the end of the round put in a written protest to the jury, who will consider the case as soon as possible. Its decision is final.

Challenge and Protest Regarding Ammunition

Any competitor has the right to put in a written protest, together with a £1 note, regarding the legality of another shooter's ammunition. A referee is also empowered to do this. Cartridges so examined and found to violate the rules can result in the user being disqualified. If the cartridges examined are found to be legal, the £1 is paid to the challengee. A set of accurate scales should always be available at shoots.

Gun Defects or Malfunctions

Gun malfunctions due to shooter negligence result in the missed target being scored as lost.

After a gun has misfired twice in any stage, further subsequent misfire will result in the target being scored lost.

Should a shooter have a gun malfunction, he must keep the gun pointing in a safe direction until the referee has examined it. Any movement of safety catch or opening of the gun before this examination will result in the target being scored lost.

Guns with ventilated recoil reducers on the barrels are not allowed in DTL shooting.

No gun is to be loaded with more than two cartridges at any one time.

At the end of the round all the squad shooters are allowed to and should check their scores. Any disagreement should be voiced immediately.

Behaviour of Spectators

The referee should try to keep the spectators quiet and well back from the firing points. It is unfortunate that the behaviour of some spectators, and even worse, a few experienced shooters who should know better, leaves something to be desired. For such people to stand close behind shooters and talk in loud voices is bad behaviour and the good and efficient referee will quietly, but firmly, put a stop to such activities.

The Skeet Disciplines

At the present time it would appear that both English and ISU rules are in a state of flux. This is nothing new as both have been changed before. It behoves referees, therefore, not only to possess an appropriate rule book but to understand thoroughly the current interpretation of these rules by the ruling body.

One of the worst aspects of these rule variations being that in ISU Skeet, two cartridges *must* be loaded before the two single targets are shot on stands 2, 3, 4, 5 and 6. Only one cartridge being loaded at a time for Station 8, high or low targets. For English Skeet only one cartridge is allowed to be loaded before shooting any single.

For American NSSA the shooter may please himself and may load one or two cartridges – a needless, unsafe complication of rules which in the interests of all Skeet shooters should be resolved.

Targets

Targets will have been put through the hoop, and also checked for distances thrown before a competition starts. The wise referee will have observed this in company with the jury.

The squads are shown targets before a competition commences. Usually a single target is thrown from each house, plus a double. Once a squad starts shooting, it is deemed to have accepted the targets and their trajectories. There should be little variation of target trajectories unless traps malfunction or club officials stupidly mix different makes of target. Even windy conditions arising during a competition should not require trap alterations, though it will cause some targets to travel farther or less distances. The traps will, or should have been, set correctly in still air conditions, and subsequently should be left alone, regardless of the distances thrown.

There will be two assistant referees, one to decide whether the high house target is killed in bounds, the other to do the same for the low house target. Targets ruled as killed out of bounds are scored as lost.

The button presser acts as chief referee and calls 'No bird', 'Kill' or 'Lost' as the case may be. This procedure may be varied at some competitions with only the 'lost' targets being called. The scorer on the visible score board will signify that he has heard the 'lost' target or targets called by raising an arm. There should also be another scorer to mark the official score card.

Squad Behaviour

The referee must be in control of the squad and should have little trouble with an experienced one. All members of the squad should shoot in rotation in the order named on the score card. They should not be allowed to move forward onto the next firing point until all have finished shooting on the previous firing point.

Irregular Targets, Fast or Slow Pulls

No claims of irregularity should be allowed where targets were actually fired on, both in singles or doubles. If the alleged irregularity consists simply of deviation from the prescribed line of flight, or in the case of an alleged 'quick' or 'slow' pull, unless the referee has distinctly called 'No bird' prior to the firing of the shot in the event of a quick pull, or prior to the emergence of the target in the event of a slow pull. Otherwise, if the shooter fires the result shall be scored.

In ISU Skeet the delay of up to three seconds after shooter's call can cause problems. The biggest being due to the target which comes out right on the button. ISU shooters are so used to waiting one, two or even three seconds, that they tend to call with a waiting complex attitude of mind. A target coming out right on the button therefore takes them by surprise. Even so, if such target(s) are shot at, the results are to be scored. Only the referee can decide on irregular targets or 'No birds'.

Gun Position

English and American gun positions, being optional, should cause no problems.

ISU Skeet

The 'gun down' position, being mandatory, can cause problems. Too high a position should result firstly in a warning from the referee; if a shooter persists or begins to mount his gun too early the referee can call 'No target', and make the shooter repeat. After two warnings in a round, the result of the next or future transgressions will be scored 'Lost'. For both disciplines the referee's decision is final in matters concerning dead, lost or irregular targets.

Visible Distraction

The referee may permit a new target to be thrown if he believes the shooter was visibly distracted. Due to rumoured changes in Skeet rules it is pointless to attempt to cover all present interpretations.

At the present time both English and ISU rules forbid straps or slings on Skeet guns. The ISU rules insist that magazine guns are plugged to prevent such guns holding more than two cartridges at any one time. For both disciplines a properly functioning gun or parts of a gun cannot be changed during a round of 25 targets. A referee may, if he decides, allow a malfunctioning gun to be changed. A total of two malfunctions per round of gun and/or cartridge is allowed. After which targets not broken due to such malfunction will be scored as lost.

The cartridge must be loaded as specified, and each round shot with cartridges of one type only. The referee may remove an unfired cartridge from a competitor's gun for inspection. This is to prevent occurrences such as the use of an excess shot charge, mixed sizes of shot and the insertion of spreader devices for close targets.

Jury Duty and Appeal

It is the duty of the jury to ensure the correct application of the regulations by both the referees and range personnel. The jury can set a fee to accompany protests. Such appeals or protests can be submitted to the jury either verbally or in writing. If the protest is upheld, the fee will be returned.

At the end of the round the scores should be checked by the shooters, and the referee will make certain that each shooter initials his score. In major ISU Championships where there is a visible score board, the results shown there will be the determining factor in deciding the final score. Failure of a shooter to sign the score sheet before it leaves the field eliminates all right to protest of scores, except for erroneous transcribing.

Spectator Behaviour

With all disciplines it is the duty of the referee to keep the spectators quiet and well back from the firing point.

Coaching

No coaching is allowed when competition shooting is in progress and the referee must make sure that this does not happen.

English and FITASC Sporting

Referees will encounter many problems peculiar to the above two disciplines.

The shooting position for English Sporting is at present optional. For FITASC Sporting the rule reads: Article 3 'The shooter adopts the standing position, his feet within the limits of the shooting stand, his gun held with two hands clearly out of the shoulder. Gun touching the body under the armpit. He will keep this position until the bird or birds are in sight.' The target or targets must be released by the referee by non-visible instructions as silent rise and with a delay of up to three seconds after the shooter has pronounced 'Ready'.

These FITASC rules still cause much annoyance on occasion. Some shooters are unfortunately 'creepers', mostly because of tension, and commence to slide their gun butt up and into their shoulder pocket as soon as they have called 'Ready' and before the target appears. The observant referee will quickly call 'No bird' and instruct the shooter to take the target(s) again. After three such incidents on one stand or firing point the target(s) will be scored zero or zero zero.

All of this is fine when the target's appearance and the shooter's gun position can be readily observed and checked by the referee as in straight forward going-away targets. Life can become difficult when the targets appear 30 to 40 yd off right or left, or perhaps the targets are being thrown from behind both referee and shooter. At such times it is often almost impossible for the referee to observe shooter movement and target appearance simultaneously.

Other complications arising in the past have been due to different referees applying varying standards, some referees even insisting that the toe of the gun butt be visible below the shooter's elbow, as in ISU Skeet, until the target or targets appear in sight. Such a ruling is incorrect, and while no one wishes to cause trouble, such inconsistencies should not be tolerated either by shooters or jury. The offence should be quietly discussed by the shooter, with first the referee, after which, as a last resort, a complaint should be placed before the jury. It has the power to make rulings on such points of law or rule interpretation and then so instruct referees. Disobeying such rulings can result in referees being removed forthwith.

In FITASC Sporting the gun must be shouldered when fired at the target, even for the rabbit clay. In other words, no firing from the hip or any gun down position is allowed. For English Sporting there is no such instruction.

Sighting Practice or Addressing the Target

This is a much misunderstood rule and very often transgressed by shooters of English Sporting, especially those shooters who have taken up English Sporting after maybe years of shooting English Skeet. In the latter and up to the present time the shooter is allowed to premount his gun and then drop it out of his shoulder pocket before calling for the target.

The Targets

Both English Sporting and FITASC targets may differ considerably from all the other disciplines. Sporting targets and firing points are set up by the shoot organizers. They try to set up sensible targets and to ensure that trappers, safety officers and referees are correctly briefed. A small percentage do no such thing.

It is not unknown for Trapper A on no. 1 layout to be throwing crossing targets which are perhaps 30 yd distance when shot. The trouble begins when Trapper B is detailed to take over from Trapper A and because of sloppy briefing has no idea where to place the clay(s) on the trap arm(s). Even more annoying is when at the same time as the trappers are changing over, so are the referees. Such a situation is fraught, to say the least, with neither new trappers or referee knowing where the targets are supposed to go. It is almost inevitable that targets will then be thrown on different trajectories than before. Some know-all among the spectators will adversely comment and at once there is the makings of much trouble.

To prevent this situation arising the organizers should have stops put on the trap arms. The traps and clays covered with a protective roof to keep everything dry. Wet targets and trap arms cause much variation in target flight, although targets with a serrated running edge will usually vary less in flight in wet conditions than those with plain or smooth running rims. Some coloured targets when wet will quickly become very slippery and this again will cause flight variation.

Targets should be of one make only. Targets of different makes may fly on slightly varying trajectories, target brand A may even travel 20 yd further than target brand B.

Traps with arms cocked against a positive stop are less susceptible to target variations in flight than those traps which are released by the trapper pushing the arm back over centre. Even so, a good trapper who always pushes the trap arm back over centre at the same tempo should have little trouble in throwing all his targets on the same flight paths.

Because of these problems the prudent referee will always insist on seeing a few targets thrown in the presence of the jury or shoot captain before a competition begins. In this way he should know well the correct trajectories. Relief referees should also insist on being shown a few targets before the referee he is replacing leaves the stand.

Trappers

The same procedure applies. The first trapper should be shown exactly where to place the target(s) on the trap arm, preferably this arm should be fitted with target stops. The relief trapper should also be briefed by the previous trapper.

Only by taking the above precautions can the referee hope to preserve the equity of a competition.

Guns

For English Sporting the shooter may use a different gun on every stand. For FITASC only one gun may be used, guns are marked at the commencement of a competition and may not be changed. However, the referee may allow a malfunctioning gun which cannot be quickly repaired to be replaced. Straps on guns are forbidden, magazine guns only loaded with two cartridges.

Cartridges

For FITASC all cartridges must be of normal loading with no spreader devices. For English Sporting desperante or spreader devices are at present legal. Maximum for English is $1\frac{1}{8}$ oz shot load, sizes English 6 to 9. Maximum for FITASC $1\frac{1}{4}$ oz pellet diameter between 2 and 2.5 mm.

The referee can at any time in either discipline take an unfired cartridge from a competitor's gun for examination. The referee can order the shooter to take another target(s) if he believes the shooter has been materially disturbed.

Gun and Cartridge Malfunction Not Due to Shooter

For English Sporting three malfunctions are allowed on any stand or firing point. The fourth or any subsequent malfunction of either gun or cartridge is considered excessive and will be scored lost.

For FITASC Sporting the rules are clear. Rule 25 states the fourth and subsequent malfunctions during a series of 25 pigeons shall be scored zero.

Spectators and Squads

For English Sporting the referee is charged with keeping the spectators quiet, preventing any coaching by other competitors or onlookers.

For FITASC Sporting only one squad and no spectators, except jury members, are allowed on a layout at any one time. Therefore the referee has only to keep the rest of the squad members quiet and prevent them giving any coaching.

The referee should call 'Kill', 'Lost' or 'No target' clearly so that scorer and shooter hear his decision. He should let the shooter check his score at the end of that shooter's stint on the firing point. The referee's decision on 'Lost', 'Killed' or 'Irregular targets' is final and cannot be overruled by the jury.

Protests

These are best done as a short written and signed notice for either discipline. However, for English Sporting the written protest must be accompanied by £1, non-returnable if the protest is lost.

Olympic Trap, Universal Trench and Automatic Trap

The referee will encounter many problems peculiar to these three disciplines.

The shooting position adopted by the shooter on call for his target is optional.

There is only one target taken at any one firing point or station, shooters are therefore walking from one firing station to the next almost continuously. No shooter is allowed to move to the next station on his right until the shooter there has called for and fired at his target. After each shooter fires at his target from Station 5, he will open his gun, remove any unfired cartridges, and keeping his gun open and empty, walk quietly back behind the rest of the squad to the waiting position behind Station 1. When the shooter on Station 1 has fired, the waiting competitor will move onto Station 1, load his gun, and after the shooter on Station 5 has shot his target, shoot in his turn.

Time Allowance

When a shooter has fired, the next shooter on his right has 15 seconds maximum to close his gun, mount it or otherwise, and call for his target. The referee will have little trouble with an experienced squad. Unfortunately, inexperienced shooters sometimes transgress, committing such offences as moving to their next firing point before the person there has fired or walking noisily along behind the rest of the squad shooters and scuffling their feet among empty cases, even doing this while carrying their gun open or closed but with a cartridge or cartridges in the chamber.

For all three disciplines target trajectories are checked each day before the competition begins. The prudent referee will be in attendance while this is being done in the presence of the jury.

For Olympic Trap and Universal Trench a different scheme is set at the commencement of each day's shooting, with an electric selector in operation to ensure all shooters receive identical targets in any one round. This selector must be changed by one notch after each round of five targets and before the shooter on Station 1 calls for his target.

Trouble can arise when the person operating the selector turns it immediately the shooter on Station 5 has called for his target. Should this target come out as a 'No bird' or should the competitor receive another target as a repeat, the whole sequence may be thrown out of balance. Therefore the referee must instruct and ensure that the selector is not turned until the shooter on Station 5 has been thrown and shot at a regulation target. Targets are thrown on command by electric or acoustic release.

Gun and Cartridge Malfunction Not Due to Shooter

For Universal Trench the shooter will have the right to a new target three times in a round of 25 targets. The fourth and subsequent malfunction will be scored zero. For Olympic and Automatic Trap the maximum is two malfunctions, the third and subsequent being scored. If both shots are fired together, the result will be scored, and this applies to all three disciplines.

If a shooter fires when it is his turn but before he gives the command, a repeat target will be allowed. However, if he fires the second shot at the original target, the result will be scored.

For Olympic and Automatic Trap, if a gun misfires on the first barrel, and the shooter does not fire the second the target will be repeated. Unless it is the third or subsequent malfunction, when the result is scored zero. For Universal Trench, it is the fourth malfunction which is scored. In any of the disciplines if the second shot is fired after the first barrel misfires, the result shall be scored.

No Birds

This is always the referee's decision and when so declared, must be taken again regardless. The new target shall be mandatory from the same trap that caused the 'No bird', both in the case of Olympic Trap and Universal Trench. But the shooter may *not* refuse it, even if he believes it was thrown from another trap.

Irregular targets shot at are deemed to have been accepted, and are therefore scored, regardless whether one or two shots have been fired.

Guns

There are rules common to all three disciplines. Not larger than 12 gauge. Straps and slings not allowed. Compensators and like devices not allowed. Changing of guns between stations not permitted, the same applying to properly functioning parts. The referee can accept a change

of gun if he decides a gun or part has developed a malfunction not due to
the shooter.

No gun to be loaded with more than two cartridges. When shooting
Olympic and Automatic Trap, magazine guns must be blocked to make
it impossible to place more than one cartridge in the magazine.

Ammunition

Maximum shot load $1\frac{1}{8}$ oz or 32 g. Shot size not larger than 2.5 in.
diameter or English size 6 shot.

The referee may remove an unfired cartridge from a competitor's gun
for inspection. Shooting and sighting practice on another competitor's
target is not allowed.

The referee's decision regarding hits, misses, or irregular targets is
final and cannot be overruled. He should make decisions quickly and
clearly and give a distinct signal for all lost targets. Where there is a
visible score board in operation, the scorer should also respond with a
visible signal to the referee on such lost targets.

Protest

Protests by shooters should be in writing. For Olympic and Automatic
Trap they have to be accompanied by the equivalent of USA $10, or
English £5. If the protest is upheld, the fee is returned. For Universal
Trench no fee is required.

The referee is charged with keeping spectators quiet, preventing
coaching by other competitors or onlookers. He can order the shooter
to take another target if he believes the shooter has been visibly
disturbed.

Photographers, Television and the Press

It is advised that assistance and guidance be given to the above on the
placement of their equipment so that it does not interfere with competitors or officials. Filming, recording or interviews should be done during
training periods of the competition or after the competition.

Some of the Referee's Problems

It has already been stated that the referee is there to preserve the equity
of the competition, also that he is not there to harass the shooter. Any
would-be referee must realize that officiating fairly can be very difficult.
Split-second decisions are essential. The referee who believes that *he*
cannot make mistakes is living in a world divorced from reality. In
top-level target shooting much prestige and money may be at stake. To
have a target disallowed through bad referee interpretation of the rules,
or worse still, through a moment's carelessness or inattention, may
prove to be the difference between success and failure as far as that
competition is concerned.

The referee must know the interpretation of the existing rules at the
time of the competition. Should the referee realize he has made a
mistake, he should be honest and admit it, apologize and amend. Only

p left   P. Stanbury with his Webley and Scott gun. In a shooting career
more than 50 years Stan shot hundreds of thousands of cartridges
rough this gun. It is bored full and full. He won many championships
th it at DTL, Skeet and Sporting. The gun is still in sound and tight
ndition.

p right   Stanbury stance and style.

ttom left   A modern exponent of Stanbury, straight front leg, lifted
ck heel, front hand with finger pointed along and under the barrels.

ttom right   A champion showing his versatility using the Churchill
nce and style. This entails shooting off a straight back leg, with the heel
the front foot lifted.

Left Stanbury style whilst shooting a semi-automatic g[u]
Above left Churchill style whilst shooting a
semi-automatic gun.
Above right The long front hand tends to pull the
barrels sideways and also block the swing, especially on
high, fast-driven targets.
Below A poor stance with both knees bent, butt low
and out of shoulder pocket, cheek off comb.

Left   Another poor stance.
Above   Muzzles held correctly for the high target.
Below left   Gun nearly premounted. To connect with a high target the muzzles will have to be swung in an arc.
Below right   A young shooter with a 28 bore successfully coping with 100 ft high targets. Since the stock is rather long, he has brought his front hand back to help his swing.

Top left   World champion J. A. R. Elliott's stance (1890).
Top right and bottom left and right   Modern stances.

Top left   Another modern stance.
Top right   Skeet, the wind back.
Bottom left   Killing the target.
Bottom right   Skeet, the aggressive stance of a lady champion.

Above left   What the coach expects to see. Muzzles out in front of the low house target which was then broken.
Above right   Sporting doubles, right to left. Shooting off the front foot, rear target shot first, swing kept going then to kill the front target. Front foot pointing left allows unchecked swing.
Below left   Another top class shooter taking the similar targets. Slight variation of feet position, rear target taken first. Both targets were broken.
Below right   The low angling incomer. Another lady champion, already she has obtained that eye, muzzle, and target relationship so essential for consistent top class shooting.

Top   A left-handed shooter's attempt at gun fitting. By mounting the butt out on the shoulder point he caused the gun to shoot right. Head lifting caused high pattern placement.
Above   When the butt was in the proper place the pattern placement proved there was no need for more cast. Head lifting still caused the pattern to be high.
Above right   What the head of a cartridge case can tell the expert. No. 1 was a reloaded cartridge. The home loader had foolishly used the wrong powder bush. The evidence of high pressures is the flattened head, the ruptured rim, the gun barrels blown off the action face. No. 2 has a good striker or firing pin indentation. There is evidence of striker pin drag.
Below   Useful equipment. The four cleaning rods are used in sequence from bottom to top of the picture. Above the rods is a Perazzi stock-removing tool and a copper-headed hammer. Below this is a trigger pull tester and pair of snap caps. Below again, two hollow ground screw drivers, socket spanner, rod and rachet to remove stockbolts. Spring cramp. Two dowels with handles to push out the retaining pins in a Remington trigger assembly. Nylon scouring pads to remove fouling. 4 × 2 flannelette cloth. Walnut stock oil. Rangoon oil, Youngs 303 oil and solvent. Mitchell X3 grease and Gun Glide grease in tubes for action joint. Cleaning cloths, Legia Spray oil, forceps and parallel jawed pliers.

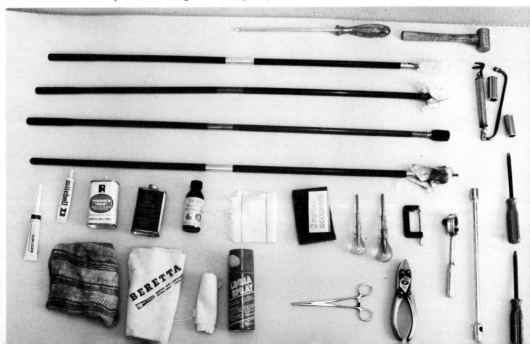

Top left English choke tubes, a design which throws fine patterns.
Left Raising the comb height by means of Blue Tack and tape.

Below left An example of the stocker's art. The stock has been lengthened, also wood has been inlet and added to provide a new comb resembling the Greener rational stock shape.

Below The low hold centre point technique. The centre target of the five placed on the rear of the trap house roof marks the place where the muzzles are held or pointed. This is regardless of the firing point which the shooter occupies.

The low hold five position gun point. The five targets placed on the roof marks the five positions or holds the muzzles. When on FP1 the hold would be on the target on the left hand corner. Every time the shooter moves to the next firing point he moves his hold to the next mark or target. When on FP5 he should therefore be holding on the target placed on the right hand corner of the trap house.

Bottom The high hold five position gun point. The tops of the five piles of targets mark the holds from the five firing points. The white marker board in the distance shows the 50 yd mark used to check the target fallout distances. The white cords angling away left and right from the trap house are placed to allow the angles of regulation targets to be checked.

in this way can he hope to keep the confidence of the shooters. He must be fair and be seen to be fair.

The Sour Squad or Shooter

At all times the referee must take care to avoid providing the reason, or worse, excuse, for shooter sourness. Most competitors are under stress and tension, a referee's mistake, quickly followed by his amendment and apology will usually avoid trouble.

In cases where the shooter protests at a referee's decision on a point of rule or law interpretation, the referee should, wherever possible, state his ruling with his reasons. He can then, if he wishes, allow the shooter to take the target again. A note with the result is put on the bottom of the score sheet, and the whole question eventually referred to the jury. Then, should the jury decide against the referee, the result of the repeat target being immediately available means a final decision can at once be taken. The alternative, where the protesting shooter has to wait until the end of a competition and then has to shoot at one specific target *cold* perhaps, can prove much more traumatic. Conditions of light and weather may have changed, any squad rhythm and feeling will have long since departed, and the shooter will have been the prey of extra and needless worry throughout a long day's competition.

Shooter's Tricks

Thankfully these are few, the great majority play fair. But there will always be the odd rotten apple.

Second Barrel Malfunction

Some shooters have second barrel malfunctions due to their not letting go of the trigger after the first shot. When this occurs, the wide boys will keep tight hold of the trigger and ask the referee to use his finger to press on their trigger finger. Naturally the gun will not fire and the referee may mistakenly allow another target. This is wrong. The referee should take the gun from the shooter and without jiggling the trigger in any way, simply press it, while keeping the muzzles pointing in a safe direction. If the gun fires, the correct ruling is gun malfunction due to the shooter.

Mechanical Triggers

Sometimes a shooter may get an alleged misfire on his first shot, if the referee then pulls the trigger the other barrel may fire. The referee's next move is to open the gun, if both cartridges are ejected and the unfired case has an indented cap the shooter may rightly claim that he had a misfire on this, his first barrel. This may be true, on the other hand, it has not been unknown in the past for a shooter to carry a cartridge which has already misfired and to load this. The idea being, in sporting targets especially, that a free practice swing is thereby obtained, and also another sight of the target before shooting at it for real. It is also possible with some o/u single selective trigger guns to load the gun, and hold the trigger back while closing it. If the shooter then attempts to fire, the first barrel will not, because the tumbler is already down. Alternatively, the shooter can hold the trigger back while closing the gun, then he will alter the firing sequence. In this manner he will fire one barrel and the second barrel will not fire. Under the old English Sporting rules with some doubles this did give the shooter an advantage; the rules have, therefore, been altered, and at present, a repeat or proof double has to be thrown with both targets to be scored for up to the three allowable malfunctions per firing point.

The prudent referee should visit a reputable gunsmith and have such tricks demonstrated. Experienced gunsmiths know which make of gun can be fiddled in this way and which not, and this knowledge should be acquired by the referee.

Finally
All problems arising during a shoot should, if possible, be settled immediately. To let a shooter or squad believe they had a grievance, if only for the remainder of a stage, is wrong, and will usually result in a sour shooter or squad. This must be avoided at all costs. Everyone will benefit from the actions of a fair, understanding referee, whose whole aim is to interpret honestly the rules for the shooters without fear or favour.

9 Forming & Running a Clay Shooting Club

The first step is to write to the CPSA requesting a supply of its booklets on clay shooting, including the excellent one called, *How to Form and Organise a Clay Shooting Club*. The enquirer will also receive, *Score with your Bird*, together with a leaflet giving some of the advantages of joining the CPSA, both as a member and also as an affiliated club.

Forming a club is relatively easy. Finding a suitable ground is difficult, and subsequently to run and keep on running a successful club is very hard and demanding work for the club officials. So much is this so that one must agree with the beliefs expressed some 20 years ago by the proprietor of a gun shop. At that time he had had some 60 years' experience of clay clubs and their problems. He put the life of a successful clay club and its committee, especially its committee, as around seven years. After which time most committee members tend to run out of steam, even if they do not, their wives do, which usually amounts to the same thing.

Today his opinions still hold true for most clubs. There are exceptions; most long-running and successful clubs have a paid secretary and treasurer who run the club as a business.

Twenty years ago the majority of even big clubs functioned actively only between Easter and the end of September, shooting practice one evening a fortnight, and running some six to eight Saturday Competition shoots for the season.

Nowadays some clubs shoot practice or training two evenings per week throughout the year, using floodlights for the dark winter evenings. One hundred target Competition shoots are also fixed to take place on most Sundays. This adds up to the club grounds being used some 150 days or evenings in the year.

Sportsmen who decide that they would like to start a club should first visit their local gun shop. The manager or owner will have a good idea of the need or otherwise for a club in the area. It is also possible that among his customers there will be landowners, farmers, or quarry owners who may be willing to provide a suitable site for the new club. Should the gun shop owner prove to be enthusiastic about the new project he may well agree to hold a meeting of kindred spirits on his premises one evening in order to explore the possibilities.

Experience has shown that most gun shop proprietors are keen to have a flourishing gun club in their locality, since it provides the chance of sales of suitable traps, together with bulk sales of clay targets and cartridges. Very often these proprietors will agree to act as club armourer, also to visit the club with a selection of guns and so on for trial and maybe purchase by club members. All in all, a friendly tie-up with a local gun shop should make life easier for the organizers, and provide useful know-how concerning guns, cartridges, and equipment.

A Suitable Site

This must depend primarily on the choice of discipline. For instance, for all the disciplines except that of Sporting, a level site with a clear background is required. The ground should face north-east, if possible, to minimize trouble from the sun. There should be no public footpaths or bridleways on the piece of ground selected. A fallout area for pellets, missed targets and pieces of broken targets is essential.

A minimum danger zone of at least 300 yd is required in front of the traps set up for the Going-Away disciplines.

Size 6 shot pellets are the largest allowed for clay shooting. Burrard gives a maximum range for no. 6 pellets when fired from a gun held at an elevation of 33°, which gives the maximum range, as 220 yd. Experiments carried out by the writer over a measured stretch of smooth water showed that with favourable following wind conditions, size 6 shot travelled 260 to 270 yd.

This, however, is only part of the story. There have been occasions when a portion of the pellets in a cartridge have balled due to cold welding or some other cause. Burrard reports a case where some pellets balled and a man had his jaw broken and some teeth carried away by this cluster of pellets. The distance was some 133 yd and the weight of pellets taken from the man's jaw was $\frac{1}{3}$ oz.

As far as this writer's research has shown there have been no accidents recorded with normal 12 gauge, size 6 shot cartridges at any greater distance. For this reason 300 yd plus is regarded as a safe distance by the CPSA and other clay shooting associations.

For Skeet ranges the CPSA gives a minimum danger zone as 300 yd in front, and 600 yd, sideways. Many clubs incorporate DTL with a Skeet range, having the DTL set up midway between the Skeet houses. Where more than one DTL range is installed there should be a minimum distance of not less than 40 yd between each layout, and the danger zone increased accordingly.

Access to the Ground

An easy access with plenty of visibility from the road is essential. Planning permission is unlikely to be obtained if the access road to the proposed ground comes out onto a busy road on say, a blind corner.

Nearby residential areas can cause much trouble, as can the presence of churches for instance. Tests should be carried out to assess the noise level. The results can be used to back up planning applications. Should a level site and clear background be unobtainable, a level site with a completely wooded background may prove satisfactory, if the targets thrown are coloured instead of black. Obviously, any wooded background should be situated outside the danger zone, or if closer, must be private woods to which the public have no access.

There should be sufficient space on free-draining level ground for the parking of members' cars.

Sporting Layouts
By their very nature and because normally only one person is shooting on a particular firing point at any one time, it is relatively easy to prepare and establish a compact shooting ground for a variety of Sporting targets. However, unless there are some contours in the ground in a Sporting layout, either one or two towers will be required. Here again there may be planning difficulties. An old unused and level-bottomed large quarry often proves an ideal site for a Sporting layout. Traps can be placed either on the quarry bottom, or back from the quarry top. Thereby providing the wide range of Sporting targets required.

Club Membership and Rules
Affiliation of the new club and its members to the CPSA is essential. By this means not only will a vast amount of clay shooting knowledge become available, but also the advantages of the CPSA's insurance scheme.

Equipment
Suitable traps and trap houses will be required. Unfortunately, not only must the trap houses be shot proof, this is easy to do, they must as far as possible be vandal-proof as well. This problem of modern times is made worse as far as clay clubs are concerned because they are usually isolated due to noise problems. Therefore, they are in thinly populated areas and vandals can wreak their destruction almost without hindrance. There is also the problem of equipment security, for it is not uncommon for traps and targets to be stolen from isolated sites. In one instance clay traps were stolen from the top of an 80 ft tower, even though the last 50 ft of the steel tower had been left without any kind of ladder. This, unfortunately, acted as no deterrent, the thieves simply climbed the tower's outside girders, unbolted the traps, lowered them in some way and departed.

For this reason as far as possible, trap houses have to be lockable and left locked. Where vandals have become a persistent nuisance, some clubs have found the only alternative is to set up the traps for every meeting. When the shoot has finished, all traps are dismantled, and taken with any unused clay targets to a safe and secure location. This may often be found on a local farm, where the farmer will act as equipment storer for the club.

Ammunition
Local bye-laws must be considered. It is almost impossible to store cartridges safely on isolated sites. Here the local gun shop will usually

prove an asset, supplying cartridges on sale or return. This arrangement makes life much easier for club secretary and member alike.

Traps

Today there is available a wide selection of traps. These range from the small, but none the less efficient, manually cocked, loaded, and released trap costing £40 to £50 to the super all-electric, and fully automatic trap, with its 300 target capacity turret, costing £3000 to £4000. It is true that such traps require an electricity supply but portable generators are easily obtainable and very efficient, therefore this poses no problem.

Clay Targets

Should adequate and safe storage be available it can be advantageous to buy targets in bulk. However, until a clay club becomes well established it may be better to collect clays from the local supplier of cartridges on the same sale or return basis.

Once a likely site has been found, and there are a sufficient number of prospective members, say 15, a general meeting can be called. The rules adopted should follow those advised in the CPSA booklet. The management will consist of a president or chairman, vice-president, field captain and/or safety officer, secretary, treasurer, armourer, and approximately five committee men or women. All should have full voting powers.

Running the Club

A bank account should be opened, preferably at the local branch, into which all monies can be paid. Only the hon. treasurer will have the power to draw on this account, and only then, after sanction on a resolution by the committee. Auditors should be appointed for the annual inspection of accounts. Copies of such audited accounts should be in every member's possession at least seven days before the annual general meeting. The cost of a member's annual subscription must be decided either with or without an entrance fee. The date for the end of the financial year must be fixed.

The club should be affiliated to the CPSA. It is also advisable to invite the Association's development officer down to the first general meeting, and indeed, to all subsequent AGMs. Unfortunately, at present there is only one development officer and with some 400 affiliated clubs it is inevitable that his attendance will not always be possible. However, as with all the CPSA executive and staff, help and advice is always willingly supplied by phone or letter. They will also give the name and address of the regional CPSA secretary, who will also help. Any rules, bye-laws, or recommendations proposed by the CPSA may be adopted by the club. A special general meeting on a petition signed by two-thirds of the members should be held within 14 days of its presentation.

Election of new members should be proposed and seconded by members of the club and considered at the first committee meeting after such application.

Unpaid Subscriptions

Privileges of membership may be withdrawn from members whose subscriptions have lapsed for more than two months.

Visitors

Members may introduce visitors, not more than two at any one meeting. No visitor is allowed to shoot more than three times in a season. Members introducing visitors shall be liable for all debts to the club incurred by him.

Unacceptable Conduct

A member may be asked to resign forthwith by the committee if it decides that his conduct warrants this. In the event of his non-resignation the committee may remove such a member's name.

Betting

No betting is allowed, under pain of expulsion. This is a difficult rule to enforce, many members often having small side bets between themselves. Most committees will accept this, but quickly put a stop to any attempt at large-scale organized betting by members or visitors.

Payment for Cartridges and Fees

Members must use such targets and cartridges as decided by the club, and pay for them before use. This rule should be strictly enforced. While most shooters today buy their cartridges in bulk, it is essential that members understand that competition fees must be paid on entering. Otherwise it may be the thankless task of the treasurer to have to ask for the fee afterwards, this can be embarassing and is best avoided.

Practice Cards

Some clubs waive the above rule at practice shoots, especially at those clubs which mainly shoot Sporting. Here a member is given a score card with his name on it. At each practice stand he gives the card to the scorer who enters upon it each target shot at. By this means the member can shoot as much or as little as he wishes at any stand or firing point. When he has finished he takes his marked card back to the entries secretary who will add up the number of targets and charge accordingly. This will also be marked as paid on the master sheet.

It is usually a condition of membership that the club will not be held responsible for any accident or injury incurred by members or visitors.

The president or chairman is responsible for having meetings called and generally chairs them. In his absence it is usual for a vice-president to officiate. The hon. secretary is responsible, with help, for keeping accurate scores and records in suitable books, attending to the clerical work incidental to the running of the club and staging of shoots.

The treasurer is responsible for collecting all subscription fees, and other monies from club members. He must keep proper records of club funds and pay only such accounts as approved by the committee.

The field captain is responsible for the care of the ground, main-tenance of traps and equipment, and the conduct of the shooting. He should ensure that sufficient targets of the required colour and size are at each trap before shooting commences. Because of variations between targets from different makers, only one make of target of the correct colour should be supplied in sufficient quantity at each trap. Before shooting commences and at any time when the change to another make of target is unavoidable, the field captain should ensure that regulation targets are being thrown. If required, he should do this in the presence of the jury. Referees and trappers must be correctly briefed by him (see Chapter 8 on the referee and Chapter 10 on traps and trappers).

The Safety Officer(s)
Unless and until all club members are safety conscious and actively co-operate, such officials have an impossible task. This is especially true of a new club.

Any well-established club will have a hard core of members of much experience of clay target shooting who, over the years, have come to realize the pitfalls. Thus they can anticipate, and check, any attempt at unsafe behaviour by new members before it can happen. A newly established club will be fortunate to have in its intake some of these mature, experienced shooters. Unhappily, it is an unpleasant fact that some newly formed clubs do not. Their grounds may have been properly equipped, safe trap houses built, safety zones clearly marked, and yet due to thoughtlessness and/or lack of knowledge, someone's life or well-being will be put at risk. For this reason the CPSA runs courses for safety officers and all members.

The safety officer(s) at any club, especially a newly formed one, will be well advised to spend all available time teaching those without clay shooting experience how to behave. Not only does this apply to members, but also to members' guests, uncontrolled dogs and children. The sight of empty and brightly coloured cartridge cases being ejected and rolling about behind the shooters fascinates the young. Unless prevented, they will quickly be running in and out among the shooters, vying with each other in catching and picking up the empties, thereby adding to the dangers. Broken bits of, or complete falling targets, are another attraction, especially at Sporting shoots. To allow any children to try and catch such objects is highly dangerous. Flying objects can cut and maim, and any fallout areas should be cordoned off. Unless the safety officials do this, it is conceivable, regardless of notices, that someone in the club may be held negligent. The safety officer will also make certain that the CPSA Ten Commandments (Rules of Safety) are fully displayed and adhered to.

The duties of a club coach, practice traps, and stands are dealt with in Chapter 11.

Licensed Bar
Alcohol and shooting do not mix. Even so, there are well-run clubs which have applied to the local Licensing Justices for permission to sell intoxicating liquors within the permitted hours. A full knowledge of the 1961 Licensing Act is essential. It is far too vast a subject to cover in this book; the CPSA as usual will be ready to advise.

First Aid
A kit should always be available on the ground. Wisely, some clubs have always had in attendance fully qualified first aid people at their shoots, though it is rare indeed for them to be called upon. Even so, it is good to see them always ready to act promptly if required.

A Move Towards Increased Member Participation
The shooting of 'targets only', recently reintroduced by the CPSA is, the writer believes, a move in the right direction. This will allow members to shoot more targets for less cash outlay than here-to-fore. The trophies and sponsored prizes can be won by all, but the member who shoots 'targets only' will not be expected to contribute £4 to £6 per 100 targets towards prize monies in a competition. Therefore he will not be eligible to receive any cash return provided by those members who shoot and provide such cash.

Pick-ups
Targets which have been shot at and missed fall on the ground, often without breaking. The wide-awake committee will organize efficient picking up of these targets at all available opportunities, for they represent a source of income for the club. These pick-ups are never again used for competition shooting but only for practice. Although unbroken, they may be chipped or cracked, and may break when thrown for a second or more time, but this does not matter for practice shooting.

Shotgun Certificates
Club members should hold valid certificates which they should carry whenever they have guns in their possession. The police have the power to confiscate a gun from anyone who cannot produce a certificate on request. Clubs can apply to the local police for an Exemption Certificate. This allows visitors who have no shotgun certificate to shoot at the club under supervision and with a borrowed gun.

Practice and Competitions
A club will not exist for very long unless it is run to meet the wishes of its members. Inevitably there will be those who are competition minded and who can afford to spend much money on competition shooting. Other members who cannot afford to shoot 100 bird competitions would like to shoot just 10 or 20 bird competitions. Again, there are those who love shooting for its own sake and are not interested in competitions.

All a committee can do is strike a balance in providing what the members like most.

Coaching Facilities

The go-ahead club will have at least one CPSA qualified coach. Such a person can be of enormous help to a club (see Chapter 11 on coaches and coaching).

Handicaps

Many clubs and their officials do not seem to understand that their bread and butter comes from the rank and file member. Out of a membership of say 50, there may well be half a dozen who will usually be in the money. The bulk of the members, i.e. the rank and file, will rarely be in that exalted and happy position. However, in a democratically run club they should be catered for and this can easily be done by the Members' Club Handicap system. There is nothing new in this.

In the live pigeon-shooting days of nearly a century ago, anyone who won money was made to shoot from a further distance from the target. This was known as giving yardage, and calculated in half-yard intervals. Today there is the CPSA classification system, with members arranged in different classes according to their averages. The Association also uses (a) handicapping by points, and (b) handicapping by distance (see the table and fig. 15). Another method used by some clubs is based on the following formula, which reads:

$$\frac{\text{Possible} - \text{Actual}}{3} \times 2 \text{ is then applied}$$

As an example, a member shooting 70 out of 100, would get $100 - 70 = 30 \div 3 = 10 \times 2 = 20$. The handicap would therefore be 20 per cent. To achieve a possible in his next competition he would have to shoot 10 per cent above his normal.

Monthly handicaps run on this formula have proved popular, in fact these clubs are simply practising a method used successfully a century ago.

The Ladies and the Young Entry

Experience has proved that clubs who cater for female members are usually more successful. The same applies to those clubs who provide classes for their young entries, the colts and/or fillies. These are the shooters of the future and their presence is an almost certain guarantee of a club's future success and its continuation in being.

Finally, there is the veteran, who deserves some consideration. Although he has had his day, he still enjoys shooting and would appreciate the opportunity of winning a small veteran's prize. Also, very often, his store of experience can prove of immense help in dealing with club problems.

HANDICAPPING BY POINTS

If handicap points are preferred for club use these can be built up from the following table:

Number of points per 100 allotted as per shooter's averages:

%		Points	%	Points
90	and over	4	79	15
89		5	78	16
88		6	77	17
87		7	76	18
86		8	75	19
85		9	74	20
84		10	73	21
83		11	72	22
82		12	71	23
81		13	70	24
80		14	69	25

%	Points	%	Points
68	26	60	34
67	27	59	35
66	28	58	36
65	29	57	37
64	30	56	38
63	31	55	39
62	32	54	40
61	33		

It may be found necessary in some clubs to adjust the figures given in the table to suit their own standard of shooting, as adherence to the table might not leave sufficient margin for the equitable handicapping of the recruits. If 80 per cent represents the best form, let this figure replace that of 90 per cent as scratch and so on in proportion.

Other Club Activities
Cartridge and gun manufacturers produce splendid films which they will lend to clubs. To begin with our home industries, the firm of Eley, has produced films on shooting and cartridges which it will lend. Hull Cartridge Co. has Remington films available on loan, and Winchester UK has Winchester films.

In addition, there are gunmakers, such as W. & C. Scott and gun importers such as Gunmark, whose experts will attend evening meetings showing and demonstrating their guns until all hours. W. & C. Scott will take club parties round their factory by appointment. Local gun shops are also keen to help with evening meetings.

BASC, previously known as WAGBI, will also supply films on shooting, and are prepared to put on one of their road shows together with shooting personalities, in almost any part of Great Britain.

Interclub shoots are another source of club activity. It is up to the

For this system of handicapping, the principle of which is to penalize shooters by distance instead of allotting points, the ground should be marked out in yards, from 12 to 23, on lines extended from those show in the diagram.

Competitors' handicap distances are based on their average percentages, and the following table will act as a guide when handicaps are being prepared:

23 yards 96% and over
22 yards 94% and under 96%
21 yards 92% and under 94%
20 yards 90% and under 92%
19 yards 88% and under 90%
18 yards 86% and under 88%

17 yards 84% and under 86%
16 yards 80% and under 84%
15 yards 75% and under 80%
14 yards 70% and under 75%
13 yards 65% and under 70%
12 yards 60% and under 65%

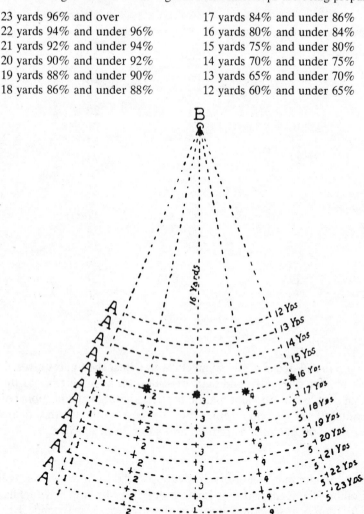

A —Firing points 1 to 5, spaced nine feet apart at sixteen yards from the trap.
B —Trap.

15 Handicapping by distance.

club, its officials and members, to explore the possibilities which are immense and endless.

Club Badge

Once a club is well established, designing and providing a badge which can be worn by the members helps to increase their participation in club affairs. Usually in a club there will be a member with artistic ability who can design a suitable badge. If not, names and addresses of badge designers and manufacturers can be found among the advertisements in the shooting press. These badges help the members to show the flag and also attract more support for the club.

Ground Inspection

Before Championships are hosted the club grounds should be inspected by members of the appropriate CPSA county committee, regional committee, or international board, for safety and for the throwing of regulation targets for the appropriate discipline.

Comprehensive Club Insurance

This is a specialist subject. The Association has a fully qualified insurance advisor. His guidance should be sought, his advice fully understood and implicitly followed, whatever insurance cover required being obtained before club activities begin. This would include insurance for club trophies, equipment, members, visitors, etc., and also for work people employed as trappers for instance.

10 Trap Houses, Traps, Trappers & Clay Targets

Trap Houses

These are many and various, and can be constructed from many materials, including steel sheeting, with wood or metal frames, concrete blocks, bricks, reinforced concrete. They may be temporary and easily transportable, made in bolt-together sections, or permanent and lockable houses. Detailed plans are shown for:

The CPSA trap house for DTL and Sporting going-away targets

High house for Skeet

Low house for Skeet

Combined high and low house for multiple Skeet installations

The essential requirements for any trap house is that it should be weatherproof, shotproof, and sufficiently roomy to allow trap installation and adequate storage of clays. Also there must be sufficient space for trapper safety, and it should be well lit and ventilated. A red flag should be provided for trapper usage.

Plans for OT, UT and ABT are shown. The trap houses for these disciplines generally consist of trenches or pits in the ground. They are open on the side facing away from the shooter, and are permanently roofed with shot proof material, such as metal sheeting or concrete. For OT and UT a tunnel is provided for access. For ABT access is usually given from the open front of the house.

The greater majority of such layouts today are designed to be used with electrical or electrical and hydraulically operated traps. Therefore a source of electricity and/or compressed air is required.

For Sporting layouts other forms of trap houses or screens are required to protect traps and trappers. Towers for high targets are designed to operate as high as 120 ft. On the Continent high towers are installed with electrically operated magazine traps. The traps can be lowered to the ground to have their target magazines filled or refilled, and then electrically elevated back up the tower to the height required. High towers in Great Britain are sometimes constructed from second-hand electric light pylons, or from mobile or fixed base cranes.

Traps

The types of trap now available are numerous (see illustrations). First

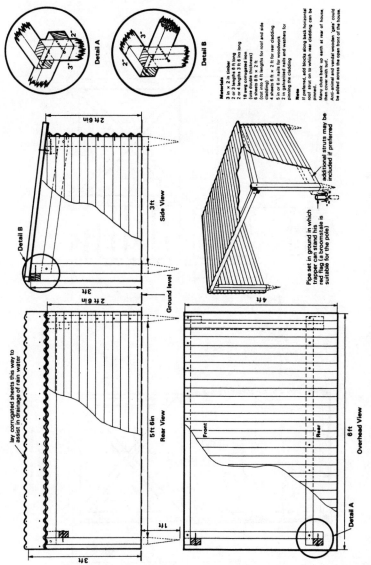

Detail A

3″ 2″

Detail B

2″ 3″

Materials

3 in × 2 in timber
2 or 3 lengths 6 ft long
2 or 4 lengths 3 ft 6 ins long
18 swg corrugated iron
6 sheets 8 ft × 2 ft
(use double thickness)
(cut into 4 ft lengths for roof and side cladding)
4 sheets 6 ft × 2 ft for rear cladding
5 in or 6 in nails for woodwork
2 in galvanised nails and washers for pinning the cladding

Note

If preferred, add blocks along back horizontal roof strut on to which rear cladding can be pinned.

Many clubs bank up earth at rear of house, then cover with turf.

Anti-animal and vandal wooden 'gate' could be added across the open front of the house.

2 ft 6 in

Side View

3 ft

Detail B

Ground level

lay corrugated sheets this way to assist in drainage of rain water

2 ft 6 in

3 ft

Rear View

5 ft 6 in

1 ft

additional struts may be included if preferred

Pipe set in ground in which trapper can stand his red flag (a broomstile is suitable for the pole)

4 ft

Front

Rear

Overhead View

6 ft

Detail A

16 Trap house suitable for Down the Line and Sporting going-away targets.

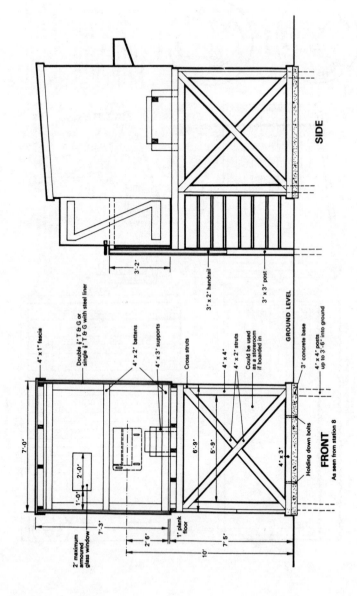

4" x 1" fascia

Double ⅜" T & G or
single ½" T & G with steel liner

4" x 2" battens

4" x 3" supports

2' maximum
armoured
glass window

7'-0"

2'-0"

1'-0"

7'-3"

2'-6"

1" plank
floor

7'-5"

10'

Cross struts

4" x 4"

4" x 2" struts

Could be used
as a storeroom
if boarded in

6'-9"

5'-9"

4" x 3"

3" concrete base

4" x 4" posts
up to 3'-6" into ground

Holding down bolts

FRONT
As seen from station 8

3" x 2" handrail

3" x 3" post

GROUND LEVEL

3'-2"

SIDE

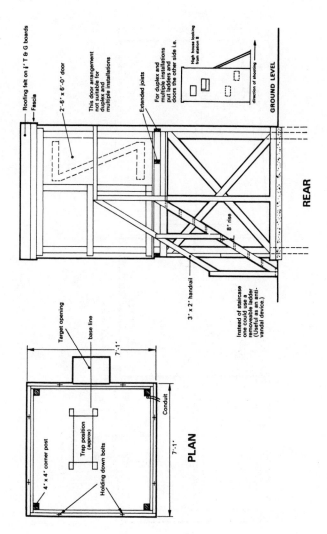

Roofing felt on ⅜" T & G boards

Fascia

2'-6" x 6'-0" door

This door arrangement not suitable for duplex and multiple installations

Extended joists

For duplex and multiple installations put ladders and doors the other side i.e.

High house looking from station 8

direction of shooting

GROUND LEVEL

REAR

8" rise

3" x 2" handrail

Instead of staircase one could use a removeable ladder (Useful as an anti-vandal device.)

Target opening

base line

7'-1"

Conduit

7'-1"

4" x 4" corner post

Trap position (approx)

Holding down bolts

PLAN

17 High house for Skeet.

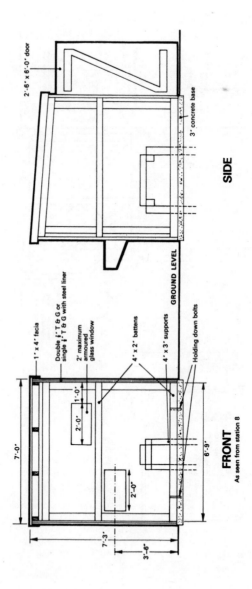

2'-6" x 6'-0" door

3" concrete base

SIDE

GROUND LEVEL

1" x 4" facia

Double ⅜" T & G or
single ⅞" T & G with steel liner

2' maximum
armoured
glass window

4" x 2" battens

4" x 3" supports

Holding down bolts

7'-0"

1'-0"

2'-0"

2'-0"

7'-3"

3'-6"

6'-9"

FRONT
As seen from station 8

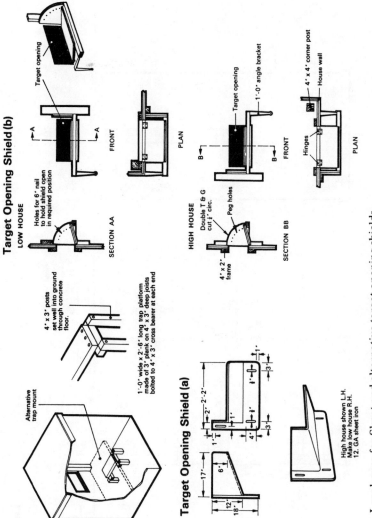

Target Opening Shield (b)

LOW HOUSE

Target opening

Holes for 6' nail to hold shield open in required position

A ◀─── A

FRONT

SECTION AA

PLAN

4' x 3' posts set well into ground through concrete floor.

1'-0' wide x 2'-6' long trap platform made of 3' plank on 4' x 3' deep joists bolted to 4' x 3' cross bearer at each end

HIGH HOUSE

Double T & G cut ¼' circ.

Peg holes

Target opening

1'-0' angle bracket

B ◀─── B

FRONT

4' x 2' frame

SECTION BB

4' x 4' corner post

House wall

Hinges

PLAN

Alternative trap mount

Target Opening Shield (a)

2'──2'──2'

1'
3'
1'
4'

1'

17'

6'

12'

18'

High house shown L.H.
Make low house R.H.
12. GA sheet iron

18 Low house for Skeet and alternative target opening shields.

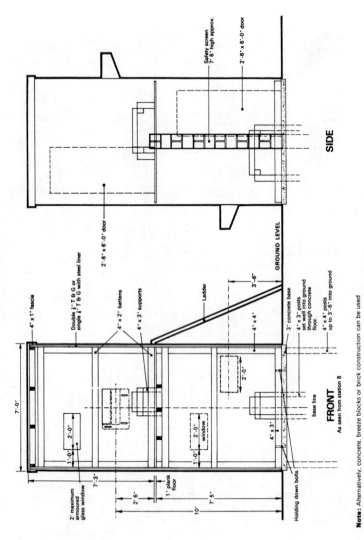

4" x 1" fascia

Double ½" T & G or single ¾" T & G with steel liner

4" x 2" battens

4" x 3" supports

2'-6" x 6'-0" door

2' maximum armoured glass window

Ladder

GROUND LEVEL

3" concrete base

4" x 3" posts set well into ground through concrete floor.

4" x 4"

4" x 4" posts up to 3'-6" into ground

7'-0'

7'-3'

2'-6'

1" plank floor

7'-5'

10'

1'-0' 2'-0'

1'-0' 2'-0'
window

base line

4' x 3'

Holding down bolts

2'-0'

3'-6'

FRONT
As seen from station 8

Safety screen 7'-6' high approx.

2'-6" x 6'-0' door

SIDE

Note: Alternatively, concrete, breeze blocks or brick construction can be used

19 Combined high and low house for multiple Skeet installations.

there are the simple manually operated traps, fitted with a singles or doubles arm. Operated by the trapper pulling the trap arm back, usually clockwise, over centre. The target(s) are placed on the arm(s) against a positive stop and for the steeply rising target, under a metal target retaining plate or spring. When the target is called for, the trapper gently pushes the trap arm back over centre and the targets are released.

Bowman produces a full range of such traps, the smallest is a single arm trap mounted on a sled type seat. This will throw a target some 50 yd. The firm's biggest trap is the Major. This can be supplied with either singles or doubles arm, spring clay-retaining clips and stops. With the singles arm and heavyweight spring, targets can be thrown 100 yd plus. These traps need little maintenance, are simple to operate and throw good targets. However, because they are released by pushing back the arm over centre, unskilled trappers may throw targets on varying trajectories. This is due to trapper inexperience. Good trappers, correctly briefed, will throw target after target on the same path.

The Bowman Pedal Trap

The original, and one of the most versatile traps made. With its built-in trapper seat, instantly adjustable main spring and arm elevations, this trap has proved easy to operate and safe to use for many years. The arm comes back to half cock after throwing the target. The throwing arm may be single or double with clay-retaining clips and stops. Unskilled operators will throw targets of varying trajectories, but the knack of using the foot pedal with the same pressure each time is soon learnt and then even teenagers of average build will throw consistent targets. This trap should be anchored to the ground with four steel pins, otherwise it has a tendency to 'go walkabout' in use.

Farey produces manual traps with single or doubles arms with clay retainers and stops. They carry on to half cock on release whether cocked by the trapper pulling on the arm, or in the case of the levermatic trap, by pulling on a lever. Both models cock against a positive stop and are released mechanically. Because of this it is easy for novice trappers to throw consistent targets. These traps can be supplied with the Farey seat base which allows the trapper to operate the trap while seated. There are also supplied two cross-bars with pegs, and on reasonably level and firm ground and with a normal weight trapper in the seat, there is little tendency for the trap to 'go walkabout'. With the heavyweight spring supplied, 100 yd plus targets can be thrown. Farey traps have been used in recent years at the Game Fair where many thousands of targets were thrown, on whatever trajectories required.

The Hewett Sporting Trap

This is another good performance manual trap, lever cocked against a positive stop, and when released the arm carries on to half cock for ease of recocking. The trap body contains a special irreversible roller bearing, and the target elevation can be altered at will without spanners. A more advanced model is the Hewett seat trap, which has the special bearing in the trap body. It is cocked by a lever, the trap with its doubles arm is fixed to a seat and base supplied. The design of this seat and base is such that with the trapper properly seated, he should then be well out of the path of the throwing arm. On firm ground these traps can be easily pegged to prevent them moving. The trap arms have spring loaded rods plus wing nuts and stud bolts in slots. This provides positive and fine adjustment for clay placement. Target throwing distance is 100 yd plus. An electric safety release using a 12 volt battery and solenoid is available as an extra. Although the trap can then be released by remote control, this cannot happen until the trapper presses a switch to energize the remote control unit. The referee is made visually aware of this by a small green light on his release unit.

An even more sophisticated trap is the Globe. Easily dismantled, the complete unit can then be stored or transported in an average car boot. It has many good points. A toggle bar allows vertical adjustment from daisy cutting targets to the almost vertical; a single or doubles arm is available, also a seat for the trapper. There is fine adjustment and positive placing for the targets. A spring tensioning disc with a thrust ballrace is incorporated to reduce friction, the ball bearings being packed with lubricant. The arm carries on after release and throwing the target until it is held at half cock. The length of target throw is 100 yd plus. All of which makes for an efficient and versatile trap.

Further up the price scale is the MCM jet trap, self cocking and reloading with a 25 target magazine. This trap is easily transportable, all working off a 12 volt car battery with, if required, a long wander lead and remote control release. The small amount of physical strength required makes this trap suitable for operation by those with only a slight physique.

The Sidewinder electric magazine traps have been developed over a number of years and are available for DTL, ABT, Sporting or Skeet. Farey also does an electric magazine trap on similar lines.

The Winchester White Flyer is imported into Great Britain by Winchester UK. This trap has been used successfully for DTL for many years; it has recently been upgraded and can be used with a large target magazine for DTL and ABT.

The Phoenix trap comes in many forms. It functions by electric power and air compression, it can be obtained with a magazine turret and may be used for DTL or ABT. Also a pair of these traps can be made up as a mobile unit in a light trailer and used for duck flushes, etc.

Finally, there are, the Danlac Farey, Le Porte and Spieth traps. Ultra sophisticated with every adjustment, they can be used for Skeet, DTL, ABT and Sporting targets of all kinds. These traps will throw targets far enough and fast enough to keep any squad on its toes.

All the foregoing are priced competitively and a clay club committee would indeed be hard to please if suitable traps could not be found to meet its requirements.

At least one club has mounted a Danlac-type ball trap in a metal house on the jib of a mobile crane. The jib is lowered and the target magazine filled with its stack of 350 clays. The crane is situated on the top of a stone quarry and 100 to 120 ft targets at approximately one per second can be thrown. There is a remote control three-button release at the end of a 100 m wander lead. The trap can be programmed to function as a 100 ft high-ball trap, or the oscillation mechanism can be controlled by the three-button switch. One button alters and holds indefinitely the horizontal traverse of the trap and target, the second button acts likewise for the vertical throw, and the third button releases the targets at will, up to one per second.

Trappers

All trappers should be treated as human beings and not as slave labour. Trapping, especially where the trapper has also to cock and load a doubles trap, is hard and monotonous work. There are local bye-laws and age limits to be observed.

All trappers must be correctly briefed. There is a correct place to put the boxes of targets, which should never be placed on the dangerous side of the trap arm. The trapper should be shown how to cock the trap with one hand and hold the trap arm in that position while he uses his other hand and arm to place the target(s) on the trap arm. His loading hand and arm must never be placed in such a position that it can be struck by the trap arm (see illustrations between pages 38 and 39). He must always keep all other parts of his anatomy well away from the trap, its arm and thrown targets. Some wise clubs provide their trappers with safety helmets and visors, then, if a target shatters on throwing and the target bits bounce on and around the inside of the trap house, the trapper's head and face is protected.

No trapper should be expected to work for long hours without relief, and on relief, beverages and food should be provided. If the trapper is working in a position exposed to the weather he should be supplied with waterproof gear. If the trap is cocked manually, a pair of properly fitting industrial gloves should be provided for each trapper.

Some traps have safety devices which should always be kept in first-class working order. These allow a trapper to immobilize a cocked trap until he has loaded it. No new trapper should be allowed in a trap house on his own until he has worked a stint as assistant to an experienced trapper. Portable radios should be forbidden in any trap house. No trap is ever to be left cocked and unattended.

A red flag on a suitable pole should be available in all trap houses, and the trapper conversant in its use. For a trapper to stick his head out of the trap house in the middle of a shoot is dangerous to say the least. In the event of trap trouble, the trapper should uncock the trap if possible, wave only his red flag outside the trap house and then sit still inside. The referee will bid competitors unload and then walk to the trap house side to deal with the problem.

Possibly the most dangerous trap being used at present is the hand-loaded automatic ball trap. This trap oscillates from side to side, also up and down. Released by someone maybe 25 yd away who cannot see the trapper, the possibilities of accidents are vast. An inexperienced trapper and a quick-calling six-man squad must be a dangerous combination.

Another trapper hazard is to have the electrical trap release in the hands of an inexperienced button presser, who, after pressing it, does not release the button quickly enough. When this happens the trap arm will simply fly round without stopping after throwing the target.

It is unfortunate that many traps are dropped almost anywhere, in any position, in small dark trap houses and with no guards around the traps to keep trappers out of trap arm dangers. If the 'man from the Ministry' is ever given the job of inspecting traps and trap houses from a safety angle one can see lots of problems arising. The sooner all traps have large-capacity target magazines, are mechanically, hydraulically or electrically operated, the better it will be for everyone. Even when this happens the master switches for the traps should be placed in a safe and sensible position. To go to a club and see, as one can, automatic loading traps with the master switch in the rear dark depths of the trap house is only creating dangers for the trapper. For, after being switched on, this trap immediately cocks the arm and loads a target on it. The unfortunate trapper has then to go past the side of this cocked and loaded trap to climb out of the trap house.

Therefore there should be two master switches, one at the inside rear of the trap house, enabling a trapper to switch on or off for trap adjustments, with another switch, say, just inside the front corner of the trap house. In this way a fully automatic and self-loading trap can have its target turret filled while switched off and with its throwing arm at rest. Then the trapper can climb out of the trap house and, while standing well out of any danger from trap arm or thrown target, can press the switch to start everything working.

Servicing Traps

This is essential to the efficient running of a club. Most trap manufacturers are well aware of the problems and if asked, will happily advise on safe and solid trap installation and maintenance. They will also advise on the upkeep of the traps and the likely wearing parts. An adequate supply of spares should be stocked by a club, and the club's trap maintenance man trained in fitting them.

The American clubs have got trap maintenance to a fine art, with complete spare traps on standby. When in the United States I saw traps taken out and replaced by a fully operational spare trap in three minutes. Some of the bigger clubs in Great Britain do this and smaller clubs could well emulate them.

Even manually operated and loaded traps eventually have to have their wearing parts replaced. Usually these are the rubber-faced target rails and the main springs. Most target rails are reversible, thus doubling their effective life. With a well-designed trap, an efficient operator will reverse or replace rails in three to five minutes. Main springs should always have their tension released at the end of a shoot, which will help to prolong their life. All nuts and bolts on the trap should be kept properly tightened, as a loose trap arm will be prone to break targets.

In all trap houses and on all traps there should be placed large notices forbidding unauthorized entry. This is essential from an insurance point of view and also to protect those helpful, well-meaning members whose willingness to trap may place them at risk through their own lack of trap knowledge.

Clay Targets

Although there are set dimensions and weights laid down for standard clay targets, there are no standards at present laid down as far as hardness of the target is concerned.

This was not much of a problem when DTL was almost the only discipline shot and the Black Diamond auto-angling trap was almost in universal use. A properly maintained Black Diamond trap was very kind to clay targets and one rarely had many breakages. Also, in those far-off days the trappers were trained to tap each target when they picked it up; if it sounded cracked it was not placed on the arm but simply discarded.

Cautionary Advice on Traps

Traps can maim or kill. Such accidents have happened but don't let them happen to you. Read and fully understand the maker's manual before going anywhere near any trap. Never, ever, work on a cocked trap whether loaded or not. Keep all parts of your anatomy well away from any of the trap's moving parts, especially the trap arm, and also from the path of thrown targets or bits of targets which may shatter on the trap arm. Do not let bystanders, especially children, come anywhere near a clay trap or its target and broken target trajectories.

Manual Traps

The majority of these traps rotate their arms anti-clockwise when released to throw a target. On such traps the further the target is placed from the spindle on which the arm rotates, the sooner it will leave the arm and the more to the right will the target be thrown. Also such a target will have less target spin and be thrown a shorter distance. (See illustrations.) It follows, therefore, that the nearer the target is placed to the arm's spindle the greater will be the spin imparted and the further the target will travel, this time more to the left.

Target Stops

Trap arms should be fitted with adjustable target stops. When a trap has been tuned the target will need to be placed firmly up against this stop.

Target Retaining Clip or Spring

The tighter such are set to hold the target the faster and more to the left the targets will fly.

Automatic Traps

These have many adjustments, described in the makers' manuals and the instructions should be followed implicitly. Some automatic traps throw slightly slower targets when cold. Such traps are therefore first tuned to throw targets to drop 2 to 3 yd short. Within a few minutes' use they will have warmed up and be throwing targets in the regulation distances.

It is impossible to cover all tuning of traps and targets, but care and caution is always required in their handling and adjustment.

These days targets are being thrown distances of maybe 100 yd instead of the old DTL or Skeet distances of 50 to 55 yd. The targets are therefore leaving the trap arm much faster and they are also being given much more spin. All of which tends to shatter the target before the shooter can. Because of this some target makers now produce targets in two grades: one normal, for DTL and Skeet, and the other in a harder grade for ABT, OT and long-throw Sporting targets.

As well as the standard targets, we now have the increasingly popular midi, the battue, the mini, etc. But there is still no standard for target hardness laid down. Therefore the clubs can only shop around and find which make of target suits their traps best. Then by sticking to the one brand they will be quick to spot a dud load. The makers will appreciate regular custom from a club and will all the more readily take action when troubles of broken targets arise.

Transportation of Targets

There is a recommended height level for boxes of targets, usually six boxes high. Boxes of targets stacked ten high and bounced along in large lorry loads, then carelessly unloaded, will inevitably result in many broken targets.

Targets should be stored in their boxes in a cool, dry place. To store targets outdoors in rain or hot sunshine will allow the rain to rot the cardboard boxes and the hot sun to warp the targets. All of which makes for poor target trajectories, more broken targets, bad-tempered trappers, officials and competitors.

11 Shooting Grounds, Coaches & the CPSA Coaching Scheme

The Grounds

There are many excellent shooting grounds in Britain, some of them are old established with a long and fine tradition of both gun fitting and the teaching of shooting sporting targets.

Some of their customers are basically live bird shooters who rightly believe in shooting sporting targets in and out of season as a means of achieving higher standards when shooting game. There are other customers who shoot clay targets as training for serious competitions and also shoot game. Finally there are the clay shooters only, whose experience has proved that periodic sessions with a professional coach is of benefit when subsequently shooting either FITASC or English Sporting targets.

Since the war we have seen the setting up of professionally run grounds where, as well as Sporting targets, there are layouts for some or all of the other disciplines. These grounds usually have a tower(s) capable of throwing high and testing targets. They have also one or more resident coaches who are capable of gun fitting, coaching and actually shooting the specialist disciplines, such as ISU Skeet, ABT and OT. At such grounds the would-be champion can train on the appropriate layout for his chosen discipline and obtain the specialist coaching required.

The Coaches

The great majority of professional coaches are expert gun fitters as well. Some have come up the hard way, beginning as trap boys at a shooting school. By dint of careful observation, many hours of work and years of experience, most have reached the top of their profession.

They are capable of producing a set of measurements resulting in a gun which will be a good and comfortable fit for the client. Because of their wide knowledge and ability to communicate, they can if required, themselves physically demonstrate how to stand, read the target, mount their moving gun and kill the bird. After such demonstrations they are then capable of 'setting up' their clients or pupils, talk them through the entire operation of safe and successful gun handling and shooting behaviour. In addition, their pupils will be taught and encouraged to call their own shots, eventually being able to do this whether coaches are present or not.

Different professional coaches have slightly varying techniques of teaching. Even so, with pupils who are willing to listen and learn, success should be achieved and pupils coached until they reach their own level of competence.

Because of the hard commercial facts of running a business, coaches are very conscious that for their pupils and themselves time is money, therefore they try to provide 100 per cent effort and value for money for every hour's coaching. What they cannot do is to produce a world class shooter from a person who believes that once a well-fitted shotgun has been acquired, all that remains is to shoot cartridges. The great majority of clay shooters, especially in their early stages, will happily shoot themselves silly if allowed.

The professional coach is well aware of this and carefully paces his pupil as required. At all times pupils are carefully watched for signs of staleness, boredom, tiredness and nervous tension. The idea is to create a consistent technique. This technique with its understanding of and confidence in the principles involved, together with its creation of muscle memory, is well worth acquiring. All the champions have it. By much work and training they try and keep it.

Clients who, after spending time and money on obtaining a suitable and well-fitting gun for their chosen discipline, negate all the fitter coache's efforts by sloppy gun mounting and unwillingness to do anything but shoot cartridges, are simply wasting everyone's time and will never reach their full potential. The professional coach will usually advise such people to take up another sport.

Most shooting grounds work to a tight timetable and expect their clients to be ready on the dot. Appointments are made by the hour. To book for an hour's tuition, turn up 20 minutes late, probably hot and bothered, and then expect to encroach on the time reserved for the next client is unrealistic. Not only will the lesson almost certainly be a waste of time, but the next client will naturally become impatient if kept waiting, and will, in turn, derive less benefit than he should.

When the writer managed a shooting ground, it was noticeable that the more successful men, of whatever trade or profession, were usually the most punctual. Coming a few minutes early, completely relaxed, and obtaining full value for every minute and upsetting no one. Conversely, there were the few who came late, bringing noisy dogs or small uncontrollable children, creating extra hazards which probably resulted in a fine crop of ulcers for both client and coach. However, if given the chance, the greater proportion of shooting grounds and coaches provide excellent value for money.

The Club Coaches' Award Scheme

The cpsa Executive, together with its Coaching Committee, has been well aware for years of the need to provide club coaches. Therefore a decade ago it instigated a Club Coaches' Award Scheme. This, I believe, has been a success. Resulting in the production to date, of more than 200 club coaches.

Inevitably since passing the examination and receiving their coaches' badges, some coaches have found other interests. The greater proportion still act as club coaches and help novice members. These coaches are an asset to their club, its members, committee and the CPSA as a whole.

One is continuously being asked as to what is required by the CPSA examiners to enable a club shooter to qualify as a club coach. The Association has kindly given permission to print its Regulations and Syllabus for the Coaches' Award Scheme.

Regulations of Application for the Coaches' Certificate
1   Eligibility
Applicants must satisfy the following conditions.
They must be:

a   18 years of age and over on the day of the examination.

b   Individual members of the CPSA.

c   Nominated by their club, which must be affiliated to the CPSA or its own National CPS Association.

2   Examination
The examination shall consist of two parts, theoretical and practical.

The CPSA Coaching Sub-Committee shall approve the theory papers and appoint a panel of examiners to mark them.

A panel of practical examiners shall be appointed by the Sub-Committee for each course.

The 'pass' mark shall be 60 per cent of the total marks available for theory and 75 per cent for practical.

The examination shall take place at centres approved by the CPSA Coaching Committee. Each examination shall be preceded by a course of instruction and preparation.

No correspondence can be entered into regarding the assessment of marks.

3   Awards
If all the conditions have been fulfilled, the Director of the CPSA will issue a certificate to each successful candidate. Cloth badges for holders of the CPSA Club Coaches' Certificate are obtainable, on payment, from the CPSA headquarters.

The CPSA Club Coaches' Award will cease to be valid if the holder's membership of the CPSA lapses.

Syllabus of Examination for Coaches' Certificate
1   Theoretical

Questions may be set on:

a   The elements of shooting skill, including gun fitting, stance and movement.

b   The principles of teaching applied to clay pigeon shooting.

c   The fundamentals of the sport in relation to:
i Skeet   ii Down the Line   iii Sporting

d   Safety in gun handling; safety in relation to layouts; the law relating to shotguns.

e   The CPSA – its organization and function.

Candidates must show a knowledge of:

a   How to convey to beginners the basic principles of shotgun handling.

b   A pupil's likely faults – their causes and corrective practices.
2   Practical
    The candidate will be required to give a series of individual lessons of not less than five minutes' duration. The lessons must be at the level of the pupils, and the candidate must be prepared to adjust the teaching to meet varied abilities and rates of progress.

    The candidate must show his ability to analyse performance, define faults and recommend appropriate remedial measures. He must be able to demonstrate the actions he is teaching.

    The idea of the coaches' course and its subsequent examinations is to provide the would-be club coach (hereafter described as the candidate) with an easy system of safe gun handling and successful shooting while teaching a novice shooter.

    As one who was closely connected with the scheme, as a member of the Coaching Committee, as the first CPSA national Coach, and now as the first senior tutor and examiner, I hope the following information may be of help to prospective club coaches.

The Courses
These are organized by the CPSA and held as required; of necessity they are highly intensive. During a three day weekend, the candidates are provided with the basics concerning the safe and efficient handling of both shotgun and novice.

    Due to the limited amount of time available, successful candidates are not expected to coach at any higher level. Much more training and coaching experience, with the ability to shoot good scores is needed to achieve the credibility essential for coaching high average shooters. The CPSA courses have had among their candidates a few people who were already established as coaches and who were also high average shooters before they ever took the coaching course. There have been others, who by dint of hard work and application while coaching at club level, have also acquired sufficient experience and credibility, to coach at more advanced levels. These rare people are a tremendous asset to their clubs.

Any candidate who prior to attending a CPSA course has had no experience of coaching is certain to find the course extremely hard work. Sometimes the information provided is more than he can assimilate in the time available, which is understandable.

Preliminary Pre-Course Training
The candidate should study and train for at least 12 months before attending a coaching course. The CPSA does not, at the present, specify any set standard of shooting ability but it is much easier for a candidate to qualify if he is a proven performer who can demonstrate as well as instruct. An A or AA average in English DTL, Skeet or Sporting must prove an asset.

Gun Knowledge
The candidate should approach a local friendly gunsmith; if this person is also the club armourer, so much the better. He will explain and demonstrate in detail how to handle safely, take down, examine for faults and reassemble all the more common types of shotguns used for modern target shooting.

The faults to look for are barrels for corrosion, dents, bulges, loose lumps, loose ribs, actions for tightness, triggers for weight of pull and creep, the mechanics of the – miscalled – safety catch, the understanding of valid English and Foreign proof marks, woodwork for soundness, and fired cartridge cases to see how the strikers or firing pins are hitting the cartridge caps.

Having acquired this gun knowledge the candidate must now learn and eventually practise the how and why of safe gun handling and coaching of novice pupils at club level. It cannot be stressed too strongly that only by practical experience can this knowledge be acquired. Theory, obtained from reading books, including this one, or even from trained teachers is fine as far as it goes. This is not far enough. Even one mistake is one too many, and can result in tragedy. As an illustration of the pitfalls, the writer knew a highly intelligent teacher whose grasp of the theory of coaching novice pupils was masterly. Yet on one occasion while coaching a novice pupil he managed to take hold of the gun in such a dangerous manner that he accidentally pulled the trigger. Fortunately the gun had a snap cap in the barrel chamber and not a live cartridge.

Because of such hazards the following is suggested as a planned progressive approach to be adopted by a candidate. As he is expected to demonstrate, the candidate should work on his own shooting until he has achieved at least A class standard. Then he can approach the nearest CPSA qualified coach and with him can attempt the following programme.

He should first watch the club coach go through the preliminaries with a novice pupil. The first session will be with a shotgun and a snap cap, well away from any firing point.

Here he will see the coach test for master eye while using a closed and unloaded gun. There are other methods of testing for master eye, using a target with its middle knocked out, a sheet of newspaper with a hole in its middle, or the old master bowman's trick of making an o with the hands outstretched in front and clasped together. These methods sometimes prove unreliable, and while the candidate will be expected to know and describe them, he will be well advised to emulate the professionals and obtain his answers with the help of a closed and empty gun.

He will then watch the coach provide a suitable gun of approximate fit, and check his diagnosis of such a fit, while premounting the empty gun in the pupil's shoulder pocket.

The candidate should then act as button presser and watch the club coach in action with his pupil while working on a simple low 2 incomer on English Skeet. He will listen while stance, reading the target, loading the gun with a snap cap is explained, seeing the coach properly premount the gun for the novice, after which the coach will talk the novice through placing the muzzles on the target, pulling out in front and pressing the trigger, all without check of swing. This, in other words, is the Wilson CPSA method of shooting, all of which has been previously described.

The candidate will observe where the coach stands to keep full and safe control of his pupil at all times. Also how the coach can see over the novice's shoulder and observe the line of the barrels in relation to the target.

Diagnosis of Mistakes and Advice on Remedies

Until the club coach is satisfied the novice is performing all the above, including pulling the trigger precisely when he intends to, no live ammunition will be used.

The candidate will eventually see the club coach allow the use of a single live cartridge and observe how for the first few shots the coach has his own right hand firmly holding the barrels. This prevents any panic shooting, or even the dropping of a loaded gun by the novice.

When the candidate has followed perhaps a dozen novice pupils through all their stages until they are capable of safe gun handling, while successfully shooting a low 2 Skeet target, it is then time for the candidate himself to act as a stooge novice for the club coach.

Beginning as before with a snap cap, he will himself be taken through all the stages up to finally loading a single cartridge and shooting low 2.

This safely accomplished, the next step is for the club coach to act as novice stooge and allow himself to be coached by the candidate. Again snap caps will be used. The club coach will take the opportunity to emulate some of the behavioural faults of the true novice. In this manner he can demonstrate the hazards which may occur and should the candidate make a wrong diagnosis can, from his experience, fully explain the fault and its remedy.

The club coach will also deliberately miss targets as follows:

Over the top because of head lifting.

Behind due to check of swing.

In front due to a simulated left master eye.

Underneath due to swinging the muzzles downwards, as well as out in front of the target.

All this in order to familiarize the candidate with the more common shooting faults which he may have to diagnose and afterwards remedy.

The foregoing training can take some months before a club coach is confident that a candidate is competent to attempt coaching novices. Then he will be allowed to act as 'stand in' club coach, but only with the use of snap caps for the first few weeks.

Candidates who carry out the foregoing progressive practical training under a good club coach should have little trouble in then taking the Club Coaches' Award course. Furthermore, they should pass with distinction.

Candidates have, in the past, worried themselves unnecessarily because they feel they may be given a novice to coach during their examination who cannot shoot or be taught. The examiners are well aware of this and always make allowances.

Should a candidate be allocated such a novice pupil, he will, as always, begin with a snap cap and a gun of approximate fit. After the preliminary, explanatory and exploratory work away from the firing point, the candidate will take the novice onto the firing point, commencing with snap cap and gun. Unless and until the pupil can put the muzzles of his premounted gun on the target, and perform the method successfully while using a snap cap, there is no sense in using and wasting live cartridges. Such uncoachable pupils are rare indeed. When a candidate is allocated one, he must back his own diagnosis, take the gun off the pupil, quietly go to the examiners and explain as kindly as possible that the pupil is not yet ready to use live ammunition, and give his reasons. In this manner, assuming his diagnosis is correct, he will be given full credit for his action by the examiners.

So far we have only dealt with the candidate, his teaching, and control of novice pupils. Inevitably among the pupils provided by the CPSA for the coaching course, will be one or two jokers in the pack. These are experienced shooters who have kindly volunteered to act as pupils but who will have developed their own set technique. Regardless of this, the wise candidate will treat such people in exactly the same manner as the complete novice. Going through all the preliminaries and taking nothing for granted that a pupil tells him until he has checked for himself.

After the preliminaries, the candidate will still begin on Station 2, using the advised sequence with gun and snap cap on the low house target. When the candidate is satisfied, and this should not take long, the use of live cartridges may be allowed.

It must be realized that the candidate is being examined on his ability to teach safely and efficiently 'the method'. If the experienced shooter pupil has never shot 'the method' and many have not, it is up to the candidate to demonstrate and sell the method to his pupil. Some experienced pupils will indeed listen and successfully adopt the method.

Others will either shoot the targets in their own way or not at all, resisting all efforts by the candidate to change their technique. When this happens the candidate must explain the situation quietly to the examiners. They, from their wide experience, will usually allow the pupil to shoot in his own way and after he has finished will find a more amenable pupil for the candidate.

Any pupil who achieves success on Station 2 low can then be moved towards Station 3 or even 4 by the candidate in an attempt to progress. While it is a waste of ammunition to allow a pupil simply to keep smoking low 2, it is equally a waste to make the target too difficult. Therefore every pupil begins on Station 2 low and is provided with increasingly harder targets as he progresses. Most candidates err on providing difficult targets too quickly for their pupils.

Finally the examiner will rightly fail any candidate who allows his pupil to behave dangerously. Also for wrong diagnosis of faults, and inevitably, the wrong remedy advised.

The examiners are not there to 'catch out' a candidate, nor do they ever attempt to do so. They expect and insist, regardless of who is holding the gun, that the candidate is solely responsible for being in full and safe control of his pupil at all times.

It is hoped that the above training programme will achieve this end.

12 Loss of Form

All shooters eventually reach their own peak of performance and for a while success may seem easy to achieve. The difficulty is to maintain one's peak performance for any length of time. Sooner or later a slump or loss of form will take place.

When this occurs it is a waste of time and money for the majority of shooters to try and shoot themselves back into top form on their own. Consideration must be given to each facet of the problem. Guns, cartridges, the shooter's physical and mental state, all these facts have to be taken into account, one at a time, in an attempt to reduce, or better still, eliminate the variables.

The Gun

A well-maintained, good-quality gun, which fits and with which previous good scores have been achieved over a period of time, is unlikely to be the cause of trouble. However, even the gun of proven performance can hiccup sometimes.

Trigger Pulls
The prudent shooter will have already carefully noted the trigger pull weights of his gun when he was shooting good scores. Sears and bents properly contoured and hardened should hold their tune for countless thousands of shots. But if the sears and bents have been carelessly altered it is possible that the sear noses or bents were softened at that time. If this has happened wear will soon occur and the pulls become light or heavy. They may also become creepy or draggy. Worse, the sear nose and bent surfaces may become roughened, allowing the nose to come almost out of the bent and stay there. This has the effect of producing a hair trigger which any jar will set off. Therefore, the trigger pulls should be checked and if at fault, put right by a competent gunsmith.

Regarding trigger pulls on poor-quality guns with soft sears and/or bents, even the shooting of a few hundred cartridges can cause wear. The majority of gunsmiths will work on such poor-quality guns only under protest and write on their invoices that their work may not stand up. The remedy is to have good-quality sears and tumblers made which is an expensive business, or, better still, sell the gun.

Vee or Coil Main Springs
Vee springs rarely 'set', but if they do, could result in the trigger pulls becoming dangerously light; vee springs snap clean, if they do anything. Coil springs do sometimes 'set', in which case the pulls will go light. The layman may think it is a simple matter to replace either vee or coil main springs. This is indeed so, but replacement springs do slightly vary in length and/or strength. Therefore, the fitting of a new main spring may often result in the trigger pulls being heavier or lighter. In such cases the gunsmith will alter sears and bents to produce the correct pull poundage as requested by the shooter from his records.

Chokes and Chokings
Lead pellets, even nickel-plated, are much softer than gun barrel steel. It is rare indeed for chokes to wear because of normal shooting, no matter how many cartridges have been shot in a particular gun. But sometimes the shooters themselves, through lack of gun knowledge, alter choke contours. More than one shooter has attempted to remove barrel leading with the aid of an electric drill, plus a length of cleaning rod and emery cloth or powder. The writer has seen barrels which have had all the choke removed by such means, and also the resulting eccentric chokings. All the above should be carefully checked by barrel gauge and pattern plate at accurately measured distances.

Loss of Form Due to a New Correctly Fitted Gun
The same criteria apply to such replacement guns.

Cartridges

Modern cartridges are rarely the cause of shooter slump. Shooters using their usual brand should ask themselves the following. Is the recoil any different than before? Are the barrels cleaner or dirtier than before? Should the answer be that recoil is the same, that the residue in the barrels is the same as before the slump, then one can rule out the cartridges as suspects. Should the recoil or the barrel residue appear different, the retailer should be approached to ascertain if others have complained. If excess pressures and maybe blown patterns are suspected, recourse can be had to either the London or Birmingham proof houses. They will test cartridges sent them by private individuals for pressures produced and variations in charges of shot or powder. The results of these tests must not be used commercially.

In fairness to the cartridge manufacturers it is suggested that when samples are sent to the proof house, samples from the same batch of cartridges are sent to the manufacturers, for their own tests. Cartridge manufacturers are rightly jealous of their reputations and in the rare event of a suspect batch occurring, their subsequent actions will be positive indeed. Faulty cartridges being replaced free of charge and the offending batch withdrawn immediately from the retailers and ruthlessly scrapped.

Having written all the above, it is fair to state the possible chances for cartridges to be at fault must be in the region of millions to one.

Gun Fit and Physical Health

Shooters who have recently gained or lost weight before a slump should always have the fit of their guns checked. Loss of weight can result in a loss of flesh on the shooter's face and in his shoulder pocket, this may alter cheek and eye position. Putting on weight can also alter eye position; in addition, previously well-fitting guns may have to have the stock toe shortened or even comb height lowered.

All checking of gun fit should be done in the presence of the gunfitter coach, with first the help of a pattern plate and then by shooting at moving targets. To attempt to check gun fit in cold blood in the gun shop rarely helps and is simply guessing.

The Shooter's Eyes

Most humans tend to strain their eyes. In a state of nature one's eyes would rarely be used for close work. To earn a living in modern times entails for most people much reading, writing, driving, all of which imposes considerable strain on one's eyes and their accommodation. In addition, watching television and such hobbies as photography must also impose strain. The use of tobacco, the consumption of alcohol and food will alter the state of one's vision. So much is this so that some of the world's shooting champions take positive steps to reduce any chance of eye strain in the days and hours before taking part in big competitions, even refusing to stay anywhere near those who smoke.

To drive many miles to a shoot and then watch targets at all times when not shooting is a certain recipe for producing eye strain, headaches, and eventual loss of visual acuity.

Whenever a slump occurs and there is any doubt about one's vision the best advice possible should be obtained. Older shooters in particular should practise 'looking to see', making absolutely certain their eyes are correctly focused on the spot in space where they expect to pick up their moving clay targets.

Shooting Psychology

Having checked and corrected all the problems arising from guns, ammunition, the shooter's physical fitness, and the quality of his eyesight, we are now left with the most complex problem of all, the shooter himself and his mental state.

All shooters, being human, are complex personalities, mostly confident in success, and tentative in failure, full of idiosyncracies, foibles, phobias, all of which will freely flower if given the chance.

Trigger Timing

We have seen how in the space of less than a second, the shooter reads his target, goes for it, and with himself and gun as a locked-up unit, is conditioned to pull the trigger when he believes his sight picture is correct. The slightest hesitation of this trigger time will result in a missed target.

One often hears a shooter bemoaning that he has lost his 'timing'. When this happens, for whatever cause, although the shooter's sight picture seems correct, his trigger timing will be faulty. After which the rot can set in and more and more targets missed.

Consistent trigger timing is a must. No matter what technique for breaking targets is favoured by the shooter, whether 'coming from behind', 'swing through', 'mount on the target and pull out', 'maintained lead' or even a mixture of all these; unless there is a consistent relationship between muzzle movement, sight picture and trigger pull timing for the technique favoured, the chances of breaking target after target will be poor.

A shooter in good form has his timing conditioned by the sight picture his eyes are used to seeing. When the picture appears to be correct, the trigger will be pulled smoothly and with confidence, the timing being the same for target after target. When this is so the shooter will be pulling the trigger without even conscious thought, in fact, he would find it extremely difficult not to pull the trigger. Suddenly, no matter which discipline is being shot, trigger timing becomes erratic. The sight picture seems right, but targets are being missed.

Causes of Poor Trigger Timing
Over-shooting and staleness.

The pressures of going straight, and trying to keep on so doing.

Counting targets and thinking how many more are left to shoot.

Shooting next to a top shooter, whose timing is faster or slower than one's own, and copying his timing.

Riding One's Targets

This can be caused by trying to make sure. With the DTL targets this riding out means they are no longer being taken on the rise, therefore one's high shooting trap gun becomes a liability.

With Skeet incomers, on Stations 1 and 2, 6 and 7, riding in means targets are taken much closer and therefore the pattern spread is much smaller.

As for Sporting targets, whether riding them further in or out, the longer they are ridden the greater the chance of missing. The second target on doubles becoming increasingly difficult.

With all the disciplines, riding targets simply ensures that one's previous sight picture is now incorrect, and the tendency is for the shooter to attempt to alter it. It is much better to try and regain one's previous good timing and keep the original and correct sight picture to go with it. Much help can be obtained from a good coach who knows the slump shooter's normal timing. He will quickly spot any variation in time between targets and advise accordingly.

Very often a few training sessions or dry runs with snap caps and a coach will work wonders. The slump shooter taking ten targets, for instance, all on the same trajectories, and using a snap cap. The coach will know whether such targets would be hit or missed. The absence of recoil and muzzle blast also helps. In this manner, and by shooting one live cartridge to ten dry runs or training efforts, the shooter should get back his sight picture, trigger timing and confidence.

The Twitch or Flinch

We now come to the worst problem of all, the 'twitch or flinch'. It is worth noting that a similar problem affects some professional golfers. Champions suddenly cannot knock a ball into the hole, some 12 in. away. Dart players find they cannot let go of their darts. As far as clay shooting is concerned, the flinch is a complex subject. Over shooting, the tensions arising in a big competition, excessive recoil, the use of single triggers, all these factors have a bearing.

The symptoms are usually as follows. The shooter sees his usual sight picture and decides to pull the trigger, a simple procedure. The trigger is not fully pulled, therefore the gun is not fired. The shooter, who was leaning into the expected recoil, finds no recoil to lean into, sometimes because of this he will even take a couple of steps forward. Some shooters try and pull the trigger three or four times before they can finally fire the gun.

The remedy, or rather remedies, for they are legion, are as follows. If the trigger pulls have been checked and are found correct, leave them alone. To have them lightened below the shooter's norm only acts as a palliative and soon the shooter is again unable to pull the lighter trigger.

Release Triggers
Popular on the Continent where they are only legal for the going-away disciplines, less popular in the United States; release triggers have found little favour in England, being banned at some clubs.

How a Release Trigger Works
The shooter, having a gun with a release trigger, will load and close his gun; on his turn to shoot, he will mount his gun and pull the trigger. This action lifts the sear out of bent, at the same time a hook drops over the tumbler head and prevents the gun from firing. When the target appears and the shooter's sight picture is correct, he eases the pressure on the trigger and the tumbler slides out from under the hook, the gun then fires.

Release triggers have been used to win World Championships, but even they are not the complete answer. The writer knows of one international shot who developed such a flinch that eventually he could not even use a release trigger.

For those who are, or who have become sensitive to recoil, the fitting of one or even two recoil reducers in the stock can help enormously. This is especially true of the disciplines which allow the gun to be premounted before calling for the target. For ISU Skeet and Sporting, the fitting of recoil reducers makes the gun butt heavy and thereby upsets smooth and accurate mounting.

Single versus Double Triggers

The difference between single and double trigger pulling by the shooter must now be considered, the writer, believing that the single trigger is possibly the most common cause of a flinch being acquired by a shooter.

The procedure with a double trigger is simple. The front trigger is pulled backwards, the hand and trigger then moves slightly backward and the rear trigger is pulled backwards, with all positive movements in the same direction. An expert shooter will get off his two shots equally as quickly with double triggers as with a single trigger.

The procedure with a single trigger is to pull the trigger backwards, then release it forwards, then pull it backwards to fire the second shot. There are therefore three movements required in two opposite directions. In times of stress it is possible for the shooter's mind to give the finger the order to pull the trigger, and then give the order to release it 'before' it has been pulled far enough back to take the sear out of the bent. Such mental short circuits resulting in the first shot not being fired.

At other times the trigger will be pulled to fire the first shot and the second order to release the trigger is forgotten. When this happens the trigger cannot then be pulled to fire the second barrel. A further complication with single triggers can arise when the shape and size of the stock grip or hand allows the shooter's hand to be placed 'anywhere' in relation to the triggers.

Shooters who are used to single triggers will have acquired muscle memory, this means their trigger finger may move only $\frac{1}{8}$ in. to fire the first barrel. If the trigger hand is placed $\frac{1}{8}$ in. too far forward, the next time the gun is to be fired, it is possible for the finger to move its usual $\frac{1}{8}$ in. and yet not succeed in firing the gun. All these factors help to produce the flinch (see illustrations between pages 102 and 103).

Furthermore, shooters often develop a flinch without actually realizing it. Although they put their finger in exactly the same place on the trigger each time, they will complain that their trigger pull has gone heavy – that it varies. A check of the trigger pull weight can easily be done with a spring balance type of trigger pull tester. Although the trigger pull pressures can thus be checked and proved unvarying, many shooters will still be unconvinced that 'they have acquired a flinch'. Until they do accept this unpleasant fact there is little one can do; unfortunately, even when it is accepted, there will still be problems.

The writer believes that once a shooter has acquired a flinch, he will have it for all time, in a greater or lesser degree. He must therefore accept the fact, and mitigate it as much as possible by use of a heavy gun and a light load. Some may find, like the writer, that a semi-automatic shotgun cuts down the apparent recoil and thereby helps to keep the problem within reasonable limits.

To Sum Up

Train under the guidance of a coach, using a snap cap and dry runs on moving targets. This should help one to acquire correct muscle memory, and positive trigger pulling by constant practice of consistent trigger hand and finger placement. This action will cut down the dangers of over-shooting and prevent the soaking up of much recoil while training.

By such means the majority of shooters can hope to live with their flinch and shoot good scores for most of the time.

13 Reloading Cartridges, Shotgun Maintenance & Patterning

Reloading Cartridges

Using common sense and care, reloading can be fun. It can also save one a certain amount of money. There are many fine machines on the market which are capable of producing consistent reloads of satisfactory performance.

In Britain reloads are not allowed in registered competitions. In the United States of America they are. In fact, at least two cartridge manufacturers there have produced cartridge cases which can be reloaded up to ten times. These are the Remington Blue Peters and the Winchester AA cases.

At shoots in the United States one sees the majority of shooters wearing a large pouch at their waist in which they place their empties. The semi-automatic guns have a cartridge case catcher on the side of the action, some of the o/us have a small lever or stud, which prevents the ejectors working. Empty cases allowed to drop on the ground are ruled to be the property of that club. The trap boys pick them up at the end of a shoot and they are then sold by the club back to the shooters for a few cents per case.

Those who wish to 'reload their own' for target practice or training sessions are advised to shop around and inspect the currently available reloading machines. Commencing with their local gun shop, they should ask to have a demonstration of whatever machine is on offer.

Claims as to the number of reloads per hour should be treated with reserve. There are indeed some large machines that will reload hundreds of cartridges per hour. Such an output only being achieved by the combined efforts of three people, one of whom will have a full-time job simply packing the reloads into boxes of 25.

It is essential that whatever machine is chosen it does a good job on the resizing of cases. Some old guns, and even some modern ones, have excessively sized barrel chambers, thereby allowing the cartridges fired in them to become oversize. Unless such cases are correctly resized, they will not subsequently be accepted in normal-sized barrel chambers. To attempt to force them in by smartly closing the gun, can be dangerous, it can also cause the gun to have its barrels forced off the face.

The recapping system of the reloader should be carefully inspected. Some early machines did not always seat the new caps correctly. Such caps if standing proud above the head of the reload may be fired simply by the action of closing the gun. It must be well understood that percussion caps are very akin to detonators and should therefore be treated with extreme care. They are carefully packed in small containers by the makers for this reason.

The matching of percussion caps to cases, powder, wads, and shot load must be carefully done. A mismatching of any two components may result in the production of reloads which produce excessive pressures.

Today there are many makes of percussion caps and powder. The makers print reloading charts containing full instructions which must be followed meticulously. Any variations from such instructions can be dangerous.

For those who desire to experiment the advice is *don't*. However, there will always be some who *will*. Here the advice must be, reload only about a dozen cartridges, send them off to the proof house and have them tested. This will cost money, but it is a wise precaution and may save blowing up a gun, or worse, the loss of bits of the shooter's anatomy.

Do not mix powders, store all components carefully, especially away from small children. Always check weigh the powder and shot loads thrown at the beginning of a reloading session, also once or twice during a session. Use some system of marking your reloads to know just what is being produced. Check weigh the powder load thrown every time a new batch of powder is being used.

Remember that to bump the machine before throwing a powder charge can cause the powder to settle. Because most reloaders throw by volume and not by weight, this bumping can mean, maybe, an extra grain of powder being loaded in some cartridges.

Stick to one kind or make of fired case, do not pick up fired cases in wet conditions. Set the crimping station carefully, so that the reloader produces correctly crimped cartridges.

Use common sense and extreme caution at all times. Keep your reloads to yourself, if you give or sell some to another person and his gun then blows up for whatever reason, you may be held liable and have to pay heavy damages.

Do remember if you are tempted to use reloads in CPSA-registered competitions and are detected, you can be disqualified. This would be a great pity if you had just produced a winning score.

Those who feel strongly about the CPSA rules on reloading have the remedy in their own hands. The Association is a democratic body and if enough members wish to have a rule changed this can be done.

The Care and Maintenance of the Shotgun

It has been said many times that more shotguns are ruined by neglect and/or slovenly cleaning than by shooting.

The greatest cause of barrel pitting and corrosion in the past was due to the old type of percussion cap. These days most cartridges claim to have non-corrosive percussion caps. Even so, a prudent owner will always clean his guns as soon as possible after use. Using the proper equipment this can be done in about 15 minutes if the gun has been used in dry weather. Guns used in wet weather will take about half an hour to clean and dry properly.

The Barrel

When a gun is fired, the lead shot leaves a thin deposit on the insides of the barrel. Any fouling from fired cartridges will be covered by the end of a day's shooting with this deposit which is called 'leading' and will be seen inside on the barrel walls as dark streaks. If plastic-wadded cartridges are used, there may also be plastic deposits left on the barrel walls, especially if the weather is hot.

Equipment

Many people use one cleaning rod and change the brushes and jags which screw into one end of the rod. It is worth while buying four good-quality rods, which can be one-piece, two-piece, or three-piece. Treated correctly they will outlast their owner. The set of four rods can each have the appropriate accessory screwed on permanently (see illustrations between pages 134 and 135).

Rod 1 should be fitted with an old, worn, but clean, phosphor-bronze brush.

Rod 2 fitted with a modern copy of the Payne-Gallwey type of phosphor-bronze brush.

Rod 3 a similar phosphor bronze brush to no. 1.

Rod 4 a clean, slightly oiled wool mop.

Other Equipment

A roll of 4 × 2 flannelette
A roll of household paper hand towelling
A couple of clean, dry, but slightly oiled gun cloths
A can of gun oil for lubrication and rust prevention
A can of powder solvent
A bottle of linseed oil-based stock finish
A can of leading remover
An old toothbrush
An aerosol spray similar to the Parker Hale Go Pro or the FN Legia spray

There are many other excellent preparations on the market and the shooter should ask for advice on these from his local gunsmith.

After shooting has finished for the day, and before the gun is taken down and put in its case, an aerosol like the Legia should be sprayed down the barrel from both ends. Also the outside of the gun can be lightly sprayed. A quick wipe-over with a slightly oiled cloth, kept in the case for the purpose, is all that is then required.

At home, rod no. 1 should have a piece of 4 × 2 placed over the end of the phosphor-bronze brush. This is pushed fully through the barrel, always from the breech end, a procedure followed with all the rods. This should remove the aerosol spray and much fouling. Then is the time to view the barrel.

To do this the barrel should be held up to the light through the gun room window. By allowing the shadow caused by part of the window frame to run up and down both inside and outside of the barrel, while slowly tilting and rotating it, the viewer can, with practice, check for scratches, leading, powder and plastic deposits, the beginning of erosion or plain rusting. Even more important, any dents or bulges will cause the straight line of the shadow to vary.

The next step is to use rod no. 2 with its Payne-Gallwey phosphor bronze brush. This should be well oiled with one of the solvents and pushed up and down the barrel. Rest the muzzle on a rubber mat on the floor to prevent the brush from coming right through. Eventually the muzzles will be lifted off the mat, and the brush and rod pushed right through and out at the muzzle end.

Rod no. 3 then has a clean piece of 4 × 2 draped over the phosphor-bronze brush and is pushed through, again from the breech.

Once more the barrel is viewed. If still showing any deposits, rod no. 2 must again be used, followed by no. 3. When the barrel is free of deposits, and clean, rod no. 4 with its lightly oiled mop can be pushed through to finish the operation.

The outside of the barrel should usually need only a wipe over with a piece of paper towelling, the exception being when the gun has been shot in the rain. In this case special care must be taken to use enough paper to dry the barrels, ribs and extractors well. The action should be wiped over with paper towelling and more used to clean the stock and fore-end if polyurethane-finished. Any dirt in the checkering should be removed by oil and the toothbrush. A final wipe over with an oily rag is then required.

If the stock is oil-finished, paper can be used to wipe off the dirt and the toothbrush used in conjunction with the linseed stock finish to clean the checkering. Finally, a wipe over with a cloth having a few drops of the linseed-oil finish is used to give a final polish.

At all times after shooting in the rain, extreme care should be taken to dry thoroughly all the gun. The case or sleeve cover must also be well dried before being used again.

Before reassembling the gun, whether side by side, o/u, or take down single barrel, the knuckle joint should be treated and there are many preparations for this purpose. The two greases most favoured by the writer are sold in tubes, and are (a) the Krieghoff Gun Glide, and (b) Mitchell X3 reel grease. Experience has proved that if an ordinary light gun oil is used on the knuckle joint, even shooting 50 cartridges may cause this oil film to be thinned to the point of removal. If this happens, especially with a fairly new gun, the two surfaces of the joint become dry and begin to 'pick up'. The surfaces will then grate on each other and become very rough, which makes the gun stiff to open. To remedy a joint which has picked up requires the services of a skilled gunsmith. The use of either grease should prevent this happening. The extractor and ejectors should be lightly oiled. Oil should not be squirted into the action as this excess oil will tend to rot the stock.

The gun is reassembled, taking care to do it with dry hands or by the use of clean oiled cloths. The gun can then be locked up in its clean well-aired cupboard until the next shoot.

The Semi-Automatic

These guns require more specialized treatment. The gun used for an example here is the Remington 1100, one of the most popular at the present time. Other semi-automatics require similar cleaning techniques.

The post shoot treatment is as previously advised. At the end of the day in the gun room, the semi-automatic should be taken down (see illustration of the tools which help to do this). Before the trigger assembly, no. 88, is removed from the receiver, the safety catch must be moved to the 'on' position. If this is not done any accidental pressure on the trigger afterwards may release the cocked hammer and cause damage to other parts of the assembly.

To remove the trigger assembly the pins, nos 92 and 93, are pushed out by the two special dowels and the assembly removed. This is cleaned by a solvent spray like Go Pro or Legia. When thoroughly cleaned of dirt and powder fouling, it should be suspended over a tray and allowed to drip-dry. Thus, there will still be a fine film of oil, where required, on the assembly.

The barrel seal, no 12, should be carefully removed, also parts 73 and 74, the piston and piston seal. The bolt-operating handle, no 69, is pulled out. A finger is pressed onto the end of the feed latch, 43, and the breech bolt 13, action bar assembly 1, and action bar sleeve 2 removed from the receiver assembly 75, and off the magazine tube.

The outside of the magazine tube is cleaned with paper towelling and solvents, and wiped dry. The same procedure is followed with parts 73, 74, 13, 1, 2 and 75. Special attention should be paid to no. 2 on its inside, any fouling being removed completely.

The inside of the receiver should be cleaned of powder residue, etc. It is best to use paper towelling and a pair of long-nosed pliers. On the inside of the receiver there is a long channel, the edge of which becomes razor sharp. Fingers carelessly pushing towelling along this channel can easily be badly cut, hence the use of long-nosed pliers.

All the parts should be reassembled in reverse order, with the trigger assembly being replaced last. Except for a very light oiling on the slide rail slots in the receiver, the parts are reassembled dry.

Barrel Cleaning

This is done as for any other shotgun barrel. There is, however, one very important addition. Underneath, and integral with the barrel, is a large piece of tube, called the gas cylinder. Parts 73 and 74 are positioned in this cylinder. The inside of the cylinder fouls in use, but this can easily be removed with steel wool and solvent and then wiped dry with paper towelling.

Inside the gas cylinder are two small holes which allow gases to bleed from the barrel and work the semi-auto action. Field and Skeet barrels have two holes. These holes must be kept clean. On some trap barrels there is also a transverse gas bleed adjustment screw. After firing about 1000 cartridges, the screw should be taken out with a small screwdriver, cleaned with solvent, the two gas bleed holes cleaned, and the screw replaced in the same position.

Barrel Bulges or Dents

It is all too easy to dent or bulge barrels. Hence the need for careful viewing when they are being cleaned. A skilled gunsmith can raise most dents or put down most bulges, and this should be done before the gun is used again.

Periodic Strip and Clean

Once a year it is a good policy to have one's gun stripped, cleaned and adjusted by a competent gunsmith. In these days of inflation it is also worthwhile having them revalued for insurance purposes at the same time.

Patterns and Patterning

In 1887 R. W. S. Griffiths, the manager of the Schultze Gunpowder Company, was actively involved in testing cartridges both for pattern quality and shot string. He is alleged to have calculated that it would take him some hundreds of years to test and pattern samples from all the then available permutations of percussion caps, cases, powders, wads, shot pellets and crimps.

Since then millions of cartridges have been fired, and millions more words written about their performances. Modern cartridges, properly matched to correct barrel chokings, produce results which are excellent. The greater proportion of clay shooters freely accept this; they simply make use of the knowledge available at any good gun shop, accepting that any poor performance is due to the man and nothing else.

There are others, of course, who derive pleasure and information from patterning their guns with various brands of cartridge in an attempt to match cartridge choke and discipline. This chapter is written for these people.

Equipment Required

A mild steel plate, 6 ft × 6 ft × $\frac{3}{16}$ in. thick. This should be mounted vertically on a frame and at right angles to the shooter.

A distemper brush on a long handle.

DETAILS OF SHOT SIZES (NOMINAL)

Desig.	Diameter		Pellets	
	mm	in	per 10 g	per oz
LG	9.1	.36	2	6
SG	8.4	.33	3	8
Spec. SG	7.6	.30	4	11
SSG	6.8	.27	$5\frac{1}{2}$	15
AAA	5.2	.20	$12\frac{1}{2}$	35
BB	4.1	.16	25	70
1	3.6	.14	36	100
3	3.3	.13	50	140
4	3.1	.12	60	170
5	2.8	.11	78	220
6	2.6	.10	95	270
7	2.4	.095	120	340
$7\frac{1}{2}$	2.3	.09	140	400
8	2.2	.085	160	450
9	2.0	.08	210	580

g = grams

SHOT SIZE EQUIVALENTS (NOMINAL)

English	Metric mm	American*	French	Belgian†	Italian	Spanish
LG	9.1	—	—	—	—	—
SG	8.4	00 Buck	—	9G	11/0	—
Spec. SG	7.6	1 Buck	C2	12G	9/0	—
SSG	6.8	3 Buck	C3	—	—	—
AAA	5.2	4 Buck	5/0	—	—	—
BB	4.1	Air rifle	1	00	00	1
1	3.6	2	3	—	1 or 2	3
3	3.3	4	4	—	3	4
4	3.1	5	5	—	4	5
5	2.8	6	6	5	5	6
6	2.6	—	—	6	6	—
7	2.4	$7\frac{1}{2}$	7	7	$7\frac{1}{2}$	7
$7\frac{1}{2}$	2.3	8	$7\frac{1}{2}$	$7\frac{1}{2}$	8	$7\frac{1}{2}$
8	2.2	—	8	8	—	8
9	2.0	9	9	9	$9\frac{1}{2}$	9

*also Swedish.   †also Dutch.

PATTERNS AT ALL RANGES

Percentage of total pellets in 75 cm circle

Boring of Gun	Range in metres							
	20	25	30	35	40	45	50	55
True Cyl.	75	63	53	43	35	28	22	18
Imprvd. Cyl.	85	74	64	53	43	34	27	22
$\frac{1}{4}$-Choke	90	80	70	58	48	39	31	25
$\frac{1}{2}$-Choke	97	86	76	64	54	43	34	27
$\frac{3}{4}$-Choke	100	93	83	70	58	47	38	30
Full Choke	100	100	90	74	62	51	41	32

Percentage of total pellets in 30 in circle

Boring of Gun	Range in yards								
	20	25	30	35	40	45	50	55	60
True Cyl.	80	69	60	49	40	33	27	22	18
Imprvd. Cyl.	92	82	72	60	50	41	33	27	22
$\frac{1}{4}$-Choke	100	87	77	65	55	46	38	30	25
$\frac{1}{2}$-Choke	100	94	83	71	60	50	41	33	27
$\frac{3}{4}$-Choke	100	100	91	77	65	55	46	37	30
Full Choke	100	100	100	84	70	59	49	40	32

Example: Charge 30 g ($1\frac{1}{16}$ oz) No. 5; find pattern at 50 yards for a half-choke barrel. Total pellets. 234 multiplied by 41 (from table above) and divided by 100. Answer 96.

A shallow pan of sufficient size to take the above brush.

A cake of whitening and a bucket of water.

A 30 in. diameter circle or hoop made from $\frac{1}{2}$ in. thick iron rod with a cross-bar.

Accurately measured distances from the plate, marked with permanent pegs at 16, 20, 25, 30, 35 and 40 yd.

Two sets of weighing scales. One capable of weighing 25 cartridges in bulk, the other capable of weighing one cartridge at a time, also the individual components, the powder, wads and shot charge.

A micrometer to measure shot diameter.

A set of tables containing details of shot sizes and diameters, pattern percentages, charge spread at various distances for different chokings. These tables are printed by permission of Eley.

DIAMETER OF SPREAD

Diameter in centimetres and inches covered by the bulk of the charge of a gun at various ranges for all calibres.

Centimetres

Boring of gun	Range in metres					
	10	15	20	25	30	35
True Cyl.	54	71	88	105	122	140
Imprvd. Cyl.	38	55	72	89	106	124
¼-Choke	34	49	64	80	97	115
½-Choke	31	44	58	73	90	108
¾-Choke	27	39	52	66	82	101
Full Choke	23	33	45	59	75	94

Inches

Boring of gun	Range in yards						
	10	15	20	25	30	35	40
True Cyl.	20	26	32	38	44	51	58
Imprvd. Cyl.	15	20	26	32	38	44	51
¼-Choke	13	18	23	29	35	41	48
½-Choke	12	16	21	26	32	38	45
¾-Choke	10	14	18	23	29	35	42
Full Choke	9	12	16	21	27	33	40

Shot sizes vary and unless one knows the approximate number of pellets in the shot charge contained in brands x or y cartridge, one cannot compare like with like.

Pattern percentages are the proportion of the pellets contained in a one-cartridge shot load which are placed on the plate within a 30 in. circle. Because of this, years ago, pellet charges for cartridges used in choke and pattern trials were always carefully counted by means of a shot-counting trowel (see fig. 20).

To test a specific brand of cartridges for patterns, one should take 25 and weigh them as one lot. The total weight should be divided by 25 to find their average weight. Each cartridge must then be individually weighed. The lightest, the heaviest, and three cartridges of average weight should then be selected and each cut open, and the powder, wads and shot weighed and carefully noted.

It is rare for there to be noticeable variations in weight of powder and wadding. The greatest variation is usually with the shot charge and pellet count.

Therefore the pellets from each cartridge should be carefully counted after weighing. A sample of pellets from each should also be miked to establish their diameter. By using the Eley tables one can establish the true English equivalent size. More important, the number of pellets per cartridge being known and recorded enables one to equate like with like when conducting future cartridge tests. The average pellet count from the above five cartridges is used as a basis for calculating pattern percentages.

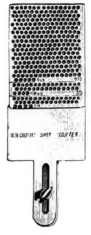

20 The shot counter.

Using the Pattern Plate
The cake of whitening should have water added to it until the mixture is of a creamy consistency. Then the surface of the plate is well coated with the mixture.

One of the remaining cartridges is fired through the barrel to foul it and remove any traces of oil.

If a permanent record of the patterns to be shot is required, the details of the cartridges being tested, together with the barrel boring and the range is all carefully written on the top right-hand corner of the plate. For instance: brand x, $1\frac{1}{8} \times 7$, 30 yd $\frac{1}{2}$ choke.

A small aiming mark should be placed in the centre of the plate. After each shot is fired, the 30 in. hoop is placed on the plate with the pattern centred in it. A sharp pointed stick is used to mark round the outside of the hoop to show the 30 in. diameter circle. The hoop is removed and a black and white photograph taken with a 35 mm camera. Then the plate should be rewhitened, except for the details of the brand, load and so on.

A second cartridge is fired from the same 30 yd mark as before. Again the hoop is used to centre the pattern and the pointed stick to mark the circle. Then another photograph is taken from exactly the same place as before.

Nine cartridges should be shot from the one barrel, using the same procedure each time.

If the other barrel has to be tested, it is fouled by firing one cartridge through it. The whole plate is rewhitened, the details of cartridge shot load and size, barrel boring and yardage marked up in the top right hand

The outer circle is the standard 30 in. The concentric inner circle is of 20 in.
Although one can check for any thickening of the pattern centre, the area of
the 20 in. inner circle is less than that of the outer ring.

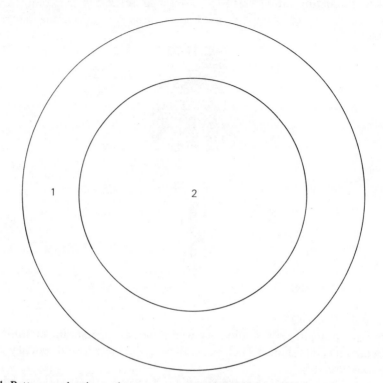

21 Pattern evaluation – the system used by Oberfell and Thompson.

corner, and the same procedure of firing nine cartridges is followed as
before. By this means one has an easily stored permanent record on
film. To then check the patterns is simple, a whole plate picture of each
pattern is printed.

The following information can then be obtained from a study of the
nine patterns per barrel.

a   the trueness of the point aim of the gun. This assumes the shooter
can centre the patterns in the same place on the plate-aiming mark each
time.

b   one can get a pellet count within the 30 in. circle while sitting in
comfort at one's desk. All one needs is a ball-point pen and patience.
Knowing the average pellet count of the shot load, the pattern
percentage can easily be ascertained.

Quality of Pattern
This can be done in many ways. Oberfell and Thompson use an inner
ring and make two counts (see fig. 21). By far the better method is the
system developed and used by the staff of the American Rifleman since
1977. This has proved highly successful for accurate comparison of

The outer circle is the standard 30 in. as used in Great Britain. The concentric inner circle is of 21.21 in. Quartering the circle provides eight equal areas. By counting the numbers of pellets in each area one can check the pellet pattern for the evenness of its distribution.

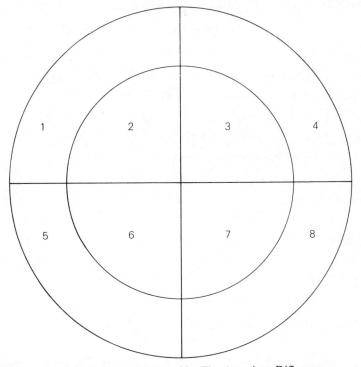

22 Pattern evaluation – the system used by The American Rifleman.

pattern distribution (see fig. 22). This shows the 30 in. circle segmented into four parts, an inner circle of 21.21 in. diameter is inscribed concentrically inside the 30 in. circle. This gives eight portions of equal size. The pattern tester simply marks this on his patterns. Knowing the percentage of pellets within the 30 in. and then recording each area, it is possible to calculate any centre thickening of pattern. Also one can easily check for unevenness.

It must be realized that shotgun patterns will vary 5 per cent either way from average. Therefore, in nine patterns produced from say, a half-choke barrel at 40 yd, there may well be one pattern open enough to be almost evaluated as $\frac{1}{4}$ choke, and yet another as $\frac{3}{4}$ choke. For these reasons one must take an average of the nine shots fired to obtain a reasonably consistent result.

So far we have considered the production of patterns, recording and evaluating them. The expert gun or cartridge maker and also the barrel regulator will by long training and personal observation note the following indications every time he patterns a cartridge.

Recoil – Is the recoil soft, normal or excessive?

Velocity – By using his ears, covered with muffs though they may be, and his eyes, his experience will enable him to differentiate between a low-, normal- and high-velocity cartridge.

Empty Case Examination – After each cartridge is fired the case will be carefully inspected and the following points noted.

Cap Indentation and Case Expansion – If pressures are excessive, the cap and case will provide evidence (see illustrations between pages 134 and 135).

Beginning ½ in. from one end a series of ⅛ in. holes are drilled in the lath. The holes are drilled at 1 in. intervals. Also required are two wooden file handles and two lengths of silver steel 3 X ⅛ in. diameter. The silver steel lengths are each driven into one of the file handles. The end of the silver steel rod is then ground to a point, thereby making two wooden handled dowels. To use, the lath is placed across the pattern on the plate and its diameter assessed. The centre of the pattern is established. One of the dowels is placed through the hole at one end of the lath and the dowel point placed on the plate at the centre of the pattern.
The other dowel is placed in the hole in the lath which is approximate to the edge of the pattern. By swinging the lath around the dowel at the pattern centre one produces a circle on the plate denoting the pattern diameter.

Wooden lath 31 X 1½ X ½ in.

Holes of ⅛ in. diameter 1 in. apart

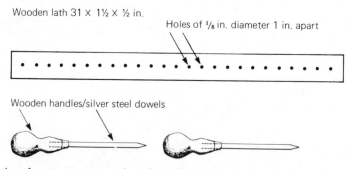

Wooden handles/silver steel dowels

23 A gadget to measure and mark out the circle showing diameter of pattern spread. A wooden lath is obtained measuring 30 × 1¼ × ½ in.

The Appearance of the Crimp – A cartridge producing high pressure and excessive recoil can be expected to iron out all, or almost all, traces of the crimp. Low-pressure cartridges will show poorly opened crimps.

After each shot is fired, the pattern placement is centralized by means of the hoop. The 30 in. circle is then marked on the plate by the pointed stick.

The marks produced by the pellets allow an assessment to be made of how hard they are striking the plate. These marks will vary in size. Well-shaped pellets of normal velocity will provide well-rounded and bruising marks. The sizes of these marks varies with shot sizes, no. 9 at 40 yd producing smaller marks than those from no. 6 shot. Badly shaped pellets of whatever shot size soon lose their velocity, and their marks on the plate will show more as pin-pricks. These pellets cannot be relied upon to break targets at 40 yd distances.

The pattern quality shown on the plate will be examined. Years of experience enables the expert to note a well-distributed pattern, a patchy pattern, or one with too thick a centre. Signs of cold welding or shot balling will also be looked for carefully. Some 3 in. chambered .410 guns are notorious offenders.

Width of Pattern Spread

The diameter of the bulk of the pattern spread is measured. It is worthwhile making up a simple gadget to do this and also to mark a circle on the plate around such a pattern (see fig. 23). By consulting the tables showing pattern spread diameter produced by various chokings at distances from 10 to 40 yd, it is possible to ascertain quickly the choke of the barrel being tested.

As an example, gun A's right barrel is alleged to be half choke. It is being shot at 30 yd distance from the plate. The bulk of the shot charge is now found to be contained in a circle of 44 in. diameter. If the nine shots fired do produce an average spread of 44 in., we then consult the tables. These show that such a spread is produced by an improved cylinder-bored barrel. A half choke barrel should place the bulk of its shot charge in a 32-in. circle at 30 yd.

By emulating the expert's methods as described above, and using the American Rifleman's 8-segment system of pattern quality comparison and evaluation, even an inexperienced person should soon become knowledgeable regarding shotgun patterns.

What the pattern plate cannot do is to provide evidence regarding shot string. This was briefly touched on in Chapter 2. For those who wish to pursue this further, their best course of action will be to experiment on the same lines as Bob Brister laid down in his book.

For those who have neither the time or money, a reasonable indication of shot string can be obtained by carefully firing a shotgun from a fixed point over a calm stretch of water. Although the length of string cannot be measured, one can see the string briefly on the surface of the water.

Penetration

The shot marks on the plate provides the knowledgeable with some information. For those who wish to proceed further a card rack on the lines of that made by Payne-Gallwey can be used.

An even more simple method is that advocated by Robert Churchill who shot at old London telephone directories at a measured distance. After which he opened the directory to see how far the pellets had penetrated.

Conclusions

After spending a lifetime patterning guns, one can only reiterate the belief that there is precious little wrong with the patterns produced by modern cartridges and correctly bored shotguns.

Those wishing to pursue this complex subject of shotgun patterns further are referred to the bibliography in this book.

14 The Future

Experience has taught the writer that most prophecies, no matter how probable they may seem at the time, eventually prove to be wrong.

At the present time there are some one million holders of shotgun certificates in Britain. The CPSA and their affiliated clubs have a combined membership of around 30,000. Yet the clay target makers claim an annual target consumption of 50 million. Based on the average member consuming 500 targets per year, and this is on the high side, we can estimate an annual consumption of 15 million targets. This figure leaves 35 million targets unaccounted for.

The shooting schools, of which there are some 60, will use approximately 15 million. The targets used by syndicates, farmers and their friends who have one or two traps set up for their own convenience and pleasure, will be around the million a year mark. The remaining 19 million are being consumed by clubs affiliated to BASC and innumerable small clubs affiliated to no one.

The writer has made many enquiries to find out why so few belong to the CPSA in relation to the huge numbers who shoot targets and do not. The answers received were as follows. 'We shoot targets for fun, or to keep our eye in for live bird shooting.' 'We cannot afford to shoot enough targets and to attain a high enough standard in order to hope of competing with the near professional international shooter, who may be spending hundreds or even thousands of pounds per year on his shooting.'

The CPSA has realized this, and as mentioned in another chapter, have now re-allowed their members to shoot 'targets only' at registered shoots. In this it has come into line with American practice. Shooters who now shoot 'targets only' neither contribute towards, or collect from any prize monies derived from entrance fees. The clubs, however, make the same profit from such shooters. The only people who regret this action are the sandbaggers who will thereby collect smaller cash prizes.

Eventually the Association may emulate the Americans and allow the use of reloads. Such a move would reduce shooting costs. Reloads have not been allowed at registered shoots in the past because of the fear that such cartridges may have heavier than legal shot charges.

The present rules allow for the challenge of any cartridge. Therefore it is surely unreasonable to believe that shooters would be so foolish as to use illegal loads and risk eventual disqualification and even banning.

Modern reloading machines turn out good quality cartridges with the correct shot load if properly operated.

The writer believes that more and more small clubs will be formed. There will always be a feeder movement from these clubs to the bigger ones by those members whose finances allow them to shoot 2000 to 5000 cartridges per annum in an effort to attain international honours.

Gun Design

There has been little change in gun design for many years. The increased use of sophisticated machinery means that good quality modern guns are excellent value for money.

The most interesting and promising development at present is the renewed interest in the screw-in choke tube. Although an old idea, the modern version, using high quality material, allows the knowledgeable shooter the means of quickly matching the patterns of his gun to suit the trajectories and distances of the targets thrown.

The Beretta, Bretton, Fabarm, Franchi, Lincoln, and Winchester guns are all fitted with screw-in, drop-in, or screw-on choke tubes. The new Caprinus O/U has normal screw-in choke tubes. Also available are choke tubes offset to throw patterns off centre by the required amount. The writer has extensively shot and patterned each of these guns, all of which produce excellent patterns when matched to suitable cartridges.

Jesse Briley in Houston has been successfully fitting screw-in choke tubes of stainless steel to many makes of guns, o/us, side by sides, and semi-automatics. This work he does without expanding the diameter of the original barrel(s).

Screw-in chokes are being produced and fitted by gunmakers in this country to both new and secondhand guns. Although our gunmaker's technique is slightly different to that used by Briley, the patterns produced by both techniques have been excellent to date. Shooters who wish to have their favourite gun so fitted should realize that the gun will then have to be submitted for English proof. The proof house procedure is to use only the tightest choke tube supplied when doing this proof test.

It must be made plain that these choke tubes can be damaged by careless handling by the shooter. Shooters who carry their choke tubes loose among their cartridges will soon ruin them. To screw a battered tube into a barrel and attempt to fire cartridges is a stupid practice and will deservedly cause trouble. The tubes should be kept lightly oiled and stored in the special boxes supplied by their makers.

Recoil Reduction

Continued absorption of recoil by the shooter can cause problems. Gun manufacturers and custom gunsmiths have been continually working on this problem since guns were first invented.

Many types of recoil reducers are now available, those fitted to the stock or to the butt pad do work, but are disliked by some shooters because the gun balance is usually altered. Muzzle brakes and compensators also work and most of these can cause shock waves which trouble nearby shooters. They are therefore banned in DTL competitions. There are numerous types of recoil pads now available. One very successful new pad is the Sorbothane. Made from a soft rubber-like material it is not easy to fit but when fitted by an expert it has proved to be very popular, especially by the ladies as a means of reducing felt recoil.

Pro-Porting

This utilizes electrical discharge machining technology and results in 22 holes being placed in a shotgun barrel. Apparently they are allowed for trap shooting in the United States, it being claimed the shock waves are thrown upwards. Certainly a barrel so treated and tested by the writer, produced less perceived recoil and muzzle flip.

Overboring

Popular in the United States. Barrels which have walls of adequate thickness are bored out from maybe .729 to .746. A similar practice was pursued by the makers of muzzle loaders, who relieved their barrels' back from the muzzles.

Overboring reduces perceived recoil, the wider bore resulting in lesser shot deformation. Barrels proofed at .729 and subsequently bored to more than .739 will need to be reproofed at .740.

Cartridges

The use of soft shot for Skeet and plated hard shot for the long going-away targets has much improved modern cartridge performance. So much so that in the United States of America, 100 straights are *now* being shot at single barrel DTL shooting, even from the 27 yd mark with 1 oz loaded cartridges. A far cry from Burrard who calculated in the 1920s that nothing less than 1¼ oz load and a full choke barrel could be relied upon to break consistently DTL targets, and this from the 16 yd distance.

Cartridges will continue to improve and in relation to other goods are now actually cheaper than they were during pre-war years.

Clay-Targets

We have recently seen the introduction of the midi or the Super 90 target. This has proved to be a superb target for Sporting competitions, travelling faster and further than a standard target. Being lighter and smaller, it takes less material to make, takes up less storage space, and is easier to transport. There would seem to be no valid reason why these targets should not eventually be used for English Skeet and DTL as well as for Sporting. It is true that automatic traps would have to be altered to take them, but this can be done.

Whatever the future may hold, one fact is certain, human nature does not change. Among those who can afford to shoot clay targets in sufficient quantity, the best shooters will come to the top as they always have. These rare few, with the will to win, and the concentration to match, will be there or thereabouts among the winners until they, in their turn, pass their peak and have to make way for the new up and coming champions.

It is also fact that although this book has dealt with the advantages of coaching and coaches at length, and any good coach *can* teach a normal person how to shoot any particular target in any discipline, no matter how much guns, applied gadgets and cartridges improve. Ultimately, it will still be up to the shooter himself to produce the guts to string his kills together in sufficient quantities to shoot straights and win championships.

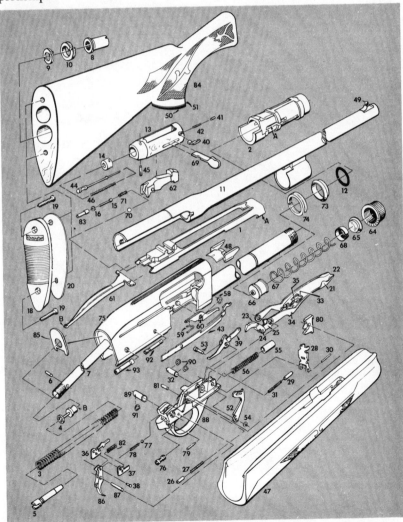

24 The Remington Automatic Shotgun Model 1100, over 3 million have been made.

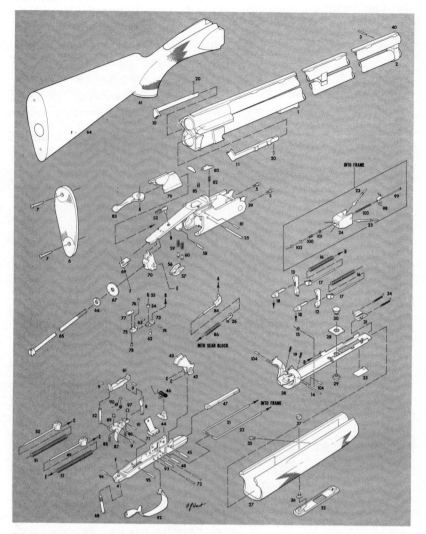

25 The Remington Model 3200 o/u gun.

2	Barrel Band – 26, 28 in.	
	Barrel Band – 30 in.	
3	Barrel Band Lock Pin	
5	Bottom Tang Screw	
6	Butt Plate	
7	Butt Plate Screw	
8	Connector	
9	Connector Pin	
12	Ejector Hammer, Right	
13	Ejector Hammer, Left	
14	Ejector Hammer Pin	
15	Ejector Hammer Pivot	
	Ring	
16	Ejector Hammer Spring	
17	Ejector Plunger	
	Assembly	
18	Ejector Sear	
19	Ejector Sear Spring	
20	Ejector Stop Pin	

21	Ejector Trip Rod, Left	
22	Ejector Trip Rod, Right	
23	Firing Pin	
24	Firing Pin Housing	
25	Firing Pin Housing	
	Assembly Pin	
26	Firing Pin Retractor	
27	Fore-end	
28	Fore-end Adjuster Plate	
29	Fore-end Adjuster Plate	
	Lock Nut	
30	Fore-end Adjuster Plate	
	Stud	
31	Fore-end Latch	
32	Fore-end Latch Cover	
33	Fore-end Latch Finger	
	Piece	
34	Fore-end Latch Spring	
35	Fore-end Screw, Front	

36	Fore-end Screw, Rear	
37	Fore-end Screw Nut	
40	Front Sight	
	Front Sight Pin	
41	Grip Cap	
	Grip Cap Screw	
42	Hammer Assembly,	
	Right	
43	Hammer Assembly, Left	
44	Hammer Cocking Cam	
45	Hammer Cocking Cam Pin	
46	Hammer Cocking Cam	
	Spring	
47	Hammer Cocking Rod	
48	Hammer Pin	
49	Hammer Plunger	
	Assembly, Right	
50	Hammer Plunger	
	Assembly, Left	

51 Main Hammer Spring
52 Rear Connector Ling
53 Safety Selector Assembly
54 Safety Selector Detent
55 Safety Selector Detent
    Spring
56 Sear, Left
57 Sear, Right
58 Sear Pin
59 Sear Spring
60 Sear Spring Plunger
61 Selector Block
62 Selector Block Guide
63 Selector Block Guide Pin
64 Stock Assembly
    Stock Assembly
    (Magnum)
65 Stock Bolt
66 Stock Bolt Lock Washer
67 Stock Bolt Washer

68 Tang Block Screw
69 Tang Block Slot Nut
70 Tang Connecting Block
71 Tang Strut
72 Tang Strut Pin
73 Toggle Block
74 Toggle Block Retaining
    Pin
75 Toggle Link
76 Toggle Link Screw
77 Toggle Slide Block
78 Toggle Slide Block Stud
80 Top Lock Latch
81 Top Lock Latch Pin
82 Top Lock Latch Spring
84 Top Lock Lever Plunger
    Assembly
85 Top Lock Lever Screw
86 Top Lock Lever Spring
87 Trigger

88 Trigger Adjusting Screw
89 Trigger Adjusting Screw
    Nut
90 Trigger Connector Spring
91 Trigger Connector Spring
    Pin
92 Trigger Guard
93 Trigger Guard Pin, Front
94 Trigger Guard Pin, Rear
95 Trigger Pin
96 Trigger Stop Screw
97 Trigger Stop Screw Nut
98 Yoke
99 Yoke Rod
100 Yoke Rod Buffer Spring
101 Yoke Rod Buffer Spring
    Washer
102 Yoke Rod Nut
103 Yoke Rod Spring
104 Ejector Sear Pin

The Remington Model 1100 (see page 161)

1 Action Bar Assembly
2 Action Bar Sleeve
3 Action Spring
4 Action Spring Follower
5 Action Spring Plug
6 Action Spring Plug Pin
7 Action Spring Tube
8 Action Spring Tube Nut
9 Action Spring Tube Nut
    Washer
10 Action Spring Tube Nut
    Lock Washer
11 Barrel Assembly
12 Barrel Seal
13 Breech Bolt
    Breech Bolt Assembly
14 Breech Bolt Buffer
15 Breech Bolt Return
    Plunger
16 Breech Bolt Return
    Plunger Retaining Ring
18 Butt Plate
19 Butt Plate Screw
20 Butt Plate Spacer
21 Carrier
22 Carrier Assembly
23 Carrier Dog
24 Carrier Dog Pin
25 Carrier Dog Washer
26 Carrier Dog Follower
27 Carrier Dog Follower
    Spring
28 Carrier Latch
29 Carrier Latch Follower
30 Carrier Latch Pin
31 Carrier Latch Spring
32 Carrier Pivot Tube
33 Carrier Release
34 Carrier Release Pin
35 Carrier Release Spring
36 Connector, Left
    Restricted
37 Connector, Right
    Restricted

38 Connector Pin
39 Disconnector
    Ejector (not numbered)
40 Extractor
41 Extractor Plunger
42 Extractor Spring
43 Feed Latch
44 Firing Pin
45 Firing Pin Retaining Pin
46 Firing Pin Retractor
    Spring
47 Fore-end Assembly
48 Fore-end Support
    Fore-end Tube Assembly
49 Front Sight – for VENT
    RIB use No. 18796
    Front Sight Base, 12 Ga.
    Front Sight Retaining
    Pin, VENT RIB
50 Grip Cap
    Grip Cap Inlay
    Grip Cap Screw
51 Grip Cap Spacer
52 Hammer
53 Hammer Pin
54 Hammer Pin Washer
55 Hammer Plunger
56 Hammer Spring
58 Interceptor Latch
    Retainer
59 Interceptor Latch Spring
60 Interceptor Latch
61 Link
62 Locking Block Assembly
    Locking Block Assembly
    (oversize)
    Locking Block Retainer
64 Magazine Cap
    Magazine Cap Detent
    Magazine Cap Detent
    Spring
65 Magazine Cap Plug
66 Magazine Follower
    Magazine Plug (3 shot)

67 Magazine Spring
68 Magazine Spring
    Retainer
69 Operating Handle
70 Operating Handle Detent
    Ball
71 Operating Handle Detent
    Spring
73 Piston
74 Piston Seal
75 Receiver Assembly
            (Restricted)
76 Safety
77 Safety Detent Ball
78 Safety Spring
79 Safety Spring Retaining
    Pin
80 Sear
81 Sear Pin
82 Sear Spring
83 Slide Block Buffer
84 Stock Assembly
85 Stock Bearing Plate
86 Trigger   (Restricted)
    Trigger Assembly
            (Restricted)
87 Trigger Pin
88 Trigger Plate, R.H.
    Safety
    Trigger Plate, L.H.
    Safety
    Trigger Plate Assembly,
    R.H. Safety
    Trigger Plate Assembly,
    L.H. Safety
89 Trigger Plate Pin Bushing
90 Trigger Plate Pin Detent
    Spring, Front (Need 2)
91 Trigger Plate Pin Detent
    Spring, Rear
92 Trigger Plate Pin, Front
93 Trigger Plate Pin, Rear

Appendix I

Useful Addresses

Shooting Organizations
The Clay Pigeon Shooting Association,
107 Epping New Road, Buckhurst Hill, Essex 1G9 5TQ.

Shooters who wish to contact
The Scottish CPSA
The Ulster CPSA
The Welsh CPSA
are advised to write to the CPSA at Buckhurst Hill, for the relevant current address.

BASC (formerly WAGBI)
Marford Mill, Rossett, Wrexham, Clwyd LL12 0HL.

Films on shooting available from:
BASC address as above.

CPSA address as above.

Edgar Bros
Catherine Street, Macclesfield SK11 6SG.

Eley
PO Box 216, Witton, Birmingham B6 7BA.

Hull Cartridge (Remington Films)
Bontoft Avenue, National Avenue, Hull HU5 4HZ.

Winchester UK
Site 7, Kidderminster Road, Cutnall Green, Droitwich, Worcester WR9 0NS.

Appendix II

The Shotgun Certificate

In law, a shotgun is a firearm with a smooth bore barrel(s) not less than 24 in. in length. To obtain a Shotgun Certificate thereby enabling one to buy, borrow, or otherwise acquire and possess a shotgun, the following procedure must be followed.

An approved form must be obtained from the police. This form is at present specified by law and no supplementary questions may be included, if they are, they need not be answered. Misleading or false information supplied by the applicant may lead to a prosecution.

When the form has been completed it must be signed by someone who is not a relation of the applicant. This person must be a British subject who has known the applicant for two years, and is a person of standing. A loose form of wording which can be construed to mean anything. In practice, people with professional qualifications, such as architects, accountants, bank managers, MPS, JPS, Ministers of Religion, doctors and lawyers are usually accepted.

At the present time one does *not* have to supply a *reason* for applying for a certificate. There is no need to provide evidence that one belongs to a clay club or any other shooting organization.

When the completed form has been signed, it should be taken in person to the local police station. The police may wish to ask questions and one should be as helpful as possible as they have a hard and difficult job to do.

The fee at the present time, 1982, is £12.

Only the chief constable may grant or refuse a certificate. Should one be refused there is a right of appeal to the Crown Court and notice of appeal must be given within 21 days of refusal. A solicitor should always be engaged in the case of such an appeal.

There are no requirements to supply information about shotguns one may own, buy or sell, once a certificate has been acquired. But those wishing to buy and sell shotguns as a business must obtain a dealer's licence.

If selling a gun one must see and note the following details on the buyer's certificate: (a) Certificate number, (b) Date of expiry, (c) County of origin and (d) Buyer's name and address. Also, a valid certificate must be produced at a gun shop when a gun is bought.

A certificate is valid for three years. Normally one receives a renewal notice from the police. It is the shooter's responsibility to ensure he always has a valid certificate. Also the police must be notified of any change of address or if the certificate is lost or stolen.

It is permissible at the present time for anyone to buy shotgun cartridges as long as he is over 17 years old. Shotgun cartridges are defined as those which contain five or more pellets, none of which exceed .36 in. in diameter.

There are no conditions applied to a shotgun certificate. It is common sense, however, to store guns and cartridges as securely as possible, and some form of security cabinet should be considered.

Appendix III

The Ten Commandments for Clay Pigeon Shooters

General

1   All guns should be: (a) nitro proofed, (b) in proof, (c) in safe and sound condition to shoot.

2   Treat every gun as if it is loaded and with the utmost respect at all times.

3   When carrying a gun it should be open and empty at all times. Pump action and semi-automatic guns should be carried with the bolts back, and with the chambers and magazines empty.

4   Avoid alcohol and horseplay when in possession of a gun.

5   When using a gun you should have on your person only those cartridges which are of the correct gauge and chamber length to match the gun. (Shot sizes nos 6, 7, 8 and 9 only.)

6   *Do not* point or fire your gun at anything other than a clay pigeon (i.e. do not point or fire your gun at any other inanimate or animate object). Failure to observe this rule can lead to disqualification and expulsion from the ground.

Behaviour on the Firing Point

7   Before loading your gun with one or two cartridges check that the barrels are free from obstruction and that they are pointing up the range.

8   Keep the muzzles pointing up the range at all times until you have opened and emptied your gun. Then (and only then) you may turn around and walk off the firing point.

Gun Malfunction

9   Keep the muzzles pointing up the range until the malfunction is identified and corrected. (If upon firing the gun the cartridge makes an unusual report, then before reloading you should check the barrels are free from obstruction.)

Remember

10   *You (and only you) are responsible for the safe handling of your gun at all times. You are also responsible for the behaviour and safety of your family, guests and animals when they are on the shooting ground.*

Glossary and Abbreviations

ABT Automatic Ball Trap.

Action The body of a gun containing most of the moving parts. May be of boxlock or sidelock construction. A conventionally designed sidelock has more moving parts and usually costs more to produce, assuming equal qualities of materials and workmanship.

Action bolt A steel bolt which fits into the bite of the barrel lump and holds action and barrel together.

Action top strap A piece of steel usually integral with the action and placed at the rear end of it.

Action bottom strap A piece of metal which may or may not be integral with the action and placed at the bottom rear end of it.

Anson & Deeley A boxlock action designed by Messrs Anson and Deeley, introduced in 1875. Even today the majority of modern actions are broadly based on this design.

Barrel The steel tube complete with lump, etc., in the chamber of which a suitable cartridge can be placed and fired, the pellets being discharged up and out through the muzzle.

Barrels Two steel tubes fastened together by various methods, in which suitable cartridges can be placed as above for the same purpose.

Barrel flats Usually in a side by side gun the breech ends of the barrels are flat where they sit on the action table.

Barrel selector Usually a catch, lever, or small button fitted to a single selective trigger double gun. Movement of this selector allows the shooter to choose which barrel he fires first.

BASC British Association for Shooting and Conservation. Founded in 1908 by Stanley Duncan as 'The Wildfowlers Association of Great Britain and Ireland'.

Bent A notch in the hammer or tumbler into which the sear nose fits when the gun is cocked.

Bifurcated As applied to the jointing of a gun, means two. A trunnion is placed on each side of the barrel replacing the one solid hinge pin underneath, resulting in a shallower action.

Bite(s) Notch(es) in the barrel lump(s), into which the bolt(s) engage.

Blacking A chemically produced black finish as applied to barrels, actions, etc.

Bolt *see* Action bolt.

Bore/gauge The inside of a barrel. The bore size or diameter for proof is measured 9 in. from the breech. This diameter is based on the number of pure lead spherical balls each fitting the bore, which go to the English 16 oz pound. A 12 bore gun would therefore accept 12 spherical balls, which weighed together would equal one pound. This holds true for all bores except the .410 calibre, which is shown in decimals of an inch as .410.

Boxlock A type of action which contains the locks internally, i.e. they are not mounted on the insides of the side plates.

Breech The end of the barrel into which a cartridge is inserted.

Calibre *see* Bore/gauge.

Calling one's shots Knowing why and where one has missed a target.

Cartridges *See fig. 26* showing the cartridge case and its components.

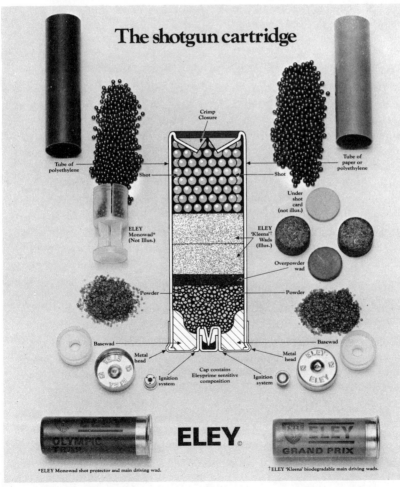

26 Eley's shotgun cartridge.

Case hardening A process whereby the outer skin or casing of the action and other parts are hardened. It may be done chemically. In Britain it is usually achieved by packing the parts in a steel pot in a mixture of, basically, ground bones and leather scraps. The whole is heated and then allowed to cool. The surface layer of the steel absorbs carbon which hardens it. This process produces colours on the hardened parts of beautiful shades of blue and brown.

Chamber That part of the barrel breech end into which the cartridge is inserted.

Choke A constriction at the muzzle end of the barrel which should produce tighter patterns than if the barrel is bored cylinder. The amount of constriction or choke is measured in thousandths of an inch and termed 'points of choke'.

5 thous: would be 5 points of choke and termed Improved Cylinder.

10 thous: would be termed $\frac{1}{4}$ choke.

20 thous: would be termed $\frac{1}{2}$ choke or American modified choke.

30 thous: would be termed $\frac{3}{4}$ choke or American Improved modified choke.

40 thous: would be termed Full choke, or American full choke.

In practice such measurements bear little relation to the tightness and more important, to the quality of the patterns thrown. Only by shooting cartridges can the layman ascertain the pattern spread and quality. Some imported guns with 40 thous: constriction are overchoked, so much so that pellets are deformed, passing through such a tight choke. The resulting patterns are poor and patchy, a skilled barrel borer can often improve such patterns and tighten them by opening the choke constriction. Therefore one can only repeat that only patterning and testing will tell a true story. Experience from the last half century has proved to the writer's satisfaction that pattern density and quality is not necessarily proportional to either the degree of constrictions, or choke shape.

Choke tubes Screw-in, screw-on, drop-in tubes which are of varying constriction and which can alter the tightness of the pattern thrown by a barrel.

Chokes, recess Where a gun is bored with little constriction and where there is sufficient thickness of metal at the muzzle end, it is sometimes possible for a skilled gunsmith to bore the barrel recess choke. About $\frac{1}{4}$ choke is the maximum that can be achieved.

Chokes, retro or trumpet Very similar to the Cutts Compensator choke system (*which see*). The barrel is expanded some 4 in. from the muzzle and then swaged in again about $\frac{1}{2}$ in. from the muzzle. This is alleged to separate the shot charge from felt or fibre driving wads. Also some of the shot pellets are distorted from the spherical thereby producing a longer shot string.

Cutts Compensator chokes Invented by Col. Cutts of the United States of America shortly after World War I. The compensator started life as a muzzle brake, slots being cut into the top of the compensator to reduce the tendency of the weapon to climb. The Lyman Gun Sight Co. applied the Cutts Compensator to shotguns. There is no doubt that the slots reduce recoil, also that various choke tubes can be screwed on the end to allow the shooter a choice of chokes. Compensators are not allowed for the going-away disciplines, such as DTL, but are allowed for Skeet.

Discipline A word used for the various types of clay target competition shooting.

DTL Down the Line discipline.

Ejectors Pieces of mechanism which throw out the fired empty cases when a gun is opened.

Engraving A pattern cut into wood or metal to make it more pleasing to those shooters with artistic tendencies.

Extractors Pieces of mechanism which partially lift either fired cases or unfired cartridges far enough out of the barrel chambers when the gun is opened to allow them to be taken out by hand.

File cut *See* Rib.

FN Fabrique Nationale. An old and famous firm of gunmakers in Liège, Belgium.

Firing pin *See* Striker.

Firing point, shooting stand, peg A position marked on the ground, usually as a square with sides measuring 1 yd or 1 m. The shooter must stand with both feet inside this square when firing his gun.

FITASC Federations Internationale de Tir aux Armes Sportives de Chasse.

Fore-end A piece of wood placed in front of the action and under and/or partially around the barrel(s). The fore-end iron is fitted into this wood in the case of single barrel side by sides or o/us. With semi-automatics and pump guns the fore-end contains the magazine tube and extraction parts. On single barrel or side by sides the wood may be of splinter or beavertail shape. On o/us it may be Sporting/snable, schnozzle, or beavertail. On semi-automatics and pumps the fore-end shape is more rounded than true beavertail.

Gauge *See* Bore gauge.

Gun canting Due to many causes. The gun barrels are canted sideways and clockwise on right-handed targets, this causes the shot charge to be thrown low.

Guns

O/U Over and Under. The barrels are placed one on top of the other. American 'Superposed'. This gives a narrow sighting plane which some shooters believe a help in seeing the target and more precise gun mounting. *Percussion* A muzzle-loading gun whose charge is fired by a percussion cap. *Pump* Single-barrelled magazine guns operated each time after firing by the shooter pumping or tromboning the fore-end backwards and forwards. In the USA the exhibition shooters filed the interceptor, this allowed them to hold back the trigger and rapid fire the gun by pumping. In this country an illegal and dangerous practice. As supplied by the makers is capable of being fired by an expert as quickly as a semi-automatic gun. For clay shooting only one cartridge is allowed to be placed in the magazine. *SA* Single-barrelled semi-automatic magazine guns which are self-loading. Pulling the trigger should fire the gun, recoil or gas pressure moves the bolt rearward and ejects the empty case, the next cartridge is then fed up from the magazine into the barrel chamber and the bolt closes, leaving the gun ready to fire the second shot. The rules for some disciplines state that the magazine must be plugged to prevent the insertion of more than one cartridge. As with pump guns some Americans file various parts thereby making these guns fully automatic. Illegal in this country and highly dangerous. *SB* Single-shot, single-barrelled guns. Very popular in the USA for Trapshooting, rarely seen in this country. *S/S* The barrels are placed side by side, not so popular these days, in the hands of an expert is still very efficient as a target breaker.

Gun position 'Clearly out of the shoulder pocket' A term used for English Sporting and FITASC Sporting. A loosely defined rule interpreted differently by various referees. Some referees insisting that the position is that for ISU Skeet. This is not so. During the past few years the gun butt position has risen higher and nearer the shoulder pocket until at some shoots it is only $\frac{1}{2}$ in. away from the shooter's cheek. Such loose wording does nothing to preserve the equity of a competition.

Gun position 'down' A term used in ISU Skeet. The gun position for which is rigidly defined. This 'down' position has to be adopted before calling for the target(s) and held until the target(s) appear in view.

Gun position 'optional' A term used for ABT, American Skeet, DTL, OT, UT. The shooter can please himself whether or not he premounts his gun before calling for the target.

Hammer/tumbler The part of the gun which hits the striker eventually to fire the cartridge. Most modern guns have hammers sited inside the action.

Hammerless A gun in which the hammers are unseen and inside the action.

Hinge pin The pin on which the barrels hinge when the gun is opened.

Hinge pins/bifurcated *See* Bifurcated.

ISU International Shooting Union.

Jointing The hinge or joint of the barrels to the action.

Kill The referee's decision alone as to whether the shooter has or has not 'killed' his target.

Lock The moving parts of the action, cocking levers or dogs, springs, sears, tumblers, etc.

Locks, box *See* Boxlock.

Locks, side *See* Side Lock.

'Locked up' When gun and shooter are swinging as one unit, butt in shoulder pocket and cheek tight to stock comb.

Lump A protrusion underneath or on the sides of the barrels into which the locking bolts engage to hold barrel and action together.

Magazine Usually a tube under the barrel on semi-automatic or pump guns in which extra cartridges are held. For clay shooting a gun must not be loaded with more than two cartridges in total, regardless of magazine capacity.

Miss and out/sudden death In tie shoots, where as soon as a shooter drops or misses a target he is out of the competition.

Mono block The barrel lumps are machined from a billet or block of steel and bored with two holes into which the barrels are inserted. They are usually soldered in place.

Monte Carlo A shape of stock comb usually parallel to the barrel top line. Was originally used at Monte Carlo for guns used to shoot live pigeons. Correctly fitted to a shooter ensures that his eye is always positioned at the same level in relation to the barrel rib, regardless where along the comb line his check is placed.

Mono wads *See* Wads.

NSSA National Skeet Shooting Association, USA.

OT Olympic Trap or Trench.

Over draft A tendency for the barrels and action to partially close themselves after being opened. This is usually due to faulty design or poorly fitted cocking mechanism. Makes loading difficult.

Over run *See* Over draft.

Overshot wad *See* Wads.

Patterns The manner in which pellets are distributed when fired from a gun onto a sheet of paper or a pattern plate. To obtain a reasonable estimate of pattern spread and quality a string of nine shots should be fired to evaluate one barrel and one type of cartridge. This should be done with the gun always fired from an accurately measured distance from the plate.

Peg *See* Firing point.

Percussion *See* Guns, percussion.

Powder charge The amount of powder used in a single cartridge. These charges are usually 'thrown' by volume. It is essential that home loaders check the amount of powder they are throwing by means of an accurate powder scale. Different batches of the same make of powder, if measured by volume, may vary in the weight of powder thrown by the same powder bush.

Rail, running A strip of rubber or similar, in a metal channel fixed to the trailing edge of a trap arm. The target runs along this, thereby acquiring spin when the arm is released.

Recoil The blow or push which a gun, when fired, gives the shooter. Based on the physics principle of 'no action without re-action'. W. W. Greener had a formula that gun weight should be 96 times that of the shot charge to avoid excessive recoil. A 6 lb gun would therefore use a 1 oz shot load. This still holds good today, assuming the gun being used has correct head space and chamber length.

Recoil pad A rubber pad on the end of the stock. May be solid, or ventilated to soften the gun recoil on the shoulder.

Ribs Metal strips brazed, pegged or soldered onto barrels.

Ribs, bottom Placed below and slightly between the barrels of a side by side gun.

Ribs, side Placed each side and slightly between the barrels of an o/u gun.

Ribs, top May be floating, parallel, raised, solid, stepped, swamped, tapered or ventilated. With a selection of top surfaces such as cross-etched, cross-milled, file-cut, matted or smooth. Some, but not all shooters, find a top rib an aid in precise pointing of the gun.

Safety catches The safeties on most guns only block the movement of the trigger. They will not prevent sear noses being jarred out of bents. Catches may be automatic, in which case they are set or returned to safe every time the gun is opened, or may be manually operated by the shooter as required.

Sand bagger One who by devious methods shoots in a lower class than his true form warrants. A difficult person against whom to legislate.

Sear The arm which holds the tumbler at full cock. Pressure on the sear by the trigger moves the sear nose out of bent, releases the tumbler, and fires the gun.

Semi-automatic *See* Guns, SA.

Shoot-offs If two or more shooters obtain equal scores in a competition, the first three places are decided by shoot-off or tie shoot between the shooters concerned. May be shot off over a number of targets, alternatively, may be shot off as first miss and out, or sudden death.

Shot string The pellets of shot after being fired travel as a long column. The length of this column or string can vary immensely due to the components of the cartridge, the chokings and internal contours of the barrels.

Shoulder pocket The shoulder is brought forward slightly, thereby providing a hollow or pocket in which the gun butt is placed.

Side lock A type of action similar to that used for hammer guns. The locks are mounted on the inside of the side plates with the hammers or tumblers also on the inside (see illustrations between pages 102 and 103).

Sights *Centre or intermediate* A small metal or white bead fitted to the top rib about 15 in. from the muzzle.   *Front* The original front sight was a round bead of metal or ivory fitted on top of the rib near the muzzle. Now front sights are available in metal, ivory, plastic and other materials. They may be bead or toothpaste-shaped, plain, coloured or fluorescent.

Silent rise A term used in Sporting shooting. When the shooter says 'Ready' the target is released by non-visible or audible instruction from the referee. The delay before target release may be up to three seconds.

Snap cap A dummy cartridge, when placed in the barrel chamber allows the gun to be closed, and the trigger pulled with no damage to the firing pin or striker.

Spread The diameter of the shot pattern. Controlled mostly by the barrel choke. By shooting a gun at a pattern plate at known distances and measuring the spread diameter it is possible to access the choking of the gun (see tables for spread diameter).

Squad hustler An energetic gentleman whose job it is to encourage squads of shooters to be ready at the proper layout at the correct time. Rarely seen except in Britain. Even here the onus is still on the shooter to be on any layout when required.

Stock Usually of wood, fitted behind the action at rear end of gun.

Stock bolt A large number of imported guns have stock and action held together by a stock bolt.

Stock boot A leather or rubber slip-over boot. Placed over the butt end of the stock to make it longer.

Stock crawling A habit common to trap shooters, the head is pushed out forward and down on the front end of the comb. This action puts extra tension on the neck muscles, the eyes have to be swivelled upwards with the eyes looking out through the shooter's eyebrows. This encourages head lifting.

Stock hand That part of the stock held by the shooter's trigger hand. May be full pistol, half pistol or straight hand shaped.

Stock head The front part of the stock in front of the hand. This part is usually an extremely close fit into the back or rear of the action.

Striker Also known as the firing pin. This is the pin which strikes the cartridge cap. The majority of British side by side boxlocks have the striker pin integral with the hammer or tumbler. Imported guns usually have separate striker or firing pins.

Stud bolt Sometimes when cast is put into a stock the stock bolt will not then go through the stock. When this occurs a bent stud bolt is made, fastened to the back of the action, the stock pushed on and a nut screwed onto the end of the stud to hold all together.

Swept out Some shooters have the face of the stock comb swept out. Very often this results in the need for cast off being reduced or eliminated.

Target ridden in Allowing the muzzles to keep swinging with the target until it is so close that successful breaking will be dangerous and difficult.

Target ridden out The opposite to the above and just as conducive to missing.

Thous: Thousandths of an inch.

Toe The point at the bottom rear end of the stock.

Top extension An extension of the barrel(s) at the breech.

Top lever A lever on the top of the action used to open the gun.

Trigger The part which the shooter pulls or presses to fire the gun. May be two on a double-barrelled gun, in which case the front trigger usually fires the right barrel on a side by side, and the bottom barrel on an o/u. Single triggers on double guns may be selective or non-selective.

Trigger guard strap A metal strip around the trigger(s) to prevent them catching on any obstructions and thereby firing the gun.

Trigger plate The plate to which the trigger assembly is fitted. A trigger plate action is one where most of the striker mechanism is fitted to the plate and may be removed as a unit.

Trigger pulls The amount of pull or pressure, usually measured in pounds and ounces, required to be exerted on the trigger to take the sear out of bent and fire the gun.

Tromboning Sliding the hand back along the barrels during the swing.

Tubes Barrels begin life as tubes, becoming barrels after they have been joined together, had loops, lumps and ribs fitted, chambered, rimmed and bored.

Tumblers *See* Hammer.

Tune A term used for setting trigger pulls. A skilled operation for an expert, who will tune pulls to be short, crisp, and take the sear nose out of bent 'at the precise poundage specified by the customer.

UT Universal or Five Trap Trench.

Ventilated rib *See* Rib.

Wads Used in cartridges to separate powder and shot; acts also as a piston when the cartridge is fired and the shot propelled up and out of the barrels. *Card* Used over the powder and/or under the shot, originally the over powder card wad was used to prevent grease from the felt wads from contaminating the powder. Under shot wads were used to prevent the bottom layer of pellets sticking to the greased felt wad. *Felt* Made of wool felt and sandwiched between the over powder and under shot card wads, the felt wad is rarely used these days. *Kleena* A vegetable fibre wad used by Eley as the main driving wad in some of its cartridges. *Mono* A plastic one-piece wad consisting of over powder cup, connecting collapsible legs and shot cup. Used by Eley in some of its clay target cartridges. *Plaswad* A British-made plastic wad highly popular with the home loader. *Various* Makers of modern cartridges such as Game Bore, Fiocchi, Hull Cartridge, Maionchi, Remington, SMI, Winchester and others have their own specially designed plastic wads to suit their particular caps, cases, powder, etc. In addition, most of them also use sophisticated combination wads made of cork, fibre, plastic and other materials, to produce cartridges of high and consistent performance.

WAGBI *See* BASC.

White line spacers White washers of plastic used to fit between recoil pad and butt end to lengthen stock and in some shooters' opinions, embellish it.

Bibliography

ACKLEY, P. O., *Home Gun Care and Repair*, 1969.

AKEHURST, R., *Game Guns and Rifles*, 1969.

ANGIER, R. H., *Firearms Blueing and Browning*, 1936.

ARNOLD, R., *Shooters Handbook*, 1955. *Automatic and Repeating Shotguns*, 1958.

ARTHUR, R., *The Shotgun Stock*, 1971.

ASKINS, Col. Charles sen., *Wing and Trapshooting*, 1922.

ASKINS, Col. Charles jnr., *Wing and Trapshooting*, 1948. *The Shotgunners Book*, 1958.

BADMINTON LIBRARY, *SHOOTING,* Articles by R. Payne-Gallwey and A. J. Stuart-Wortley, 1885.

BADMINTON MAGAZINE, The Holland and Holland Shooting School by R. Payne-Gallwey, 1896.

BAILEY, DE WITT, and NIE, D. A., *English Gunmakers*, 1978.

BASC, *A Handbook of Shooting*, 1983.

BEARSE, R., *Sporting Arms of the World*, 1976.

BEAUMONT, R., *Purdeys, The Guns and the Family*, 1984.

BERESFORD, Hon. Charles, *Beresford's Monte Carlo*, circa 1910.

BIRMINGHAM PROOF HOUSE, *A History*, 1946.

BLAGDON, *Shooting*, 1900.

BOGARDUS, A. G., *Field Cover and Trap Shooting*, 1881.

BLAINES, *Rural Sports*, 1858.

BOUGHAN, R., *Shotgun Ballistics*, 1965.

BRINDLE, J., *Shotguns and Shooting*, 1984.

BRISTER, Bob, *Shotgunning: The Art and the Science*, 1976

BROWNELL, Bob, *Encyclopedia of Modern Firearms*, 1959. *Gunsmith Kinks*, 1969.

BROWNING, J., and GENTRY, C., *J. M. Browning, American Gunmaker*, 1962 and 1982.

BROOMFIELD, B., and CRADOCK, C., *Shotguns on Test*, 1980.

BRUETTE, W. A., *Guncraft*, 1912.

BURCH, Monte, *Gun Care and Repairs*, 1978.

BURRARD, Maj. Sir Gerald, *In the Gunroom*, 1930. *The Modern Shotgun*, 1931.

CARMICHAEL. J., *Gunsmithing: Do-It-Yourself*, 1977.

CHAPEL, C. E., *Field Skeet and Trap Shooting*, 1949.

CHURCHILL, R., *How To Shoot*, 1925–27–38. *Game Shooting*, 1955. *Churchill's Shotgun Book*, 1955.

COOPER. C., *Annie Oakley.*

CURTIS, P. A., *Guns and Gunning*, 1934.

CRUDGINGTON, I., and BAKER, D., *The British Shotgun*, 1979.

DANIEL, Rev. W. B., *Rural Sport*, 1801.

DOBSON, W., *Kunopaedia. The Art of Shooting Flying*, 1817.

DOUGALL, J. D., *Shooting Simplified*, 1865.

DUNLAP, R. F., *Gunsmithing*, 1963. *Gun Owner's Book*, 1974.

EAST SUSSEX, *The Shotgun and its Uses*, 1914.

ELEY, *Layouts for Clay Target Shooting*, 1971. (M. Rose) *Shooting Technique*, 1978. *Sporting Clays*, 1964. *The Shooter's Diary*

ELLIOT, A. & G., *Gun Fun and Hints*, 1946.
The Encyclopaedia of Sport, 1911.

ETCHEN, F., *Commonsense Shotgun Shooting*, 1946.

EXPERT, *Notes on Shooting*, 1915.

GARNER, P., *Shotguns*, 1963.

GARRARD, D., *Cartridge Loading*, 1978.

GARWOOD, Gough Thomas, *Shotguns and Cartridges*, 1963. *Gun Book*, 1969. *Shooting Facts and Fancies*, 1978.

GREENER, W., *The Gun*, 1834.

GREENER, W. W., *The Breechloader and How to Use It,* 1892 and 1905. *The Gun and Its Development*, 5th edition 1892. 9th edition 1910.

THE GUNMAKERS ASSOCIATION, *Gun Sense.*

THE GUNMAKERS COMPANY AND THE GUARDIANS OF THE BIRMINGHAM PROOF HOUSE, *Rules of Proof*, 1954.

THE JOINT AUTHORITY OF THE WORSHIPFUL COMPANY OF GUNMAKERS OF THE CITY OF LONDON AND THE GUARDIANS OF THE BIRMINGHAM PROOF HOUSE, *Notes on the Proof of Shotguns and Other Small Arms*, 1960–76–81.

HARRISON, E., *Guns and Shooting*, 1908.

HARTMAN, B., *Hartman on Skeet*, 1967.

HAWKER, Col. P., *Instructions to Young Shooters*, 1833. *The Diary*, 1893.

HEARNE, A., *Shooting and Gunfitting*, 1946.

HINMAN R., *Golden Age of Shotgunning*, 1971.

HOLTS, *Holts Shooting Calendar*, 1883.

HOOD, A., *Shooting*, 1909.

HOWE, J., *The Modern Gunsmith* (2 vols), 1934.

HUMPHREYS, J., *The Shooting Handbook*, Annual.

ICI *The Stringing of Shot*, 1926. *Skeet*, 1934.

JENNINGS, M., *Instinct Shooting*, 1965.

JOHNSON, P., *Parker*, 1961.

KEITH, E., *Shotguns*, 1950.

KENNEDY, M., *Checkering and Carving Gunstocks*, 1952.

KYNOCH LTD, *Shooting Notes and Comments*, 1910.

LANCASTER, C., *Art of Shooting*, 1889.

LAVIN, I., *History of Spanish Firearms*, 1965.

LEE BRAUN, *Trap Shooting*, 1969. *Skeet Shooting*, 1969.

LIND, E., *Complete Book of Trick and Fancy Shooting*, 1972.

LONSDALE LIBRARY, *Shooting*, 1929.

MACINTYRE, D., *Memories of a Highland Gamekeeper* Circa 1926.

MARCHINGTON, J., *The Complete Shot*, 1981.

MARCHINGTON, J., *Book of Shotguns*.

MARKSMAN, *The Dead Shot*, 1860.

McFARLAND, F., *Clay Pigeon Shooting*, 1964.

MIGDALSKI, E., *Clay Target Games*, 1978.

MISSELDINE, F., *Skeet and Trap Shooting*, 1968.

MONTAGUE, A., *Successful Shotgun Shooting*, 1971.

MORETON and OTHERS, *Gun Talk*, 1973.

NEWELL, D., *Gunstock Finishing and Care*, 1949.

NICHOLLS, R., *Skeet*, 1939. *The Shotgunner*, 1949.

NOBEL INDUSTRIES, *The Versatile Clay Bird*, 1921.
    A Handbook of Clay Target Shooting, 1927.

OBERFELL and THOMPSON, *The Mysteries of Shotgun Patterns*, 1960.

PARKER, E., *Elements of Shooting*, 1924.

PAYNE-GALLWEY, R., *Letters to Young Shooters*, 1895.

PETREL, *Approach to Shooting*, 1954.

POLLARD, H., *Shotguns*, 1923.

PURDEY, T. & J., *The Shotgun*, 1936.

PURPLE HEATHER, *Something about Guns and Shooting*, 1891.

RAYMONT, M., *Modern Clay Pigeon Shooting*, 1974.

RILING, R., *Guns and Shooting*, 1951.

RUFFER, Maj. J. E. M., *Art of Good Shooting*, 1976.

SEDGEWICK, N., *The Young Shot*, 1940.

SELL, F., *Sure-Hit Shotgun Ways*, 1967.

SERVICE, *Shooting* (no date).

SHARP, R., *The Gun*, 1903. *Modern Sporting Gunnery*, 1906.

The SHOOTING SPORTS TRUST, *Buying a Shotgun*, 1981.

SMITH, L., *Trap Shooting*, 1925. *Modern Shotgun Shooting*, 1935.
    Shotgun Psychology, 1938.

SPORTING ARMS, *Handbook on Shotgun Shooting*, 1940.

STACK, R., *Shotgun Digest*, 1974.

STANBURY, P., and CARLISLE, G., *Shotgun Marksmanship*, 1962.
    Clay Pigeon Marksmanship, 1962.

STONEHENGE, *The Sporting Gun*, 1859.

TEASDALE BUCKELL, G. T., *Experts on Guns and Shooting*, 1900.
    The Complete Shot, 1907.

TWENTY BORE, *Practical Hints on Shooting*, 1887.

THORP, R., *Doc Carver*, 1937.

WAGNER, Doc. F., *The Art of Shooting,* circa 1926.

WALLACK, L., *American Shotgun Design and Performance*, 1977.

WALSH (STONEHENGE), *Rural Sports*, 1881.

WINSBERGER, G., *The Standard Directory of Proof Marks*, 1975.

ZUTZ, D., *Modern Hand Loading*, 1977. *The Double Shotgun*, 1978.

Magazines

American	**British**
American Rifleman.	*Guns Review* (monthly).
American Shotgunner.	*Sporting Gun* (monthly).
Field and Stream.	*Shooting Magazine* (monthly).
Guns and Ammo.	*Shooting Times and Country*
	Magazine (weekly).
American Annuals	*Game and Gun*, 1926–1946
Gun Digest.	
Guns and Ammo.	

Video Films

Clay Pigeon Shooting with Brian Hebditch.
The Sporting Shotgun, by James Douglass and Chris Cradock.
Game Shooting – Holland and Holland/Shooting Times

Index